TIBERIUS
AND THE
ROMAN EMPIRE

BY

CHARLES EDWARD SMITH

KENNIKAT PRESS
Port Washington, N. Y./London

TIBERIUS AND THE ROMAN EMPIRE

Copyright 1942 by Louisiana State University Press
Reissued in 1972 by Kennikat Press by arrangement
Library of Congress Catalog Card No: 74-159060
ISBN 0-8046-1683-3

Manufactured by Taylor Publishing Company   Dallas, Texas

PREFACE

In writing a general history of the reign of Tiberius the author was fully cognizant of the value of the late Professor Frank Burr Marsh's *The Reign of Tiberius*, as well as of the excellence of the studies by M. P. Charlesworth in *The Cambridge Ancient History* and M. Gelzer in the *Real-Encyklopädie*. Yet few topics in ancient history offer wider opportunities for the exercise of judgment on questions of emphasis and interpretation or present more critical problems in the use of ancient authorities. Many of the most controversial issues cannot be definitively settled by the utilization of epigraphical or numismatic evidence and, hence, continue to engender interpretative variation.

Since the appearance of the works of Stahr and Freytag, many monographs and articles have demonstrated the need for critical caution in the study of Tacitus' *Annals*, which of necessity must remain the basic source for the history of the period. It is hoped that this book will indicate that its author is not unfamiliar with the literature on Tiberius' reign. Not all recent views and interpretations have been accepted, however, simply because they happen to be challenging or novel. Indeed, many interpretative suggestions advanced within the past few years were advocated (and in some instances refuted) long before in doctoral dissertations, inaugural lectures, and gymnasia programs. The author, therefore, has attempted to avoid the mistake of considering the last word as necessarily the true one, and has endeavored to present an account of the reign which to him seems most closely to approximate the truth.

The author was fortunate to enjoy the benefit of the counsel of the late Professor Marsh in the preparation of the first five chapters of this study. Professors A. E. R. Boak of the University of Michigan and W. E. Caldwell of the University of North Carolina read critically the entire manuscript and contributed many helpful suggestions for its improvement. In acknowledging his debt to these scholars the author accepts undivided responsibility for errors of fact or judgment.

Dr. Fred C. Cole, editor of the *Journal of Southern History*, extended indispensable editorial assistance in the preparation of the manuscript for printing. The author's work was greatly facilitated by the efficiency of Mrs. Rubie Hanks and other members of the Louisiana State University library staff, who secured much material not locally available.

Quotations from the *Loeb Classical Library* translations are used with the permission of the Trustees and Fellows of Harvard College.

C. E. S.

May, 1942

TABLE OF CONTENTS

		PAGE
	Preface	iii
	Introduction	1
I.	The Accession of Tiberius	12
II.	The Mutiny of A.D. 14	36
III.	The German Campaigns	57
IV.	Germanicus in the East	80
V.	The Trial of Piso	103
VI.	Sejanus	116
VII.	The Retirement to Capri and the Fall of Sejanus	133
VIII.	*Lèse Majesté* Prosecutions under Tiberius	166
IX.	War and Peace in the Provinces	182
X.	Relations with the Senate and the Administration of Italy	214
XI.	Economic Conditions During the Reign of Tiberius	233
	Bibliography	257
	Index	271

INTRODUCTION

Octavian's victory at Actium was tantamount to the establishment of his unchallenged mastery of the Roman world. After a leisurely progress through the eastern provinces, distinguished by his reorganization of Egypt, he returned to Rome in 29 B.C. The Senate immediately ratified his eastern settlements and voted him the honor of a triple triumph. "The joy that greeted him was sincere. It was genuine not only because of the rich booty, of which a portion was distributed in cash among the populace of the capital according to the old custom; it sprang from the feeling that now the era of civil wars was terminated and a time of tranquillity was at hand." [1]

Octavian lacked the incisive genius of Julius Caesar, as well as "the reach and grasp of his intellect [which] alarmed the dull and timid"; [2] yet his caution, moderation, and abstinence from a brusque cleavage with the republican tradition enabled him to rule without abrogation of time-honored institutions and without excessive offense to the sensibilities of those devoted to the old order.

About a year after his return to the capital Octavian assumed censorial powers in order to purge the Senate of members who owed their inclusion to Caesar's deliberate policy of diminishing the prestige of the body. The senators, grateful for this evidence of Octavian's intention to restore them to an important place in the government, awarded him the title of *princeps senatus* which gave him,

[1] H. Dessau, *Geschichte der römischen Kaiserzeit*, 2 vols. in 4 (Berlin, 1924 ff.), I, 25–26.
[2] T. S. Jerome, *Some Aspects of Roman History* (New York, 1923), 202.

as a *primus inter pares,* the right to speak and vote first; this distinction in reality vested in one person the old republican concept of the *principes civitatis.*[3]

The *princeps* had brought peace, stability, and order to the Roman world. His censorial action had purged the Senate, and he had ensured the prohibition of intermarriages between freedmen and members of the senatorial aristocracy. These measures, interpreted as evidences of his determination to preserve the status of Italy as the ruling center of the Roman empire as well as to restore the dignity of the Senate, earned popular approval. Although there was little disposition to question his authority, his status demanded clarification, unless he wished to rule with no apparent sanction save the loyalty of his legions. It was therefore his sensibility to constitutional exigencies that impelled him to appear before the Senate in January of 27 B.C. to renounce all powers except those normally vested in the consulship. The Senate, hardly without some previous understanding, responded to this "abdication" by granting him proconsular powers for Syria, Egypt, Gaul, and the Two Spains, which he henceforth governed by his legates and procurators; the older and peaceful provinces remained under senatorial administration, with Asia and Africa under proconsuls and the rest under propraetors. The Senate also bestowed upon him the title of *Augustus,* or the "Revered One," and this title was destined to be the underlying foundation for the imperial cult.

Proconsular authority was subject to a fundamental weakness in its theoretical inapplicability within the *pomerium.* The collegiate nature of the consulship likewise was an embarrassment. Then, too, successive con-

[3] E. Herzog, *Geschichte und System der Römischen Staatsverfassung,* 2 vols. in 3 (Leipzig, 1887), Vol. II, Pt. I, 130–31.

INTRODUCTION   3

sular terms, reminiscent of the Marian era, were in strong
contravention to republican precedent. In a second abdication ceremony in 23 B.C. Augustus accordingly renounced the consulship and received investment with
tribunician powers. Now, as proconsul, his continued
command of the troops was legalized; indeed, as shown
by the famous Cyrene Edicts, he did not hesitate to issue
edicts applicable to a province nominally under the Senate, and at least small contingents of troops were stationed
in the senatorial provinces.[4] His tribunician powers extended him inviolability and invested him with the power
to summon the *Comitia Tributa*. He also possessed the
veto power (*intercessio*) which enabled him to annul the
acts of the Senate or those of any magistrate. Further, his
tribunician position strengthened the appearance that he
was the direct representative of the populace, legally the
ultimate source of the *imperium*.

He had evolved a compromise between Caesar's dictatorship and Sulla's conservative regime; his government
was that of "a monarchy in the framework of a republic." [5] He had no colleagues in the tribunician office save
those whose designation he himself procured as an indispensable feature of his arrangements for the succession.[6]

[4] I agree with D. McFayden, "The Princeps and the Senatorial Provinces," *Classical Philology*, XVI (1921), 37–38, who holds that Augustus was not granted a *maius imperium* in the senatorial provinces. Yet he issued edicts applicable to them. See, J. G. C. Anderson, "Augustan Edicts from Cyrene," *Journal of Roman Studies*, XVII (1927), 42–48. For troops in senatorial provinces, see, E. Ritterling, "Military Forces in the Senatorial Provinces," *ibid.*, 29. The praenomen *imperator* had no practical significance in the West. D. McFayden, *The History of the Title Imperator under the Roman Empire* (Chicago, 1920), 1–56.

[5] E. Kornemann, "Die Römische Kaiserzeit," in A. Gercke and E. Norden (eds.), *Einleitung in die Altertumswissenschaft*, 3 vols. (Leipzig, 1923), III, 213–15.

[6] *Id.*, *Doppelprinzipat und Reichsteilung im Imperium Romanum* (Leipzig, 1930), 1–16.

His proconsular powers were not limited to any given area,[7] and, as prince of the Senate, he was in a position to exert pressure on the Fathers. Although the electoral rights of the *comitia* were nominally operative, he submitted lists of approved candidates and in large measure ordained the decision by granting or withholding his support. He refused the title of dictator in 22, and three years later refused to assume the *cura legum et morum*. In A.D. 2 the Senate, upon motion of a former republican, conferred upon him the title of *Pater Patriae* to signalize the ostensible reconciliation between the old aristocracy and the new regime.

Although in the *Monumentum Ancyranum* Augustus stated that "I bequeathed the direction of public affairs from my power to that of the Roman people,"[8] "he was not willing to give up even a portion of the power for which he had begun to fight while still almost a boy and for which he had warred with both honest and dishonest means."[9] "When Rome did homage to him he renounced title and pomp; one could call him neither dictator nor lord; it was enough for him to be master."[10]

One of Augustus' major problems naturally was that of the succession, the determination of which seemed all the more imperative in view of his chronic ill-health. Theoretically, he governed the state co-operatively with the Senate, which had bestowed powers upon him presumably for limited terms. Upon his death the Senate

[7] Cf., E. Meyer, "Kaiser Augustus," *Historische Zeitschrift*, LV (1903), 385 ff.
[8] VI, 13.
[9] Dessau, *Gesch. der röm. Kaiserzeit*, I, 32.
[10] W. Drumann, *Geschichte Roms in seinem Übergange von der republikanischen zur monarchischen Verfassung*, 2nd ed., 6 vols. (Leipzig, 1908), IV, 279. See, T. R. Holmes, *The Architect of the Roman Empire* (Oxford, 1928), 179–86.

ostensibly would have complete freedom in the subsequent disposition of the proconsular and tribunician powers which were the basis of the principate. Never for a moment, however, did Augustus contemplate senatorial assumption of such discretionary authority, with its attendant risk of precipitating another era of civil war. From the beginning he planned to confine tenure of powers vital to the continuance of the principate to the Julian *gens,* as the dynastic marriages and adoptions which accompanied his succession arrangements clearly demonstrated.

Augustus' only child was a daughter, Julia, born of Scribonia, his second wife. He divorced Scribonia in order to marry Livia, wife of Tiberius Claudius Nero, a former adherent of Lucius Antonius, who had fled from Italy with his wife and the two-year-old son Tiberius. The permission extended to the elder Tiberius to return to Italy was probably contingent upon his willingness to connive at Octavian's marriage to Livia. A second son, Drusus, was born to Livia, a few months after her marriage to Octavian.

Augustus' first choice of a successor fell upon his nephew, Marcellus, who accordingly was married to Julia in 25 B.C. After his premature admission to the Senate at the age of nineteen the youth held the aedileship, a position which enabled him to court popularity by sponsoring lavish games and spectacles. His bitterly lamented death in 23 B.C. forced the emperor to reorder his plans. Agrippa, the faithful general whose talents had been so largely responsible for Augustus' rise to power, was wedded to the widowed Julia and invested with proconsular *imperium* and tribunician powers for five years. These powers were renewed in 13 B.C., but Agrippa died the following year, leaving two infant sons, Gaius and Lucius, and the posthumously born Agrippa.[11]

Augustus then turned to Tiberius as his apparent choice for the succession. At the age of nine, Tiberius, after the death of his father, entered Augustus' household. He received a good education and retained an interest in learning in later life. His first military experience was gained as a tribune in Octavian's army that operated in Spain against the Cantabrians (27–24 B.C.). He began the *cursus honorum*, for which his military service had been a necessary prerequisite, by tenure of the quaestorship in 23 B.C. He then accompanied Augustus to the East (22–19 B.C.) and received from King Phraates of Parthia the standards lost by Crassus in the disastrous battle of Carrhae (53 B.C.). He also officiated at the installation of Tigranes III as king of Armenia.

After his return from the East he served with Augustus in Gaul in campaigns that resulted in the crushing defeats of the Sugambri, Tencteri, and Usipites, and he gained additional experience as governor of the Three Gauls. In 16 B.C. he held the praetorship, and upon expiration of his term he was sent to join his brother Drusus in campaigns against the Vindelici, north of the Alps. The victories gained by the two young commanders, coming as a sequel to Drusus' conquest of the Rhaeti, made possible the organization of the provinces of Rhaetia and Noricum in 8 B.C.

Tiberius held his first consulship in 13 B.C. as a colleague of the ill-fated Varus, who later fell in the disastrous battle of Teutoberg Wood, a victim of German ambush. Upon the death of Agrippa in 12 B.C. Augustus

---

[11] Kornemann, *Doppelprinzipat und Reichsteilung im Imperium Romanum*, 14–15, believes that the tribunician power was equivalent to making its recipient a colleague of the emperor, whereas adoption was necessary for designation as successor.

required Tiberius to divorce his dearly loved wife, Vipsania, Agrippa's daughter, in order to marry Julia.

Tiberius, having complied with the marital condition prescribed by Augustus, was sent to succeed Agrippa in Illyria. Here his campaign from 12 to 9 B.C. resulted in the subjugation of Pannonia and Dalmatia and the establishment of the Drave as the northern boundary of the empire. At the same time, Drusus was fighting four memorable campaigns in Germany between the Rhine and the Elbe, and his successes, synchronizing with Tiberius' victories in Pannonia and Dalmatia, constituted one of the most remarkable chapters in the history of Roman expansion. In the year 9 B.C. Drusus succumbed to injuries sustained in a fall from his horse, and Tiberius was sent to succeed him. Tiberius' German operations, however, were confined to the area between the Rhine and the Ems and had for their apparent purpose the stabilization of Roman control over part of the area conquered by Drusus.

In 7 B.C. Tiberius was rewarded with his second consulship which he held as a colleague of Gnaeus Calpurnius Piso, and the following year he was granted tribunician powers for a five-year term. There was evidence, however, that the distinctions accorded him were merely precautionary, and that he was to be replaced in the succession plans by Gaius and Lucius. It was doubtless the embarrassment of this position, coupled with the disgraceful conduct of Julia, that induced him to go into voluntary exile at Rhodes in 6 B.C. Here he lived a simple life, devoting much time to scholarly pursuits. When Julia was banished in 2 B.C., Tiberius requested permission to return to Rome. The succession of Augustus' grandsons seemed assured, and Tiberius' tribunician powers were nearing expiration. Despite these considerations and the importunities of Livia, Augustus, who had been greatly angered by Tiberius' withdrawal, refused to allow his return.

In 5 and 3 B.C., respectively, Gaius and Lucius had been permitted prematurely to assume the *toga virilis*, and the occasion was pointed in each instance by Augustus' tenure of the consulship. Minimum age qualifications of the *cursus honorum* also were set aside in favor of the youths so that each might hold the consulship in his twentieth year. In A.D. 2, however, Lucius was fatally stricken with a fever while he was in Spain, and two years later Gaius succumbed to the aftereffects of a wound suffered while he was carrying out an important diplomatic mission designed to ensure tenure of the Armenian throne by a pro-Roman king.

Tiberius, who, in response to Livia's pleas, finally had been permitted to return to Rome as a private citizen in A.D. 2, now was recalled from retirement by the emperor. Not long after Gaius' death he was adopted by Augustus, along with Agrippa Posthumus, last surviving son of Agrippa and Julia. Tiberius alone, however, received investment with tribunician powers. He then was sent to the Rhine frontier, where he conducted a successful campaign between the Weser and the Elbe.

A campaign against the Marcomanni, designed to conquer the territory between the Upper Danube and the Elbe, then was planned. Tiberius was to move northward from the Danube, while Gaius Saturninus was to march eastward from the Rhine. Before this campaign could be begun, however, the great rebellion in Dalmatia and Pannonia in A.D. 6 forced abandonment of the plans.

The uprising, caused by severe Roman exactions and army levies, was carefully and intelligently planned. It began in Dalmatia where Bato, chief of the Desidiates, marched on Salonae. The Breuci, under a leader also named Bato, then attacked Sirmium. Salonae held out, and Aulus Caecina, legate of Moesia, saved Sirmium. Tiberius pressed the rebels down the valley of the Save. The two rebel forces, nevertheless, effected a junction and took up a strong position near Sirmium, where they were held in check by Thracian cavalry under Rhoemetalces. With the approach of winter (6–7) Tiberius fell back to Siscia. In the spring of 7 he marched up the valley of the Drave and defeated the two Batos.

Germanicus, son of Drusus, then subdued Dalmatia, aided by a famine that swept that region in A.D. 8, and Bato, leader of the Breuci, was driven to negotiate with Tiberius. The following year Tiberius suppressed the last rebellious elements, and Bato of the Desidiates surrendered after his defeat at Anderitum, near Salonae. Tiberius' victories were of paramount importance in view of the great disaster that overtook Varus in Germany. The ambush of the Roman forces by Arminius in the Teutoberg Wood in A.D. 9 resulted in the annihilation of the three legions under Varus' command. If this disaster had been coupled with success of the rebellions in Dalmatia and Pannonia the catastrophe would have subjected Italy to the gravest danger since the Hannibalic invasion.

Tiberius was hurriedly sent to Germany to reorganize the Rhine defenses after the Teutoberg disaster. The Rhine frontier was reinforced in 9–10 by the construction and enlargement of fortresses and the building of strong points in conformity with Augustus' momentous decision to adhere to a strictly defensive policy. With the defensive line secure, Tiberius led an army across the Rhine in 11, primarily as a demonstration to deter the Germans from interpreting reversion to defense as a sign of weakness.

In 13 Tiberius' tribunician powers were renewed, and

his proconsular *imperium* probably was made coequal with that of Augustus. He was now, in effect, a co-regent,[12] but, as part of the new arrangement, he was required to adopt Germanicus, son of Drusus and Agrippina. This stipulation was enlightening, for it showed that Augustus emphasized blood relationship with himself in his succession plans. Tiberius had a son by Vipsania, named Drusus, but his claims were set aside in favor of Germanicus, husband of Agrippina, daughter of Agrippa and Julia and a direct descendant of Augustus. Agrippa Posthumus apparently no longer figured in the succession plans, for he had been banished at the emperor's command because of conduct suggesting mental derangement.

It is doubtless true that Augustus' choice of Tiberius was a choice of necessity. From the beginning the succession schemes had emphasized blood relationship, and Augustus personally had little in common with Tiberius who "was a man of an earlier generation, dignified in bearing, hating flattery, frugal in his personal habits, and cordially detesting the frivolous luxury then common in high society." [13] Furthermore, the emperor had been virtually alienated from his stepson during the years of the latter's residence at Rhodes. Yet his outstanding services after his return, particularly his brilliant campaigns in Germany and Illyria, unequivocally demonstrated his ability and loyalty, and the apparently genuine letters quoted by Suetonius [14] indicate that cordial personal relations finally prevailed between Tiberius and Augustus. While "Augustus originally had not selected so differently natured a stepson as heir to the throne, nonetheless, under the stress of circumstances and in view of the undeniable com-

[12] Cf., H. Dieckmann, "Die effective Mitregenschaft des Tiberius," *Klio*, XV (1918), 339–75.
[13] F. B. Marsh, *The Reign of Tiberius* (Oxford, 1931), 47.
[14] Suetonius, *Lives of the Twelve Caesars: Tiberius*, XXI–XXII.

petence of Tiberius, he had overcome his inclination." [15] Yet, Tiberius "too long had been watched when he should have been trusted; he had too much been made to feel that the charm and social virtues of others counted for more than the real ability and effective work of a shy and silent man," [16] and this goes far to explain the aloofness he evinced as emperor.

[15] B. Niese, *Grundriss der römischen Geschichte*, 5th ed. (Munich, 1923), 305.
[16] G. P. Baker, *Tiberius Caesar* (New York, 1928), 72.

Chapter I

THE ACCESSION OF TIBERIUS

Augustus died on August 19, A.D. 14, at Nola, at the age of seventy-five years, ten months, and twenty-six days.[1] Charges of poisoning, so common in the writings of Roman imperial historians, apparently were circulated. According to Tacitus, the emperor, shortly before his death, had gone to Planasia to visit Agrippa Posthumus, banished by the Senate at his command. "There tears and signs of affection on both sides had been plentiful enough to raise a hope that the youth might yet be restored to the house of his grandfather." [2] It was further alleged that Fabius Maximus had accompanied the *princeps* on the visit. He had informed his wife of the impending restoration of Agrippa to favor, and she, in turn, divulged the situation to Livia, the empress. Maximus, fearing the emperor's wrath at the premature disclosure of his plans, may have committed suicide, for his wife allegedly reproached herself at his funeral "as the cause of her husband's destruction." [3] Dio states that Livia was suspected of having poisoned Augustus "because of the rumor that he had become reconciled with Agrippa." [4] These rumors of poisoning apparently were wholly unfounded. Augustus, who succumbed to dysentery, had suffered from a number of chronic ailments, including dropsy, a diseased hip, and liver disorders. In view of his advanced age and physical frailty, his demise certainly could be attributed to natural

[1] Dio, *Roman History*, LVI, xxx, 5.
[2] Tacitus, *Annals*, I, 5.
[3] *Ibid.*
[4] Dio, *R.H.*, LVI, xxx, 1–3.

causes, whatever the truth of the reports of the imminence of his reconciliation with Agrippa.[5]

Tiberius was in Illyricum at the time the emperor's illness took a grave turn. A letter from Livia caused him to hasten to Nola, but it is not known whether he found his stepfather still alive.[6] Suetonius states that an interview took place between Tiberius and the dying emperor, upon the termination of which Augustus was heard to cry, "Alas for the Roman people to be ground by jaws that crunch so slowly." [7] In view of the statements of the other authorities, however, this version at best is doubtful.

Livia acted with promptness and resolution upon receipt of the news of the emperor's fatal illness. In addition to urging Tiberius to hurry to his side, she posted guards around the house at Nola and concealed the true state of Augustus' condition by the issue of optimistic bulletins until after his death. The report of his demise could be issued simultaneously with the announcement of Tiberius' accession.[8] There apparently was some reason to fear an uprising against Tiberius' succession.[9] It was especially necessary to forestall any attempt to proclaim Agrippa,[10]

---

[5] Drumann, *Gesch. Roms in seinem Übergange von der republikanischen zur monarchischen Verfassung*, IV, 293-98. Tacitus' treatment of Augustus' death resembles his description of that of Claudius. H. Willrich, "Augustus bei Tacitus," *Hermes*, LXII (1927), 76-77. M. P. Charlesworth, "Livia and Tanaquil," *Classical Review*, XLI (1927), 55-57, likewise points out similarities in the Tacitean accounts of the accessions of Tiberius and Nero. K. Glaser, "Bemerkungen zu den Annalen des Tacitus," *Mitteilungen des Vereines Klassischer Philologen in Wien*, VI (1929), 34-35, does not think that Tacitus was influenced by Livy, I, 41, in his account of Tiberius' accession. The story of Tanaquil was well known, and this facilitated circulation and belief of the rumor of poisoning.

[6] Tacitus, *Ann.*, I, 5; Dio, *R.H.*, LVI, xxxi, 1.
[7] Suetonius, *Tib.*, XXI.   [8] Tacitus, *Ann.*, I, 5.
[9] Dio, *R.H.*, LVI, xxx, 1.
[10] Tacitus, *Ann.*, I, 6; Suetonius, *Tib.*, XXII. Both Tiberius and Agrippa had been adopted. Adoption was an important feature of the succession arrangements. Agrippa, however, never received tribunician

and the legions along the Rhine, commanded by Germanicus, obviously were a potential menace.[11]

Tiberius exhibited equal energy and initiative. He sent dispatches to all the legions and provinces from Nola,[12] and upon his return to the capital gave the watchword, or countersign, to the praetorian cohorts and posted sentries. He was attended by men-at-arms and was invested with other prerogatives and symbols of power.[13] The consuls, Sextus Appuleius and Sextus Pompeius, took oaths of allegiance to him. Seius Strabo, commander of the praetorians, and Gaius Turranius, curator of grain, in turn swore allegiance before the consuls, while the senators, soldiers, and general populace followed with similar oaths.[14] "He was administering in reality all the business of the empire." [15] In view of these manifestations of resolution and vigor, the statement of Tacitus, that "in every action of Tiberius the first steps had to be taken by the consuls as though the old republic were in being and himself undecided whether to reign or not," is exaggerated.[16]

Agrippa Posthumus was put to death immediately after

---

powers, the basis of coregency. Kornemann, *Doppelprinzipat und Reichsteilung im Imperium Romanum*, 13–14, 34–35.

[11] *Infra*, 45–55.   [12] Dio, *R.H.*, LVII, ii, 1–3.

[13] Tacitus, *Ann.*, I, 7. Tiberius acted "promptly, efficiently, and constitutionally." E. Hohl, "Wann hat Tiberius das Principat übernommen?" *Hermes*, LXVIII (1933), 111. Herzog, *Gesch. und System der Röm. Staatsverfassung*, Vol. II, Pt. I, 234, maintains that these acts constituted usurpation.

[14] Tacitus, *Ann.*, I, 7. For the form of the oath, see, *Corpus Inscriptionum Latinarum*, II, 172. It is hard to explain why such oaths were taken if one agrees with M. Hammond, *The Augustan Principate* (Cambridge, Mass., 1933), 73–74, that the consuls were exercising the chief executive authority. For Sextus Appuleius, see, A. F. von Pauly, G. Wissowa, and W. Kroll (eds.), *Real-Encyklopädie des classischen Altertumswissenschaft*, 25 vols., 7 supp. (Stuttgart, 1894 ff.), II, 259.

[15] Dio, *R.H.*, LVII, ii, 3. See, P. Fabia, "L'avénement officiel de Tibère," *Revue Philologie*, XXXIII (1909), 28.

[16] Tacitus, *Ann.*, I, 7.

Augustus had expired.[17] His death doubtless was ordered to remove him as a pretender and to prevent disaffected elements from rallying around him to undo the succession arrangements of the late emperor. Tacitus narrates that Tiberius pretended that instructions had been left by Augustus directing the tribune, in whose custody Agrippa was held, to execute the captive as soon as he received word of the emperor's death.[18] Suetonius also mentions letters of a like tenor and expresses similar doubts as to their authenticity.[19] Although Agrippa allegedly was "innocent of virtue, and confident brute-like in his physical strength," and Augustus, by "his frequent and bitter strictures of the youth's character," had secured his banishment, Tacitus declares that "at no time did he harden his heart to the killing of a relative, and it remained incredible that he should have sacrificed the life of a grandchild in order to diminish the anxieties of a step-son." [20]

There was reason to ascribe the deed to the direct orders of Tiberius or Livia. A centurion allegedly reported to Tiberius that his orders had been carried out, whereupon the emperor disavowed responsibility and declared that a report would have to be made to the Senate.[21] No action, however, was initiated before the Fathers. Tacitus claims that Sallustius Crispus, "a partner in the imperial secrets," feared that he would be involved and urged Livia to use her influence with her son to prevent him from carrying out his intention of reporting the affair to the Senate.[22] Tacitus, an unfriendly witness, brings out this point in further disparagement of Livia and Tiberius; yet the log-

---

[17] Suetonius, *Tib.*, XXII; Dio, *R.H.*, LVII, iii, 5; Tacitus, *Ann.*, I, 6.
[18] Tacitus, *Ann.*, I, 6.
[19] Suetonius, *Tib.*, XXII. Dio, *R.H.*, LVII, iii, 5–6, states that there were some who believed that Augustus had ordered the execution of Agrippa.
[20] Tacitus, *Ann.*, I, 6. [21] *Ibid.*; Suetonius, *Tib.*, XXII.
[22] Tacitus, *Ann.*, I, 6.

ical inference seems to be that Tiberius seriously contemplated the inauguration of senatorial action in the case, and this fact would tend to exculpate him from personal responsibility for the execution. The execution doubtless was impelled primarily by the desire to safeguard the new regime. It is hardly likely that either Tiberius or Livia would have shrunk from the issue of an order for the removal of one so potentially dangerous to them, even if no instructions to this effect had been left by the late *princeps*. Rumors of the alleged reconciliation of Augustus with his grandson made the threat all the greater. Since Tiberius apparently was sincere in his desire to secure senatorial investigation of the affair, Livia's guilt seems more strongly indicated.[23]

[23] G. R. Sievers, *Studien zur Geschichte der Römischen Kaiser: Tacitus und Tiberius* (Berlin, 1871), 14–15; A. Spengel, "Zur Geschichte des Kaisers Tiberius," *Sitzungsberichte der philos.-philog. und historische Klasse der K. Bayerische Akademie der Wissenschaft* (Munich, 1904), 11, maintains that Livia and Sallustius naturally did not want an investigation because they were guilty. See, L. Freytag, *Tiberius und Tacitus* (Berlin, 1870), 57–58; W. Ihne, *Zur Ehrenrettung des Kaisers Tiberius* (Strassburg, 1892), 11; V. Gardthausen, *Augustus und seine Zeit*, 2 vols. in 6 (Leipzig, 1904), Vol. I, Pt. III, 1251–53, 1270. W. Willrich, *Livia* (Leipzig, 1911), 35, thinks that Crispus would not have acted on Livia's orders. He holds that Augustus ordered the execution for the good of the state. B. R. Motzo, "I commentari di Agrippina madre di Nerone," *Studi di Storia e Filologia*, I (1927), 28, 31, argues that Tacitus' account is based on the memoirs of Agrippina the Younger and, therefore, accuses Tiberius and Livia. There was no mention of Agrippa in Augustus' will. Even if a reconciliation had taken place Augustus never would have permitted Agrippa's accession to the throne. C. C. Barini, "La tradizione superstite ed alcuni giudizi dei moderni su Livia," *Rendiconti della R. Accademia Nazionale dei Lincei*, Series V, Vol. XXXI (1922), 29–30. Arguments that Crispus ordered the execution on his own responsibility are most fully summarized in J. Ritter, *Die taciteische Charakterzeichnung des Tiberius* (Rudolstadt, 1895), 5. M. P. Charlesworth, "Tiberius and the Death of Augustus," *American Journal of Philology*, XLIV (1923), 145–57, holds that there was no reconciliation with Agrippa. He points out that there is reason to doubt that the visit to Planasia was made because it hardly could have been accomplished without the knowledge of Livia. C. Sallustius Crispus was the grandnephew and adopted son

THE ACCESSION OF TIBERIUS

Fears that Agrippa was dangerous to the new regime were well founded. Clemens, Agrippa's faithful slave, vainly attempted to rescue his master when he learned of Augustus' death. He planned to spirit him to the legions in Germany which he hoped could be induced to support Agrippa's candidacy for the throne. Before he reached Planasia, however, Agrippa was slain.[24]

Two years later Clemens caused reports to be circulated that Agrippa was still alive, and he appeared in a number of places posing as his former master. Ultimately he dared to appear at Ostia, where he was welcomed by a great crowd, and he covertly visited Rome on several occasions while the capital buzzed with excitement. Tiberius hesitated to employ the soldiery to suppress the plot of a mere slave. He finally sent Crispus and several trusted men-at-arms to the usurper to whom they represented themselves as secret supporters. An opportune moment finally arrived for them to have the pretender seized and taken before the emperor, who ordered his secret execution.[25] The fact that a usurper, posing as Agrippa, could secure a following two years after Tiberius' elevation is an indication that the emperor's position might have been precarious had Agrippa succeeded in reaching the legions in the fall of 14.

Augustus' body had been brought from Nola to the capital. The foremost men of each city through which the cortege had passed had borne the bier with all respect and honor. Because of the heat, travel had been confined to night-time, and the body had reposed in temples during the day. At Bovillae, near Rome, the procession had been met by the *equites*, and the day after the arrival of the

---

of the historian Sallust. Although he enjoyed the friendship of Maecenas and Augustus he did not attain senatorial rank. See, Tacitus, *Ann.*, III, 30; Horace, *Odes*, II, 2.

[24] Tacitus, *Ann.*, II, 39.   [25] *Ibid.*, 40.

procession in Rome the Senate met to make the funeral arrangements.[26] Tiberius called the Senate session by virtue of his tribunician powers in a terse edict characterized by moderation of expression.[27] His tribunician power was a vital point, for it was this that had enabled him to take many of the measures that had been carried out since Augustus' death.[28]

The late emperor's will was brought before the Senate by the Vestal Virgins. It was read by an imperial freedman, after witnesses to the document, all of senatorial rank, had acknowledged the authenticity of their seals.[29] Two thirds of Augustus' estate was bequeathed to Tiberius, and one third was assigned to Livia who was adopted into the Julian *gens* and honored with the name of Augusta. Legatees in the second degree were the grandchildren and great-grandchildren; since Agrippa's death, of course, no grandchildren survived save Agrippina, wife of Germanicus. A number of prominent nobles also received legacies, and Tacitus charges that the emperor's bounty toward them was designed to secure the "applause of posterity," for he actually had "detested most of them." [30]

[26] Suetonius, *Augustus*, C; Dio, *R.H.*, LVI, xxvi–xxxv. See, T. Mommsen, *Römisches Staatsrecht*, 3 vols. (Leipzig, 1877), Vol. I, Pt. III, 263.

[27] Tacitus, *Ann.*, I, 7; Suetonius, *Tib.*, XXIII. J. Kromayer, *Die rechtliche Begründung des Principats* (Marburg, 1888), 40, considers the convocation of the Senate an unwarranted use of tribunician powers.

[28] Dieckmann, "Die effective Mitregenschaft des Tiberius," in *loc. cit.*, 352 ff. Hammond, *The Augustan Principate*, 78, states that "The value of the tribunician power lies rather in its sentimental association than its practical usefulness." Yet he points out that a tribune could veto any act of the Senate or a magistrate, annul judicial sentences, consult Senate and *populus*, exercise the power of *coercitio*, and enjoy inviolability by virtue of his office. The importance of the tribunician power is further proved by Tiberius' practice of dating the years of his reign by the years of his tribunician power. *C.I.L.*, II, 2037, 2062, 2181; III, 2972; VI, 903; X^1, 207, 1414; X^2, 8088; XI, 2647, 3782, 3784, 3786; XIII, 1036, 4481; XIV, 2592, 2910b, 2911, 3488, 4086.

[29] Tacitus, *Ann.*, I, 7; Suetonius, *Tib.*, XXIII. [30] Tacitus, *Ann.*, I, 7.

THE ACCESSION OF TIBERIUS

Special bequests were not above the customary civic scale. A total of 43,500,000 *sesterces* was allocated. Each member of the praetorian cohorts received 1000 *sesterces*. Half that sum was given to each man of the urban troops, while the legionaries and members of the Roman cohorts received 300.[31] Heirs whose estates had been held in trust by the late emperor were paid in full.[32]

Reading of the will was followed by the submission of Augustus' instructions for his funeral. The *Res Gestae Divi Augusti*, a summation of his reign, was then presented.[33] A third document was a comprehensive report as to the state of the empire, with information in regard to the number of troops under arms, the number of fleets, and the strength of the allies.[34] The state of the provinces and protectorates received adequate attention, and a full financial report was included. The fourth document submitted to the Fathers contained admonitions to Tiberius and to the Roman state. Manumission of slaves was discouraged, as was further extension of the citizenship. Augustus also advised that public business be entrusted to all who had the ability to understand and transact it rather than that it be permitted to fall into the hands of one person. The document closed with advice to refrain from attempts to expand the territories under the control of Rome.[35]

---

[31] *Ibid.*, 8. For description of urban troops, see, *ibid.*, IV, 5.
[32] Tacitus, *Ann.*, I, 8.   [33] Dio, *R.H.*, LVI, xxxiii, 2.
[34] *Ibid.* Tacitus, *Ann.*, I, 11, implies that this report was read later.
[35] Dio, *R.H.*, LVI, xxxiii, 5–6. There is no justification for Tacitus, *Ann.*, I, 11, to imply that this advice was founded on fear or jealousy. It may well be that this document was an appendix of the third. Fabia, "L'avénement officiel de Tibère," in *loc. cit.*, 33. See, T. Mommsen, "Der Rechenschaftsbericht des Augustus," *Historische Zeitschrift*, LVII (1887), 390; Hohl, "Wann hat Tiberius das Principat übernommen?" in *loc. cit.*, 113. Tacitus' famous summary of the reign of Augustus, *Ann.*, I, 4–6, 9–10, includes an account of coincidences in the life of the late emperor, a list of favorable comments, and a num-

Discussion of honors to be paid to Augustus followed the reading of these documents. Asinius Gallus proposed that the funeral train should pass under a triumphal gateway. Lucius Arruntius suggested that the mortuary couch should be preceded by titles of the laws, the passage of which the late emperor had secured, as well as the names of peoples he had conquered. Senators offered to carry the body to the pyre on their shoulders, but Tiberius, "with haughty moderation," excused them from that duty. He also issued an edict warning the people not to indulge in the excesses that had marked the funeral of Julius Caesar by demands that the cremation should take place in the Forum rather than in the *Campus Martius*.[36]

The funeral ceremonies were carried out in accordance with senatorial decisions. On top of the ivory and gold couch, which contained the coffin, rested an image of the deceased in triumphal garb. Another image was borne from the palace by high officials, while a gold likeness was carried from the Senate House. Tiberius delivered the eulogy,[37] but, according to Suetonius, "suddenly groaned aloud, as if overcome by grief, and with the wish that not only his voice but his life as well might leave him, handed the written speech to his son Drusus to finish." [38] After priests, knights, and soldiers had paid their last respects around the bier in the *Campus Martius*, centurions lighted the funeral pyre with torches. Livia remained on the site for five days, after which she gathered

---

ber of adverse criticisms. Most of the comment is based on historic fact, as shown by comparison with the *Monumentum Ancyranum*. The adverse criticisms, however, are colored by the historian's prejudices against Tiberius. L. E. Lord, "Note on Tacitus' Summary of the Reign of Augustus," *Classical Review*, XLI (1927), 41.

[36] Tacitus, *Ann.*, I, 8.
[37] Dio, *R.H.*, LVI, xxxv–xliii. The text is, of course, apocryphal.
[38] Suetonius, *Tib.*, XXIII.

up the ashes and placed them in the mausoleum.³⁹ Danger of disorder seems to have been imminent, but the observation of Tacitus that "an aged prince, a veteran potentate, who had seen to it that not even his heirs should lack means to coerce their country, must needs have military protection to ensure a peaceable burial" seems to be a malicious exaggeration.⁴⁰

Augustus was deified on September 17, and priests and sacred rites were assigned.⁴¹ A shrine, subsequently built by Tiberius and Livia, was voted to his cult in Rome, and many municipalities paid similar honors. Livia, already honored by the names of Julia and Augusta, was made high priestess of the cult.⁴² It was further proposed that she be called "Mother of the Country," and that Tiberius be named "Son of Julia," but he forbade the employment of these titles on the grounds that "official compliments to women should be kept in bounds." He likewise refused

---

³⁹ Dio, *R.H.*, LVI, xlii, 4. For the significance of the various parts of the ceremonies, see, E. Bickermann, "Die Römische Kaiserapothéose," *Archiv für Religionswissenschaft*, XXVII (1929), 8–9, 12.

⁴⁰ Tacitus, *Ann.*, I, 8. See, Ritter, *Die taciteische Charakterzeichnung des Tiberius*, 6–7.

⁴¹ Augustus was considered to have been "the perfect and absolute expression of humanity—a man par excellence who attained his divine majesty by his dignity and the immensity of his creative work." M. St. Poplawski, "L'apothéose de Sylla et d'Auguste," *Eos*, XXX (1927), 329. The *Victoria Augusti*, responsible for his success and the establishment of the empire, was eternal. J. Gagé, "La Victoria Augusti et les auspices de Tiberè," *Revue Archéologique*, XXXII (1929), 1–2.

⁴² Dio, *R.H.*, LVI, xlvi, 1–2. Vows were taken in her name, and her birthday was honored. She enjoyed the rights of a Vestal Virgin. She could make a will, testify in the courts, give games, award dowries to young girls, own slaves, and pay for public works in provincial towns. F. Sandels, *Die Stellung der Kaiserlichen Frauen aus dem Julische-Claudischen Hause* (Darmstadt, 1912), 42–49, 67–70. The third day of the annual eight-day ceremonies at Gythion, in Laconia, was devoted to "Julia, fortune of our nation and of our town." M. Rostovtzeff, "L'empereur Tiberè et le culte impérial," *Revue Historique*, CLXIII (1930), 4–5. See, *Année épigraphique, 1929*, 99, 100. For a survey of her enormous properties, see, Willrich, *Livia*, 71–75.

to permit Livia to have a lictor,[43] although she probably was so attended while performing her official duties.[44]

Tiberius doubtless resented Livia's position; yet she strengthened his own legitimacy. The action of the Senate "had decided the future and in large measure the form of the imperial cult. By the conservation of the founder it assured a divine prestige for the imperial institution; indeed, it prolonged the human work of Augustus. . . . The *Divus Augustus* had all the elements of a posthumus reign." Henceforth, the important factor in the early imperial period was not the Julian *gens*, but the house of Augustus. "Across the intrigues of palace and praetorians it seems as though a tacit law from Tiberius to Nero regularly devolved the empire to the nearest or most capable relative of the house of Augustus." [45] Tiberius refused to

[43] Tacitus, *Ann.*, I, 14. There are many inscriptions in which Livia is entitled "Mother of Tiberius," or "Mother of Augustus." Most of them are listed in C. A. Holtzhausser, *An Epigraphic Commentary on Suetonius' Life of Tiberius* (Philadelphia, 1918), 39.

[44] Dio, *R.H.*, LVI, xlvi, 2. In all the succession arrangements the title of Augustus was held only by Octavian. The name emphasized his unique position. F. Haverfield, "The Name Augustus," *Journal of Roman Studies*, V (1915), 249-50. The grant of the Augustan title to Livia was significant, but Tiberius prevented her from exercising any material influence in governmental affairs. Kornemann, *Doppelprinzipat und Reichsteilung im Imperium Romanum*, 36-40. See, *id.*, "Neues von Kaiser Tiberius," *Forschungen und Fortschritte*, V (1929), 342. See, *Inscriptiones Graecae ad Res Romanas Pertinentes*, III, 1344, and *Année épigraphique*, *1927*, 158, for joint dedications to Tiberius and Livia.

[45] J. Gagé, "Divus Augustus," *Revue Archéologique*, XXXIV (1931), 13-14. Coins were issued in a number of cities, including Sardis, Mitylene, and Magnesia, bearing the figures of *Pietas* and *Salus* with the features of Livia. Special funerary coins, bearing her likeness and her title of Augusta, also were struck. V. Kahrstedt, "Frauen auf antiken Münzen," *Klio*, X (1910), 293. A coin minted at Rome in A.D. 22-23 shows that Livia was honored by the right to ride in a *carpentum*. Other Roman mintings show her as *Salus Augusta* and priestess of the Augustan cult. H. Mattingly, *Coins of the Roman Empire in the British Museum*, 2 vols. (London, 1923), I, xxxv-xxxvii. For the procedure in the deification ceremonies, see, Bickermann, "Die Römische Kaiserapothéose," in *loc. cit.*, 8-9, 15-16. W. S. Ferguson, "Legalized Ab-

take the title of *Augustus,* for he did not wish to be considered divine in his relations with the Senate. Nevertheless, he employed the title in some of his correspondence with eastern rulers, and the inscriptions, including some for the West, show that the title was frequently employed. The praenomen *imperator* seldom appears in the inscriptions, and the rare appearance of the title *Pater Patriae* likewise indicates the emperor's unwillingness to accept this distinction.[46]

As we have seen, Tiberius had conducted himself as Augustus' successor. He had employed his tribunician powers and exercised command of the troops by virtue of his proconsular power. Receipt of oaths of allegiance from the consuls likewise was significant. He also procured senatorial action authorizing the dispatch of proconsular powers to Germanicus, whom apparently he had informed of Augustus' death from Nola.[47] In view of these actions, his conduct before the Senate at the session de-

---

solutism en Route from Greece to Rome," *American Historical Review,* XVIII (1913), 33, rightly points out that a primary purpose of deification was to safeguard the social and political regime established by the ruler.

[46] Tacitus, *Ann.,* I, 72; IV, 37-38; Dio, *R.H.,* LVII, viii, 1. See, K. Scott, "Tiberius' Refusal of the Title of Augustus," *Classical Philology,* XXVII (1932), 43-50. Some inscriptions in which Tiberius is called *Augustus* are these: *C.I.L.,* II, 1660, 2037, 2062, 2181; III, 2972, 3148, 3198, 3201; V, 6416; VIII, 10018, 10568; X^1, 207, 1414; X^2, 7226, 8088; XI, 2647, 3872; XIII, 1036, 4481, 4635; XIV, 2592, 2911, 3448, 3943a, 4635. Most of the milestones from Spain and *Gallia Narbonensis* likewise include the title. The praenomen *imperator* appears in *C.I.L.,* III, 8512, 10918; VIII, 685; *Année épigraphique, 1914,* 172; *1921,* 3. This title in Tiberius' reign was a military one and was not equivalent to "emperor." McFayden, *The History of the Title Imperator,* 56. The military distinction was awarded eight times, as many inscriptions point out. See, for example, *C.I.L.,* II, 1660, 2037, 2062, 2181; VI, 903; X^1, 1414; X^2, 7226, 8088; XI, 2647; XIII, 1036, 4481; XIV, 2911, 2952. The *Pater Patriae* title appears in *C.I.L.,* V, 6416; XI, 3085; *I.G.R.R.,* I, 853.

[47] Tacitus, *Ann.,* I, 14. See, Kornemann, *Doppelprinzipat und Reichsteilung im Imperium Romanum,* 14-15.

voted to the deification of Augustus on September 17, A.D. 14, has been the subject of considerable controversy.[48] According to Tacitus:

> Then all prayers were directed towards Tiberius, who delivered a variety of reflections on the greatness of the empire and his own diffidence: Only the mind of the deified Augustus was equal to such a burden: he himself had found, when called by the sovereign to share his anxieties, how arduous, how dependent upon fortune, was the task of ruling a world! He thought, then, that in a state which had the support of so many eminent men, they ought not to devolve the entire duties on any one person; the business of government would be more easily carried out by the joint efforts of a number. A speech in this tenor was more dignified than convincing. Besides, the diction of Tiberius, by habit or by nature, was always indirect and obscure; even when he had no wish to conceal his thought; and now, in the effort to bury every trace of his sentiments, it became more intricate, uncertain, and equivocal than ever. But the Fathers, whose one dread was that they might seem to comprehend him, melted in plaints, tears, and prayers. They were stretching their hands to heaven, to the effigy of Augustus, to his own knees.[49]

[48] A. Lang, *Beiträge zur Geschichte des Kaisers Tiberius* (Jena, 1911), 22-26, believes that there were three Senate sessions. The first was devoted to the discussion of funeral arrangements; the second to the deification of Augustus; the third, at which the Senate's offer of the throne was met by Tiberius' apparent refusal, was held late in September, or early in October, after the suppression of the mutiny of the legions. Hohl, "Wann hat Tiberius das Principat übernommen?" in *loc. cit.*, 106-107, has, in my opinion, successfully refuted these views. The apotheosis ceremonies were held on September 17. The *iustitium*, or public mourning period during which no sessions could be held, ended with the deposit of Augustus' ashes in the mausoleum on September 16. Mommsen, *Staatsrecht*, Vol. I, Pt. III, 263. Five days elapsed between the cremation and the gathering of the ashes for entombment. The session devoted to the discussion of last honors to Augustus could not have taken place before September 11. Hohl, "Wann hat Tiberius das Principat übernommen?" in *loc. cit.*, 104-108.

[49] Tacitus, *Ann.*, I, 11.

THE ACCESSION OF TIBERIUS 25

The account of Suetonius is basically the same. He informs us:

> Though Tiberius did not hesitate at once to assume and to exercise the imperial authority, surrounding himself with a guard of soldiers, that is with the actual power and the outward sign of sovereignty, yet he refused the title for a long time, with barefaced hypocrisy now upbraiding his friends who urged him to accept it, saying that they did not realize what a monster the empire was, and now by evasive answers and calculating hesitancy keeping the senators in suspense when they implored him to yield, and fell at his feet.[50]

Both Tacitus and Suetonius accuse Tiberius of hypocrisy in this renunciation. His position doubtless was critical, and his misgivings seem to have been abundantly justified; indeed he was "holding a wolf by the ears," as Suetonius alleges he observed.[51] Clemens, a former slave of Agrippa, apparently had organized a revolt to avenge his slain master.[52] Germanicus had been adopted by Ti-

---

[50] Suetonius, *Tib.*, XXIV.

[51] *Ibid.* Lang, *Beiträge zur Gesch. des Kaisers Tiberius*, 22, believes that the throne was first offered to Tiberius by the Senate at the session devoted to the funeral plans.

[52] Suetonius, *Tib.*, XXV. This could have been serious if Clemens, posing as Agrippa, could have reached the Rhine legions. Freytag, *Tiberius und Tacitus*, 117. Suetonius, *Tib.*, XXXV, declares that one of the causes of Tiberius' hesitation was the plot of Lucius Scribonius Libo. This is described in detail by Tacitus, *Ann.*, II, 27-32, but not in connection with the question of the acceptance of the throne. The plot probably was not fomented until late in the year 15. W. Schott, *Die Kriminaljustiz unter dem Kaiser Tiberius* (Erlangen, 1893), 25-26. In any event, it was not as dangerous as Freytag considered it. See, A. von Domaszewski, *Geschichte der römischen Kaiser*, 2 vols. (Leipzig, 1909), I, 277-78. No widespread support was secured. Marsh, *Reign of Tiberius*, 58. Yet "there could not fail to be an opposition of a personal nature, contemplating not so much to attack the imperial throne as to overthrow the person of the prince." V. Strazzulla, "Il processo di Libone Druso," *Rivista di Storia Antica*, XII (1908), 69. "Tacitus, in telling of attempts at republican reaction on the part of some patricians under Augustus and his immediate successor, and in referring to the invectives which some senators directed against the

berius at the express orders of Augustus, and, moreover, he was married to Agrippina, granddaughter of the former emperor.[53]

There was some reason to fear that Germanicus, "backed by so many legions, the vast reserves of the provinces, and a wonderful popularity with the country, might prefer the ownership to the reversion of a throne."[54] There is, however, no evidence that hostility existed between Germanicus and Tiberius, nor can the charge that Germanicus feared Tiberius and Livia be substantiated.[55] The promptness with which Tiberius sent proconsular powers to his nephew, however, probably was at least partially dictated by the desire to ensure his continued good will. A dangerous mutiny of the legions in Pannonia and along the Rhine broke out; this disturbance may have begun sufficiently early to serve as a cause of the apparent hesitancy of Tiberius,[56] but it was not an evidence of the hostility of the legions to his elevation.[57]

It must be remembered that Augustus had gone through two ceremonies of abdication, or simulated abdication, each of which had been followed by prompt senatorial

---

representatives or even the person of the emperor, indeed evaded splendid opportunities to mirror the importance and extent of that anti-Caesarinian propaganda." V. Casagrandi, "Germanico Cesare secondo la mente di Tacito," *Storia e Archeologia Romana* (Genoa, 1886), 171.

[53] This was a factor of great importance. A. Viertel, *Tiberius und Germanicus* (Göttingen, 1901), 4. Drusus was not born before the legal marriage of Augustus and Livia. J. Carcopino, "Le mariage d'Octave et de Livie," *Revue Historique*, CLXI (1929), 225 ff.

[54] Tacitus, *Ann.*, I, 7; Suetonius, *Tib.*, XXV; Dio, *R.H.*, LVII, iii, 1. C. Ferber, *Utrum metuerit Tiberius Germanicum necne quaeritur* (Hamburg, 1890), 7–9, makes much of the alleged danger. Cf., Freytag, *Tiberius und Tacitus*, 63.

[55] W. Liebenam, "Zur Tradition über Germanicus," *Jahrbücher für classische Philologie*, CXLIII (1891), 720–22; H. Willenbücher, *Tiberius und die Verschwörung des Sejans* (Gutersloh, 1896), 4.

[56] Suetonius, *Tib.*, XXV.   [57] *Infra*, 36–39.

investment with important powers enabling him to continue the appearance that a "dyarchy" existed, while at the same time retaining in his own hands the indispensable proconsular and tribunician powers. The most superficial study of the reign of Tiberius shows his strong reliance on precedents established by his predecessor, and it doubtless would have greatly strengthened his position to be "regarded as the called and chosen of the state rather than as the interloper who had wormed his way to power with the help of connubial intrigues and a senile act of adoption." [58]

The emperor's authority at best was "ill-defined and uncertain, rendered indeed more powerful by its obscurity." [59] Legitimacy seemed to demand investment with powers by the Senate, but just how was this to be brought about? There was, after all, no clearly established succession procedure. Caesar and Octavian in reality had been raised to power by their soldiery, and their positions subsequently had secured nominal senatorial ratification. This, however, was a time of peace, and the Senate thus was called upon to act in behalf of the Roman people, theoretically the ultimate source of authority.[60]

[58] Tacitus, *Ann.*, I, 7.
[59] J. Boissier, *L'opposition sous les Césars* (Paris, 1875), 68.
[60] Sievers, *Studien zur Gesch. der Röm. Kaiser: Tacitus und Tiberius*, 50–51. "Only from the hands of the Senate and people, and in response to the pressing appeals of the highest body, did the succession to the extraordinary office of Augustus secure legitimacy." O. T. Schulz, "Das Wesen des römischen Kaisertums der ersten zwei Jahrhunderte," *Studien zur Geschichte und Kultur des Altertums*, Vol. VIII, Pt. II (1916), 34. "If, at the death of Augustus, the Senate, the magistrates, and the army refused the oath of fidelity to the designated successor they were entitled to do so, and thus the continued existence of the new regime would be questioned." Gardthausen, *Augustus und seine Zeit*, Vol. I, Pt. III, 1261. "Augustus had assumed the guidance of the state because it found itself in a precarious position from which only an extraordinary man could deliver it; he continued in power at the request of the Senate.... With Augustus dead, according to this fiction, the empire was at an end." O. Seeck, *Kaiser Augustus* (Leip-

Tiberius doubtless realized the difficulty of inaugurating a new regime when there was every likelihood that any mistake would subject him to disparaging comparison with Augustus, and that every success would be attributed to the policies and counsels of his illustrious predecessor. Then, too, the apparent renunciation of the imperial power certainly gave him an opportunity to measure the strength of the opposition and to identify its potential leaders.[61]

There is no reason to credit the claim that Tiberius wished to renounce the rule of the empire because of his age, since he was only fifty-six and virtually in full possession of his physical and mental powers. Failing eyesight hardly could have been serious enough to impel such a step, in view of his activities preceding the death of Augustus and of his subsequent career.[62] To be sure, he was not a ready speaker,[63] but there is little evidence to support Tacitus' charge that he was habitually vacillating.[64]

---

zig, 1902), 119. "History shows that in the administration and the management of public business the part of the prince was preponderant, and upon its personal character depended, in substance, the power of the Senate." L. Cantarelli, "La diarchia Romana," *Studi Romani e Bizantini* (Rome, 1915), 183. L. Hahn, *Das Kaisertum: Das Erbe der Alten*, 6 vols. (Leipzig, 1913), VI, 5, likens the *princeps* to a Greek tyrant whose primary function, he holds, was to protect the masses against plutocracy. See also, Kornemann, "Die Römische Kaiserzeit," in Gercke and Norden (eds.), *Einleitung in der Altertumswissenschaft*, in *loc. cit.*, III, 214–15, 277.

[61] V. Casagrandi, "Il partito dell'opposizione repubblicana sotto Tiberio," *Storia e Archeologia Romana* (Genoa, 1886), 187. See, Dio, *R.H.*, LVII, iii, 3.

[62] Dio, *R.H.*, LVII, ii, 4. J. Bergmans, *Die Quellen der Vita Tiberii (Buch 57 der Historia Romana) des Cassius Dio* (Heidelberg, 1903), 21, thinks Dio's statements are attributable to misreading of Suetonius, *Tib.*, XXIV, or Suetonius' source.

[63] Tacitus, *Ann.*, I, 11.

[64] *Ibid.* C. Merivale, *History of the Romans under the Empire*, 8 vols. (London, 1865), V, 132, thinks Tiberius lacked confidence in himself. See, H. Hentig, "Über den Cäsarenwahnsinn die Krankheit

Disinclination to accept the burdens of sovereignty might well have been sincere. His withdrawal to Rhodes,[65] while dictated primarily by the desire to avoid the impossible situation created by the births of Gaius and Lucius, also was motivated to some degree by his wish to free himself from the cares, the incessant intrigues, and the arduous labors incident to his position at the imperial court. Toward the close of his life he again left Rome to live in virtual seclusion at Capri.[66] "He had a right to seek repose. Eighteen years of unflagging industry, the fatigues and arduous labor of many campaigns in the most distant parts of the empire, misery and soul-searing sorrow in the most intimate relations of family life, the loss of his brother, and the gathering attack of the hostile members of the ruling family had weakened his strength, bent his spirit, and filled his heart with bitterness." [67]

The pleas of the Senate continued unabated. Close reading of the texts of Tacitus and Suetonius shows that "Tiberius never committed the mistake of categorically refusing, even for effect, all participation in the imperial power. What was the good of running the risk, as little as it was, of being taken at his word?" [68] He already had gone too far in the exercise of ruling authority to withdraw.[69] Up to this point, while the Senate presumably had importuned him to accept the imperial position, it had made no proposal that would impart the appearance of constitutional legitimacy comparable with that enjoyed by Augustus.[70]

---

des Kaisers Tiberius," *Grenzfragen des Nerven und Seelenlebens*, CXIX (1924), 32–33, for an attempt to psychoanalyze Tiberius and account for his "irresolution."
[65] *Infra*, 7–8.
[66] Lang, *Beiträge zur Gesch. des Kaisers Tiberius*, 23.
[67] A. Stahr, *Tiberius* (Berlin, 1863), 23.
[68] Fabia, "L'avénement officiel de Tiberè," in *loc. cit.*, 30–31.
[69] *Ibid.*   [70] F. Abraham, *Tiberius und Sejan* (Berlin, 1888), 9.

Tiberius then suggested his willingness to rule in conjunction with colleagues.[71] When nothing came of this proposal he broached the prospect of partition of the empire. He observed that "unequal as he felt himself to the whole weight of government, he would still undertake the charge of any one department that might be assigned to him." [72] It will be remembered that the admonitions of Augustus, read before the Senate, had advised against concentration of authority in the hands of one person. This, of course, would have given Tiberius adequate reason to suggest the selection of colleagues or the partition of the empire.[73] It would seem likely that the precepts of the late emperor were read along with the other documents submitted to the Fathers. Tacitus, however, declares that the reading of the report on the state of the empire and the admonitions were a prelude to Tiberius' offer to assume control of part of the empire.[74] If this is correct, the transition from his ostensible refusal to assume power to his expression of willingness to accept a share of responsibility would have been smoothed.[75]

Dio reports details of the partition plan under the terms of which the empire was to be divided into three parts. One portion was to embrace Rome and Italy; the second part was to include the provinces and the command of

---

[71] Suetonius, *Tib.*, XXV.

[72] Tacitus, *Ann.*, I, 12; Suetonius, *Tib.*, XXIV. Lang, *Beiträge zur Gesch. des Kaisers Tiberius*, 22, believes that these proposals came with the reopening of the discussion of Tiberius' position begun at the funerary session. L. Levy, *Quo modo Tiberius Claudius Nero erga senatum se gesserit* (Paris, 1901), 26, 33, 34–35, thinks Tiberius really wanted to share his powers with the Senate, hence his proposal for division. Perhaps he had in mind a commission of senators such as had served as an advisory council in the last years of Augustus' reign.

[73] W. Pfitzner, *Das Verhalten des Tiberius im Senate bei der Uebernahme der Herrschaft* (Parchim, 1877), 11.

[74] Tacitus, *Ann.*, I, 11.

[75] Fabia, "L'avénement officiel de Tiberè," in *loc. cit.*, 34–35.

THE ACCESSION OF TIBERIUS   31

the legions; and the third portion was to comprise control of subject peoples and vassal kingdoms.[76]

Matters came to a head when Asinius Gallus suddenly asked Tiberius which portion he wished for himself. Tiberius apparently was surprised that his suggestions for partition met with a disposition to carry out such a plan, and for a moment he was at a loss to frame a suitable reply.[77] He finally pointed out the impropriety of accepting any part of the ruling authority which he was resolved to renounce in its entirety. Gallus perceived that he had given offense, and hastily claimed that his question was intended merely to emphasize the unity and indivisibility of the empire. To this statement he added praise of the reign of Augustus and exhorted Tiberius to live up to his predecessor's glorious achievements and to the splendid record he had thus far made for himself. Tiberius was not mollified. He had several reasons for hating Gallus. In the first place, the senator had married Vipsania, the beloved wife Tiberius had been forced to divorce at the behest of Augustus to pave the way for his marriage to the worthless Julia. Aside from the jealousy engendered in view of his continued love for Vipsania, Tiberius regarded Gallus' marriage to her as presumptuous.[78]

Lucius Arruntius likewise compromised himself by speaking along the same lines as Gallus. Tacitus describes

---

[76] Dio, *R.H.*, LVII, ii, 5. Hohl, "Wann hat Tiberius das Principat übernommen?" in *loc. cit.*, 114–15, rejects this version. Bergmans, *Die Quellen der Vita Tiberii*, 23, labels the statement of Dio as a "foolish" identification of the constitutional divisions of the empire with Tiberius' proposal for sharing the ruling power.

[77] Tacitus, *Ann.*, I, 12; Suetonius, *Tib.*, XXIV; Dio, *R.H.*, LVII, ii, 6. Fabia, "L'avénement officiel de Tiberè," in *loc. cit.*, 37, thinks that Gallus was sincerely trying to bring matters to a successful issue. E. Bunting, "The Stoic Opposition to the Principate as Seen in Tacitus," (Ph.D. Dissertation, Yale, 1932), 134–37, points out that the opposition was not concerted and was not attributable to Stoic ideals.

[78] Tacitus, *Ann.*, I, 12; Dio, *R.H.*, LVII, ii, 7.

him as "rich, enterprising, greatly gifted and correspondingly popular, and so suspect." He states further that Augustus, in discussing possible successors, once had remarked that while Asinius Gallus was eager for power, he was unfit to receive or exercise it. Arruntius, on the other hand, he had judged "not undeserving, and bold enough to venture should occasion arise." [79] It is perhaps of some significance that Germanicus was not mentioned as a possible contender who would challenge the position of the new regime.[80] Tacitus' accusation that those who displeased Tiberius on this occasion "were soon entrapped on one charge or another, prompted by Tiberius," is palpably false.[81]

The awkward discussion, which had almost reached the stage of altercation, continued. Quintus Haterius said, "How long, Caesar, will you permit the state to lack a head?" Mamercus Scaurus observed that since Tiberius thus far had not used his tribunician power to veto consular acts there was hope "that the prayers of the Senate would not be in vain." [82] Haterius was immediately answered by Tiberius with invective, whereas the emperor's greater anger against Scaurus smoldered.[83] Scaurus had blurted out the truth in calling attention to Tiberius' possession of tribunician power, which thus far had enabled him to exercise imperial power in fact if not in theory. If Tiberius sincerely wished to renounce the rule of the empire, abdication of his tribunician powers was clearly in order.[84]

---

[79] Tacitus, *Ann.*, I, 13.
[80] Spengel, "Zur Gesch. des Kaisers Tiberius," in *loc. cit.*, 18.
[81] Tacitus, *Ann.*, I, 13. See, Freytag, *Tiberius und Tacitus*, 64–67; R. S. Rogers, "Lucius Arruntius," *Classical Philology*, XXVI (1931), 37–43. For Asinius Gallus, see, Tacitus, *Ann.*, VI, 23; for Scaurus, see, *ibid.*, 9, 29.
[82] Tacitus, *Ann.*, I, 13.   [83] *Ibid.*
[84] Fabia, "L'avénement officiel de Tiberè," in *loc. cit.*, 41. Tribunician

THE ACCESSION OF TIBERIUS 33

Suetonius describes a more defiant attitude on the part of the Senate. He alleges that one of the Fathers cried out, "Let him take it or leave it," while another voiced the taunt that "while some men were slow to carry out what they promised, Tiberius was slow in promising that which he already was doing." [85] There was doubtless considerable impatience on the part of the Senate.[86] To be sure, there was reason for the senators to doubt the sincerity of Tiberius' protestations, and the proposals for the partition of the empire and the nomination of ruling colleagues introduced the ominous note of a possible triumvirate.[87] It is difficult, however, to reconcile open manifestations of hostility with the servility of the Senate as described by Tacitus and Suetonius.

Tiberius finally agreed to accept sole ruling authority. "Wearied at last by the universal outcry, and by individual appeals, he gradually gave ground, up to the point, not of acknowledging that he assumed the sovereignty, but of ceasing to refuse and to be entreated." [88] Suetonius agrees in substance by declaring that "At last, as though on compulsion, and complaining that a wretched and burdensome slavery was being forced on him, he accepted the empire." [89] He adds the important qualification, however, that the acceptance was "in such fashion as to suggest

---

power had given Tiberius the position of coregent. Adoption was a prerequisite to succession. The first instance of coregency coupled with the promise of succession, signalized by adoption, was the adoption by Augustus of Tiberius and Agrippa Posthumus. Kornemann, *Doppelprinzipat und Reichsteilung im Imperium Romanum*, 24–28.

[85] Suetonius, *Tib.*, XXIV.

[86] Fabia, "L'avénement officiel de Tiberè," in *loc. cit.*, 46. J. Asbach, *Römisches Kaisertum und Verfassung bis auf Traian* (Cologne, 1896), 12, dismisses the whole procedure as a farce.

[87] Lang, *Beiträge zur Gesch. des Kaisers Tiberius*, 22. O. Kuntz, *Tiberius and the Roman Constitution* (Seattle, 1924), sees evidence of strife between "imperialists and irreconciliables." She believes that Tiberius sincerely desired to restore the Republic.

[88] Tacitus, *Ann.*, I, 13.   [89] Suetonius, *Tib.*, XXIV.

the hope that he would one day lay it down. His own words were 'Until I come to the time when it may seem right to you to grant an old man some repose.' " [90]

Tiberius thus accepted the imperial position with the appearance of deferring to the wishes of the Senate—certainly a major objective of his conduct from the beginning. It is quite likely that his acceptance was made conditional upon a reservation that he would be permitted to retire at some future time. This reservation introduced at least a semblance of time limitation on the powers he was exercising, and, at the same time, facilitated the transition from his initial refusal to undertake the rule of the whole empire.

The emperor doubtless was in some measure guilty of hypocrisy. There is no reason to believe that he was sincere in his protestations of unwillingness to rule, for, it will be noted, he never directly offered to relinquish his tribunician powers nor his command of the troops; and these powers were the basis of the principate. The episode in the Senate was basically an attempt to repeat the abdication ceremonies of Augustus in 27 and 23. His chief objective was to make it appear that he held authority with constitutional sanction implemented by senatorial action. "His conduct, under the circumstances, was inspired by the nature and the very condition of existence of the imperial regime. The system of Augustus represented at one time a reality—the military power—and a fiction—the appearance of civil government. The policy of Tiberius

---

[90] *Ibid*. Although no definite term was fixed, the fiction inaugurated by Augustus, to the effect that the tenure of the principate was limited, was preserved. Herzog, *Gesch. und System der Röm. Staatsverfassung*, Vol. II, Pt. I, 235. Ritter, *Die taciteische Charakterzeichnung des Tiberius*, 8, suggests that Tiberius wanted to have the senators openly acknowledge that he alone was fitted to rule the empire.

THE ACCESSION OF TIBERIUS   35

at the time of his accession was a double one: to seize the realities and safeguard the appearances." [91]

[91] L. Homo, *L'empire Romain* (Paris, 1925), 31. Hohl, "Wann hat Tiberius das Principat übernommen?" in *loc. cit.*, 110, points out that the initiative really belonged to the Senate. He thinks senatorial bestowal of the title of *princeps* would have been the proper way to accord legitimacy to the new regime. Gardthausen, *Augustus und seine Zeit*, Vol. I, Pt. II, 535, rightly points out that the Senate might well have been puzzled as to just what was expected of it. O. T. Schulz, *Vom Principat zum Dominat. Das Wesen des römischen Kaisertums des dritten Jahrhunderts* (Paderborn, 1919), 10-11, insists that senatorial action was necessary to legitimate the succession from the beginning of the empire to the third century.

Chapter II

THE MUTINY OF A.D. 14

Augustus' death submitted the regime he had established to a severe test. The promptness of Tiberius' actions, based on the tribunician powers he exercised, in large measure was responsible for the frustration of possible efforts to reopen the succession issue. Opposition to Tiberius there doubtless was, and the Senate certainly had done little to facilitate the new emperor's attempts to comply with what he properly regarded as necessary constitutional amenities. Much more formidable, however, was the mutiny of the legions that followed the emperor's accession.

News of Augustus' death and his successor's accession was the immediate cause of the outbreak of dangerous rebellions among the legions in Pannonia and along the Rhine. These uprisings were not manifestations of opposition on the part of the soldiery to the advent of the new regime. The grievances that precipitated the rebellions were of long standing, and the discontented soldiers naturally hoped that the elevation of a new emperor would present an opportunity to demand concessions.[1]

The Pannonian legions were the first to revolt. Three

---

[1] Tacitus, *Ann.*, I, 16; Dio, *R.H.*, LVII, iv. Gardthausen, *Augustus und seine Zeit*, Vol. I, Pt. II, 532, holds that the soldiers wanted to make their allegiance to Tiberius conditional upon his compliance with their demands. Tiberius probably anticipated trouble, which accounts for his decisive and resolute conduct immediately after Augustus' death. Liebenam, "Zur Tradition über Germanicus," in *loc. cit.*, 726. See, Hohl, "Wann hat Tiberius das Principat übernommen?" in *loc. cit.*, 107. Kuntz, *Tiberius and the Roman Constitution*, 46, considers the revolt a reaction against nonexpansion policy.

THE MUTINY OF A.D. 14

legions under the command of Junius Blaesus were stationed in summer quarters when the reports of Augustus' demise arrived. Blaesus suspended the ordinary military routine in order that the late *princeps* might be mourned and Tiberius' accession might be suitably marked.[2] In the light of what ensued it was a mistake for the commander to furnish so convenient an opportunity for the voice of dissent to be heard, but any officer would have taken measures to signalize such important events in the absence of evidence of imminent mutiny.

Efforts to restore discipline and the normal routine of camp life were unsuccessful as agitators fanned the flame of discontent. A former actor named Percennius utilized his scurrilous tongue and histrionic talents to enhance the disaffection, and groups of the legionaries covertly rehearsed grievances which tended to seem progressively more insufferable.

The length of service was one of the leading grounds for complaint. Upon expiration of the twenty-year term of enlistment, the soldiers were kept under the *vexillum* as a reserve of seasoned fighting men. Theoretically the attainment of this status brought exemption from the routine work of the legions, but, according to the disgruntled soldiery, "they endured the old drudgeries under an altered name." After their discharge the former soldiers received land allotments, but they complained that they were "dragged once more to the ends of the earth to receive, under the name of a farm, some swampy morass or barren mountain side."[3]

[2] Tacitus, *Ann.*, I, 16. Q. Junius Blaesus had served as governor of Sicily and as consul. He also served as proconsul of Africa in 21-22 during the war with Tacfarinas. *Ibid.*, III, 35, 58, 73, 74; IV, 23; V, 7.
[3] *Ibid.*, I, 17. In A.D. 6 Augustus had increased the term from sixteen to twenty years. The soldiers therefore were demanding return to the old conditions of enlistment. H. M. D. Parker, *The Roman Legions* (Oxford, 1928), 212-13.

Equally vehement complaint was made in regard to the pay. The legionaries received ten *asses* per day, and out of this meager income they were required to purchase their own clothes, weapons, and tents. Then, too, experienced soldiers frequently found that it was expedient to bribe their centurions as a precaution against bullying, and that monetary payments could secure immunity from much of the fatigue duty imposed on the troops. The leaders of the mutiny therefore demanded a definite contract restricting the period of service to sixteen years and fixing the pay at one *denarius* per day.[4] The special status of the Praetorian Guard also occasioned bitter criticism. Stationed in the vicinity of the capital, where they were not called upon to face the ferocity of barbarian enemies, they received two *denarii* per day and were released from service upon the expiration of sixteen years. The harsh discipline to which the troops were subjected also played a large part in arousing the resentment that culminated in mutiny.[5] Flogging, even of officers, was common. The legionaries were beaten with rods, while auxiliaries were scourged. Tribunes, centurions, and *principes,* or labor foremen, had the right to flog the soldiers. Death by crucifixion, burning at the stake, beheading, or torture were

---

[4] Tacitus, *Ann.*, I, 17. Dio, *R.H.*, LVII, iv, summarizes the same demands. Augustus had paid 225 *denarii* to the legions per year, in three installments of 75 *denarii* each. In the late Republic the legionaries received an annual pay of 120 *denarii*, but were required to purchase their provisions. Allowing 45 *denarii* for provisions, the actual pay was 75 *denarii*, which was raised to 150 by Caesar and to 225 by Augustus. A. von Domaszewski, "Der Truppensold der Kaiserzeit," *Neue Heidelberger Jahrbücher*, X (1900), 218–23. See also, Parker, *The Roman Legions*, 76–77; Gardthausen, *Augustus und seine Zeit*, Vol. I, Pt. II, 636, for discussion of the pay question. J. Marquardt, *Römische Staatsverwaltung*, 4 vols. (Leipzig, 1881–1885), II, 95 ff., shows most clearly how payment of the praetorians in silver and the legionaries in copper aggravated the grievances of the legions.

[5] Tacitus, *Ann.*, I, 17.

the penalties inflicted on deserters and those guilty of treason.[6]

As the excitement continually mounted, the three rebellious legions virtually merged, and a mound was raised upon which to plant their standards. Blaesus vainly attempted to restore order. He declared that he was willing to perish in resisting the rioting, and that it would be a lesser crime to murder him than to continue in revolt against the emperor.[7] Ultimately the work of raising the mound was brought to a halt, and the commander was able to secure a hearing. He pointed out that the soldiers could hardly expect to secure compliance with their demands in response to mutiny and riot, and that it was particularly reprehensible to embarrass an emperor who had just succeeded to the throne by demands that they had refrained from submitting to his predecessor. Although Blaesus clearly was opposed to the demands of the soldiery, which he characterized as "claims unasserted even by the victors of civil wars," he recommended that emissaries be instructed in his presence and sent to the emperor.[8] The rebels responded by insisting upon the appointment of his son, who thereupon was instructed to ask for the discharge of the soldiers who had served sixteen years, with the understanding that their other grievances subsequently would receive attention. Upon the departure of the emissary the turmoil was allayed.[9]

[6] A. Müller, "Die Strafjustiz in römischen Heere," *Neue Jahrbücher für das klassische Altertum-Geschichte und Deutsche Literatur*, XVII (1906), 557, 563-65, 569, 570.

[7] Tacitus, *Ann.*, I, 18. Marius had given the legions separate identity, signified by their silver, later gold, eagles. The eagles, mounted on poles, were kept in the *aerarium* in Rome in time of peace, or in chapels in the camps. Preservation of its eagle was equivalent to the survival of the legion; its loss was the greatest ignominy. Parker, *The Roman Legions*, 36-42.

[8] Tacitus, *Ann.*, I, 19.   [9] *Ibid.*

The comparative quiet was short-lived. Several companies had been sent to Nauportus (Ober-Laybach) to repair roads and bridges, and upon receipt of the news of what had occurred in the summer camp they also rebelled. Their centurions were subjected to violence, and the camp-marshal (*praefectus*), particularly unpopular because he had risen from the ranks and become a stern disciplinarian, was heavily laden with baggage and was driven at the head of the column on the return march to the camp.[10]

Fresh impetus was given to the mutiny with the arrival of this contingent. Blaesus ordered the arrest and flogging of a few who had been guilty of looting, but the prisoners were rescued from the guardroom in which they had been confined.[11] Passions were further aroused when Vibulenus, a common soldier, was hoisted to the shoulders of the mob milling before Blaesus' tribunal. He charged that the gladiators whom Blaesus employed as a bodyguard had killed his brother, who, he claimed, had been sent as an emissary from the legions in Germany to arrange concerted measures of rebellion with the Pannonian troops.[12]

This dramatic accusation evoked immediate response. The gladiators were taken into custody, and a search for the body of the alleged victim was begun. Even under torture, however, the accused gladiators stanchly denied the

---

[10] *Ibid.*, 20. The prefect was usually a promoted centurion. He laid out the camp, and, with the necessary surveyors and laborers, kept it in order. He also had general supervision of the maintenance of the siege engines. Parker, *The Roman Legions*, 192. Augustus had created the position. It was particularly necessary to have such an officer, since the tribunes frequently were members of the aristocracy with little interest in military routine. H. Delbrück, *Geschichte der Kriegskunst im Rahmen der politischen Geschichte*, 2 vols. in 3 (Berlin, 1902), Vol. II, Pt. I, 166.
[11] Tacitus, *Ann.*, I, 21.
[12] *Ibid.*, 22.

murder, and eventually it was learned that Vibulenus had fabricated the whole story.

Rioting and plundering continued. The marshal and tribunes were driven from the camp, and their effects were confiscated. A centurion, hated because of the severe floggings he had meted out to the soldiers, was slain. Only one centurion was permitted to remain in camp, and he was spared because it was believed he might be employed to prosecute effectively the claims of the mutineers.[13]

Tiberius acted promptly after receipt of reports of the Pannonian outbreak. Two cohorts, as well as most of the cavalry of the Praetorian Guard, were reinforced by picked troops and a contingent of Germans. The whole force was placed under the command of Drusus, the emperor's son, whose instructions apparently gave him considerable latitude in dealing with the situation. In addition to the nobles of his staff, the young prince was accompanied by Aelius Sejanus, who was serving as a colleague of his father Seius Strabo, in command of the Praetorian Guard. Sejanus was expected to act as a trusted adviser and monitor in view of Drusus' inexperience, and the confidence thus reposed in him was an intimation of the emperor's favor that was to carry him to the pinnacle of power and ultimately to his death.[14]

No overt resistance was offered to Drusus and his troops upon their arrival at the Pannonian camp,[15] but when the prince entered the gates the mutineers posted sentries and stationed picked troops at strategic places. Drusus proceeded to the camp tribunal before which most of the rebellious troops had gathered, and he ultimately succeeded in quieting the clamor. He then read a letter from his father in which the legions were praised for their past

[13] *Ibid.*, 23.   [14] *Ibid.*, 24.   [15] *Ibid.*

campaigns, in many of which the emperor had taken part. Drusus, according to the letter, was authorized to grant such concessions as might be made without further reference to Rome. Other grievances the emperor promised to submit to the Senate for consideration.[16]

The soldiers thereupon appointed the centurion they had reserved for the purpose as their spokesman. He summarized the demands of the legionaries, but Drusus responded by insistence that such matters would have to be referred to the emperor and the Senate. An uproar greeted this plea. "Why had he come, if he was neither to raise the pay of the troops nor to ease their burdens; if, in short, he had no leave to do a kindness?" When Tiberius had been their commander, the soldiers charged, he had evaded their just requests by pleading the necessity of referring them to Augustus. Drusus was merely resorting to old stratagems to frustrate attainment of their desires. Senatorial action was not requisite to compel the soldiers to undergo punishment or the ordeal of battle; it was strange that the Fathers had to be consulted when benefits and concessions were in question.[17] This taunt was justified, for there is no evidence that the Senate had authority over the legions.

Violence again flared up when Drusus left the tribunal.

[16] *Ibid.*, 25.
[17] *Ibid.*, 26. T. H. Abele, *Der Senat unter Augustus* (Paderborn, 1907), 18-21, contends that the Senate had authority over the army. He relies primarily on Dio, *R.H.*, LIII, xi, 5; LIV, xxv, 5-6. R. S. Rogers, "Tiberius' Reversal of an Augustan Policy," *Transactions and Proceedings of the American Philological Association*, LXXI (1940), 534-35, emphasizes what he regards as the sincere intention of the emperor to submit the issues to the Senate. Such an interpretation is plausible if we acquiesce in the author's view that Tiberius was "by background and conviction a Pompeian and a Republican. His government was a Republican reaction against the Augustan regime." *Ibid.*, 536. See also, R. Syme, *The Roman Revolution* (Oxford, 1939), 344, 418, 424.

THE MUTINY OF A.D. 14

Gnaeus Lentulus, a former consul renowned for his campaign on the Danube against the Getae, was stoned by the rebels, who apparently believed that he was urging Drusus to resist their demands. He was rescued by members of Drusus' retinue. Drusus was in a precarious position. His response to the demands of the mutineers had accentuated the danger that violence would culminate in an attack on his person. The forces under his command were inadequate to combat three legions, unless some of the rebels first could be induced to return to obedience.[18]

On the night of September 26, "The moon suddenly was seen to be losing light in a clear sky. The soldiers, who had no inkling of the reason, took it as an omen of the present state of affairs: the labouring planet was an emblem of their own struggles, and their road would lead them to a happy goal if her brilliance and purity could be restored to the goddess!" [19] Superstitious fears goaded the soldiers into frenzied efforts to arrest the eclipse by shouts, trumpet blasts, and the ringing of bells, and they were terrorized when the eclipse became complete. Drusus realized that almost incredible fortune had put a powerful weapon in his hand, and trusted officers hurriedly were sent through the camp to augment the fears of the rebels. The enormity of their crime in rebelling against the emperor was stressed, as was the futility of expecting concessions to ensue. Jealousy of Percennius and Vibulenus, who had taken leading roles in the uprising, was skillfully fomented. "The leaven worked; and under the influence of their mutual suspicions they separated once more re-

---

[18] Tacitus, *Ann.*, I, 27.

[19] *Ibid.*, 28. Tacitus shows his skepticism in regard to the intervention of the gods in human affairs. R. von Pohlmann, *Die Weltanschauung des Tacitus*, 2nd ed. (Munich, 1913), 25. Cf., however, Tacitus, *Ann.*, VI, 12, 27.

cruit from veteran, legion from legion." The sentries at the gates abandoned their posts, and the standards that had been grouped on the mound raised during the course of the mutiny were restored to their proper places.[20]

At daybreak Drusus called another meeting. He insisted that he could not be intimidated, but that if the soldiers immediately returned to their duties he would write to his father to request that he "lend an indulgent ear to the prayers of the legions." [21] The soldiers begged him thus to intercede for them, and a deputation, including the younger Blaesus who had represented them before, thereupon was dispatched to Rome. Drusus' officers were not in unanimity in regard to the subsequent course to be followed. Some advised that he await the return of the deputation, keeping the troops quiet by a show of leniency; others urged immediate application of stringent measures. The prince decided in favor of the latter suggestion and ordered the execution of Vibulenus and Percennius. Their conduct during the revolt would have forfeited their lives before any military court; their execution is no proof that "Drusus had a natural bias towards severity." Other leaders of the mutiny vainly attempted to flee from the camp, only to be cut down by the expelled centurions, who had returned with Drusus to the camp, or by the praetorians. The legionaries, in an effort to expiate their guilt, handed over a number of alleged leaders for execution.[22]

Preparations then were begun to transfer the legions to winter quarters. Continuous rain and the early approach of cold weather made the change welcome to the soldiers, many of whom were still terrified by the eclipse they had witnessed. The eighth and the fifteenth legions left for

[20] Tacitus, *Ann.*, I, 28.   [21] *Ibid.*, 29.   [22] *Ibid.*

winter quarters in good order. For a time the ninth insisted upon awaiting the return of the emissaries sent to the emperor, but the departure of the other two legions virtually compelled it to follow.[23]

Drusus' conduct had been courageous and firm. Although his forces were inadequate to suppress the mutiny, he made no promises to the rebels in his first speech. The discovery that he was not authorized to deal with any of the chief grievances, coupled with the appearance of the hated praetorians, fanned the passions of the troops, and it is hard to see how disaster could have been averted if the eclipse had not terrorized the rebels as a preliminary to their submission. There is no evidence that the prince was guilty of excessive severity after the spirit of the rebels was broken. Apparently, the death penalty was inflicted only on ringleaders. Retaliation was not permitted to get out of hand; the cowed legionaries did not dare kill alleged leaders of the mutiny themselves, but handed them over to centurions and praetorians. This was in sharp contrast to scenes enacted later in the suppression of the Rhine mutiny.

The Pannonian mutiny alone was dangerous, but the gravity of the general military situation was tremendously accentuated when the Rhine legions, impelled by the same grievances, revolted about the same time. There were two armies along the Rhine in the fall of 14. The Upper Army was commanded by Gaius Silius, while the Lower was under Aulus Caecina. Germanicus, who was commander-in-chief of the entire force, was engaged in taking the census in Gaul at the time of the outbreak of the mutiny. The Upper Army did not participate in the revolt, although there was danger that it would succumb

[23] *Ibid.*, 30.

to the temptation to emulate the example of the Pannonian and Lower Rhine legions.

The twenty-first and the fifth legions in the army of Caecina took the initiative in precipitating the Rhine revolt. They were stationed in summer camp near Cologne when the news of Augustus' death arrived. Many of the soldiers were recent recruits drawn from Rome. Unaccustomed to the rigors of the camp, they yearned for the pleasures of the city, or at least for a material abatement of their hardships. No single leader arose to urge the claims of the mutinous soldiery for higher pay and the discharge of the veterans; "It was a sedition of many tongues and many voices." [24]

Caecina, overawed by the threatening mien of the troops, did not attempt to crush the rebellion. The mutineers, gathering courage, attacked the centurions, whom they threw to the ground and lashed, administering sixty strokes to each, one for every centurion in camp. The unfortunate officers, cruelly lacerated and bruised, then were thrown into the Rhine. One of them was pulled away from Caecina's feet, where he had hoped to find refuge, and slain, but another, Cassius Chaerea, saved himself by boldly drawing his sword and forcing his way through the menacing throng. The officers were impotent, and all pretense of discipline and camp routine was abandoned. The danger was aggravated by the fact that the legionaries

[24] *Ibid.*, 31. Caecina had served as consul in 6 B.C. He was governor in Moesia at the time of the great Pannonian rebellion of A.D. 6. Dio, *R.H.*, LV, xxix, 3; Velleius, *Roman History*, II, cxii, 4. For a sketch of his career, see, Pauly, Wissowa, and Kroll (eds.), *Real-Encyklopädie*, III, 1241–43. In Lower Germany, Legions I (Germanica) and XX (Valeria) were at Cologne; V (Alaudae) and XXI were at Xanten. In Upper Germany, II (Augusta) was at Strassburg; XIII (Gemina) was at Windisch, and XIV (Gemina) and XVI were at Mainz. About 80 per cent of the complements of the Rhine legions were made up of Italians at this time; virtually all the remainder came from highly Romanized *Gallia Narbonensis*. Parker, *The Roman Legions*, 176.

THE MUTINY OF A.D. 14

presented an apparently solid front, with no dissenting voices or divided counsels.[25]

Germanicus received the news of the mutiny shortly after swearing fealty to Tiberius and administering a similar oath to his officers and the people of the Belgian municipalities. He hastened to the rebellious camp, where his arrival was greeted with a flood of complaints. He ordered the troops to assemble in military formation, but was able to secure only partial and grudging compliance. When a semblance of order had been secured, he eulogized the memory of Augustus and paid tribute to Tiberius' military exploits. He further emphasized the absence of disaffection in Italy and the loyalty of the Gallic provinces.[26]

When he reproached the rebellious legions, the soldiers bared their bodies to exhibit the scars of wounds and the weals of the lash. They bitterly complained of the miserable pay and the onerous labor from which exemption could be secured only by the payment of monetary compositions. Veterans, some of whom had served in thirty or more campaigns, begged for their discharge. The rebels also indicated that if Germanicus desired the throne they were ready to support him, but the prince leaped from the rostrum lest he seem to condone treason.[27] The sol-

---

[25] Tacitus, *Ann.*, I, 32.   [26] *Ibid.*, 34.
[27] *Ibid.;* Dio, *R.H.*, LVII, v. Tacitus "builds a gripping drama as the hero saves the throne for the emperor who persecutes him." Liebenam, "Zur Tradition über Germanicus," in *loc. cit.*, 723. Tiberius did not take the offer of the throne seriously or he would have recalled Germanicus as soon as possible. *Ibid.*, 727. The centurions and tribunes did not participate in the offer, or Tacitus surely would have emphasized this. Spengel, "Zur Gesch. des Kaisers Tiberius," in *loc. cit.*, 13. Subsequent conduct of the troops certainly revealed no particular affection for Germanicus. *Ibid.*, 14. Ferber, *Utrum metuerit Tiberius Germanicum*, 11, in advocating his thesis that Tiberius feared the prince, holds that Germanicus' loyalty did not allay the emperor's misgivings, for he now had proof that the troops might support Germanicus' candidacy for the throne. Dessau, *Gesch. der röm. Kaiserzeit*, Vol. II,

diers pressed about him, however, and endeavored to force him to resume his place on the platform. He exclaimed that he would rather die than be a traitor; snatching his sword from his side, he pressed it to his breast, but his arm was held by bystanders. The suicide gesture was not effective, however, for some of the rebels urged him to drive home the blade, and one drew his own sword and offered it to Germanicus with the explanation that he would find it sharper. The incident created enough of a diversion to enable the prince and his officers ultimately to reach their tents.[28]

As the prince and his officers subsequently discussed measures to be employed, it was reported that a mission was going to be dispatched by the mutineers to secure the aid of the Upper Army. They planned to destroy Cologne and proposed to invade and pillage the Gallic provinces. Abandonment of the Rhine defenses would almost surely entail Germanic inroads. If Gallic auxiliaries were recruited and turned against the legions, civil war was inevitable. It seemed equally dangerous to employ severe measures or to treat the mutineers with indulgence. It was therefore decided to prepare a letter, ostensibly from the emperor, in which veterans of twenty years' service would be granted their discharge, and the legacies granted to the legions by Augustus would be paid in double amount.[29] This was indeed an ignominious stratagem, but, in view of the precarious position of the prince, it may have been justified as a desperate expedient to allay the re-

---

Pt. I, 9, says that Germanicus had held the destiny of the empire in his hands on this occasion. It is doubtless significant that after Germanicus' recall in 17, control of Gaul and the Rhine legions never again was vested in a single person. O. Hirschfeld, "Die Verwaltung der Rheingrenze in den ersten drei Jahrhunderten der römischen Kaiserzeit," *Kleine Schriften* (Berlin, 1913), 371.

[28] Tacitus, *Ann.*, I, 35.
[29] *Ibid.*, 36.

THE MUTINY OF A.D. 14 49

bellion for the time being, at least until the disposition of the Upper Army could be accurately ascertained.

The soldiers were not gulled by the spurious letter, but insisted upon immediate compliance with their demands. Discharges therefore were granted to the veterans, but the prince attempted to delay payment of the promised legacies until the legions moved into winter quarters. The fifth and twenty-first legions refused to move until the legacies were paid out of the money-chests of the prince and his entourage. Germanicus then was able to lead the first and twentieth legions to Cologne, while Caecina conducted the fifth and twenty-first to Xanten.[30]

Upon arrival at the camp of the Upper Army, Germanicus secured oaths of allegiance from the second, thirteenth, and sixteenth legions without demur; the fourteenth followed their example after some hesitation. The same concessions then were made to the Upper Army as had been extorted by the rebellious legions.[31]

About this time a detachment drawn from the disaffected legions for service against the "Lesser Chauci," between the Ems and the Weser, again revolted. Manius Ennius, the camp-marshal, ordered the execution of two of the leaders. His action, although extralegal, temporarily cowed the rebels. When the disorders recurred, the marshal, after vainly attempting to flee, bravely confronted his men and excoriated them for their insurrection against prince and emperor. He then turned the standards toward the Rhine and ordered the contingent to march, proclaiming that anyone who failed to heed the command would be regarded as a deserter. His audacity succeeded, and he

---

[30] Tacitus is mistaken about the identity of the legions. He says the first and the twentieth were under Caecina, whereas, of course, the fifth and the twenty-first were the ones in question. G. Kessler, *Die Tradition über Germanicus* (Berlin, 1905), 22.

[31] Tacitus, *Ann.*, I, 37.

was able to lead the disgruntled soldiers back to winter quarters.[32] The incident indicates that, had Caecina been resolute, the uprising of the Lower Army might have been quelled before it assumed such serious proportions; indeed, Germanicus, with a prompt and unflinching demonstration of authority immediately after his arrival at the mutinous camp, likewise might have been able to suppress the revolt without resort to the expedients of the bogus letter and the dangerous concessions to the demands of the troops that ensued.

In the meantime, a deputation from the Senate arrived at Cologne, where the first and twentieth legions had settled in winter quarters. The soldiers, convinced that the arrival of the senatorial mission meant the revocation of the concessions they had extorted, charged that Munatius Plancus, an ex-consul who served as chief of the legation, had initiated efforts to annul them. During the ensuing night the veterans, who were quartered in the city, rushed to the headquarters of Germanicus and compelled him, in imminent danger of death, to hand over the *vexillum*, which they ostensibly thought would indicate their status and save them from retaliatory action by the embassy. Shortly afterward, soldiers roving through the streets encountered members of the mission, who had been aroused by the clamor raised by the attack on Germanicus, and immediately attacked them. Plancus was the special target of their wrath. He fled to the quarters of the first legion, where he attempted to avail himself of the sanctuary afforded by the standards and eagle of the legion. The passion of the troops was so great, however, that they were ready to ignore the customary rights of sanctuary as well as the traditional immunity of an emissary, but the standard-bearer heroically protected him.[33]

[32] *Ibid.*, 38.   [33] *Ibid.*, 39.

THE MUTINY OF A.D. 14

The following morning Germanicus entered the camp and proceeded with Plancus to the tribunal. He explained to the assembled troops the reasons for the dispatch of the senatorial embassy and bemoaned their violation of the rights of the ambassadors, which would leave an indelible stain on the honor of the legions. He then withdrew from the tribunal and provided the emissaries with a cavalry guard.[34]

Members of his suite reproached him for not hurrying to the Upper Army, whose loyalty could be counted on, to secure help in disciplining the rebellious legions. "Discharges, donations, and soft-hearted measures had done more than enough mischief." If he spurned this advice, he was exhorted at least to take measures to ensure the safety of his wife and child. According to Tacitus, Agrippina, after first greeting with disdain the proposal that she should leave, ultimately was persuaded by her husband to depart.[35] Accompanied by wives of officers and friends of the prince, bearing her infant son Gaius in her arms, she led a melancholy procession toward the gates of the camp. The soldiers allegedly were shamed by the spectacle of the granddaughter of Augustus, obviously pregnant, forced to seek refuge among the Treveri. She was taking with her Gaius, whom they had affectionately nicknamed Caligula and who had been a great favorite with them. They thereupon clamored that she should stay.

Germanicus, according to Tacitus, subsequently delivered a harangue to the troops in which he bitterly denounced their conduct. They had ignored the privileges and immunities due even to any enemy when they had attacked the senatorial deputation; they had assaulted and killed centurions and other officers. It would have been far better had they permitted him to kill himself, he main-

[34] *Ibid.*   [35] *Ibid.*, 40.

tained; under another commander perhaps they would have turned against the Germans to avenge the defeat of Varus rather than leave this task to the loyal Belgians. The speech, if correctly summarized by the historian, was shrewdly designed to shift the passion of the mutineers against the Germans. The hint that the Belgians were ready to undertake a campaign to avenge Varus was as effective an appeal to the pride of the legions as could have been made. Encouraged by signs of wavering among his auditors, the prince exhorted those who would return to obedience to segregate themselves from the malcontents.[36]

The soldiers abandoned their threats and menaces, and as suppliants implored him to punish the guilty and spare the innocent. Above all, he should recall his wife and child; Caligula must not fall as a hostage into the hands of the Gauls. Germanicus responded that his wife could not return because of her impending confinement; Caligula, however, would be restored to them.

It is virtually impossible to accept this account. Why should the prince speak of the return of Agrippina when, according to Tacitus, she had not left the camp? In describing the attack on the quarters of Germanicus, Tacitus states that they were in the city; yet in telling of the departure of Agrippina she leaves from the camp. Why should she go on a long journey in view of her imminent parturition? "That the soldiers, those uncouth and rough fellows whose work was killing, who killed their centurions, pulled their commander out of bed, and threatened him with death, suddenly were overcome by a sentimental urge of the heart and became irresolute because they saw a woman leaving the camp with her children" [37]

---

[36] *Ibid.*, 43.
[37] Spengel, "Zur Gesch. des Kaisers Tiberius," in *loc. cit.*, 20. Kessler, *Die Tradition über Germanicus*, 25–26, thinks that Tacitus and Dio followed a common source except for the material on the alleged exodus.

THE MUTINY OF A.D. 14

is intrinsically implausible. No child was born to Agrippina until November of A.D. 15. She may have suffered a miscarriage, but it is more likely that Tacitus or his source has confused this incident with the story of the action of Agrippina in preventing the destruction of the bridge across the Rhine in the fall of 15.[38]

Lynch law ensued as the prince declared that "what was to be done they could do for themselves." The soldiers seized ringleaders of the uprising and brought them before Gaius Castronius, legate of the first legion. The accused were displayed one at a time on the platform by a tribune. If the soldiers cried that one was guilty, he was thrown down and butchered by the first ranks of the legions standing before the tribunal. "The troops revelled in the butchery, which they took as an act of purification; nor was Germanicus inclined to restrain them—the orders had been none of his, and the perpetrators of the cruelty would have to bear its odium." [39] When the massacre was over the legions were ordered to Rhaetia, ostensibly to defend the provinces against the Suevi, but actually to remove them from a camp so fraught with memories of treason and death. The centurions were subjected to an unheard-of referendum by the troops. Each was called before the commander and required to give his name and company, as well as the number of campaigns he had fought and the distinctions and decorations he had earned.

[38] T. Mommsen, "Die Familie des Germanicus," *Gesammelte Schriften*, 6 vols. (Berlin, 1906), IV, 286.

[39] Tacitus, *Ann.*, I, 44. Germanicus seems to be a mere spectator of these proceedings. Liebenam, "Zur Tradition über Germanicus," in *loc. cit.*, 733. The action of the tribunes in this incident does not mean that they ordinarily exercised judicial powers in the army. By this time their functions were mostly clerical. They had charge of the muster rolls, which probably accounts for the part they played in the punishment of the mutineers. A. von Domaszewski, "Die Rangordnung des Römischen Heeres," *Bonner Jahrbücher*, CXVII (1908), 39–42.

If the tribunes and his legion approved the integrity and competence of the centurion, he was retained in his post; if he was charged with avarice and cruelty, he was dismissed.

Only the fifth and the twenty-first legions remained to be dealt with. They were wintering in what was known as the Old Camp, near Xanten. They had been the first to revolt, and had not as yet returned to unqualified obedience. Germanicus accordingly arranged to send troops by boat down the Rhine.[40] He sent a letter to Caecina informing the latter of his impending arrival and threatening that, unless the soldiers themselves executed the leaders of the rebellion, he would put all to the sword. Most of the soldiers proved reasonably loyal, and Caecina therefore ordered picked men to strike down the unsuspecting victims who had been previously marked for death as leading participants in the mutiny.[41] When the massacre began, however, the cries of the victims aroused the whole camp. Those who had played prominent roles in the rebellion realized that they were lost, but they sold their lives dearly by fighting to the last. No officer attempted to restrain the murderous mob. Germanicus, upon his arrival in the camp, was justified in saying that "this is not a cure but a calamity." [42]

The danger of further outbreaks was by no means past. To allay the spirit of rebellion the prince decided to cross the Rhine to begin a campaign against the Germans. This developed into a much more ambitious undertaking, as will be described in the ensuing chapter.

Germanicus' handling of the crisis left much to be desired. His theatrical threat of suicide had made him appear ludicrous. The transparent device of the fraudulent letter did not deceive the soldiery, and the concession of

---

[40] Tacitus, *Ann.*, I, 48.   [41] *Ibid.*, 49.   [42] *Ibid.*

the legacies in response to threats was virtually tantamount to abdication of authority. Tacitus' account seems to imply that the troops were somewhat penitent the morning after they had seized the standard from the commander-in-chief's headquarters, but the prince apparently made no effort to turn this to advantage. It is unlikely that the exit of Agrippina so graphically described by Tacitus occurred or was even seriously considered. How an unguarded group of women could be considered seeking "safety" by striking out through the wilderness to Treves defies reasonable explanation. The prince openly had connived at sheer lynch law; indeed, he deliberately ordered such a procedure to be employed against the twenty-first and fifth legions. Certainly many of the victims deserved the death penalty; it is equally certain that many of the innocent suffered with the guilty.[43] The success of Manius Ennius in quelling the uprising of the contingent under his command inclines one to the conclusion that the commander-in-chief, a member of the ruling house, invested with the *imperium*, could at least have had as much success had he attempted sterner measures immediately after his arrival at the mutinous camp.

Tiberius' conduct during the course of the mutiny was severely criticized by Tacitus who accused him of "hypocritical hesitation." He charged that the emperor was derelict in the performance of his duty because he refrained from going in person to suppress the uprisings.[44] In large measure the historian refuted his strictures by the presentation of the explanations Tiberius gave for his decision to remain in the capital.[45] By relying on the princes

---

[43] *Ibid.*   [44] *Ibid.*, 46.
[45] *Ibid.*, 47. S. C. Tuxen, *Kejser Tiberius* (Copenhagen, 1896), 106–107, believes that Tiberius' conduct during the mutiny was deserving

both mutinies could be dealt with simultaneously, and there was still opportunity for them to refer to the emperor to secure such concessions for the troops as expediency might dictate. If either or both princes failed in their mission, and an attack on Italy ensued, the emperor still was in position to organize its defense, and, in the last extremity, to defend the capital. If, on the other hand, he went in person, either to Pannonia or to the Rhine, the fate of the government virtually would have depended on his reception by the soldiery. Failure to restore order would have been tantamount to the overthrow of the Julio-Claudian dynasty.

of censure. He is one of the few writers, since the works of Stahr and Freytag appeared, who accept Tacitus' judgment on this point.

Chapter III

THE GERMAN CAMPAIGNS

Germanicus believed that the suppression of the mutiny had not permanently allayed the disaffection of the troops. Nothing could be better calculated to revive their *esprit de corps* and restore discipline than a campaign against the Germans. Varus' defeat was unavenged, and it could be argued from purely defensive considerations that it was necessary to re-establish Roman prestige to deter possible Germanic inroads into Gaul. Tiberius apparently gave no direct orders to Germanicus to assume the offensive; certainly he did not approve the campaigns which ultimately were launched for the apparent purpose of establishing the Roman frontier at the Elbe.[1]

Signs of restlessness had begun to be apparent among the Germans after the death of Augustus and the subsequent mutinies in the Roman armies. The Roman forces, however, succeeded in passing through the Caesian Forest, along the left bank of the Lippe, and reached the defensive line that had been set up by Tiberius some years before. There a camp was pitched, possibly as a base for the ensuing operations to the south. The troops pushed through the wilderness along a route which the Germans had left undefended. Scouts reported that the enemy were making ready to celebrate a pagan holiday. In order to take advantage of this situation, the Roman advance,

[1] Tacitus, *Ann.*, II, 14, 26; Dio, *R.H.*, LVII, vi. F. Knoke, *Die Kriegzüge des Germanicus in Deutschland* (Berlin, 1922), 23-24. See, W. Oldfather and H. Canter, *The Defeat of Varus and the German Frontier Policy of Augustus* (Urbana, Ill., 1915), 19-20.

facilitated by Caecina's work in clearing the road, was accelerated. As had been anticipated the Marsi were found virtually defenseless, since no outposts had been set up, and the warriors were lying about the camp in a drunken stupor.[2]

Germanicus then divided his forces into four columns to extend the area of Roman devastation. A strip of territory fifty miles in extent was pitilessly harried; "neither age nor sex inspired pity: places sacred and profane were razed indifferently to the ground." [3]

The Bructeri, Tubantes, and Usipites were goaded into action by the Roman attack on the Marsi. They occupied the forests along the routes that Germanicus had to traverse on the return to his winter camp, and the prince therefore was forced to exercise the greatest vigilance. The cavalry and a force of auxiliaries served as the vanguard of the column. Next in line was stationed the first legion, after which came the baggage train. The left and right flanks were guarded by the twenty-first and the fifth legions, respectively, while the twentieth legion and the rest of the auxiliaries brought up the rear.

The Germans waited until the column was nearly out of the wilderness. They then feinted an attack on the front and flanks of the Romans, but concentrated their assault on the auxiliaries in the rear. These soon were thrown into confusion by the savage attack. Germanicus brought up the twenty-first legion as a support and called to the le-

[2] Tacitus, *Ann.*, I, 50. K. Müllendoff, *Deutsche Altertumskunde*, 2nd ed., 5 vols. in 8 (Berlin, 1890-1908), II, 222, places the Caesian Forest between Werden and Essen. For other identifications see, Pauly, Wissowa, and Kroll (eds.), *Real-Encyklopädie*, III, 1311.

[3] Tacitus, *Ann.*, I, 51. The army marched east then south. The Marsi dwelt in the valley of the Ruhr. Knoke, *Die Kriegzüge des Germanicus*, 29-32. See also, O. Dahm, "Die Feldzüge des Germanicus in Deutschland," *Westdeutsche Zeitschrift für Geschichte und Kunst*, XI (1902), 21-24.

THE GERMAN CAMPAIGNS 59

gionaries that the time had arrived for them to expiate their guilt in the mutiny. The troops enthusiastically responded to this appeal. They fell upon the Germans, drove them into the open, and cut them down. In the meantime, the head of the Roman column emerged from the forest, and a camp was pitched on open ground. The march from this camp to winter quarters was uneventful.[4]

Tiberius, according to Tacitus' account, was torn by mixed emotions when he received the news of the recent events. He was gratified that the German legions had been reduced to obedience, but he deprecated the concessions that had been made to them. Nevertheless, he ordered that the same concessions that had been extorted by the Rhine legions should be extended to the rest of the troops, although the action was subsequently rescinded with all the legions affected.[5] Tacitus' charge that the emperor resented the military renown won by Germanicus is absurd. Surely Tiberius' military reputation was sufficiently established to obviate any fear that it would be eclipsed by a mere harrying expedition. Early in A.D. 15 a triumph was decreed to Germanicus which could with justice have been withheld; this hardly indicates that the emperor desired to disparage the achievements of his nephew.[6] Tacitus admits that the emperor praised Germanicus more highly for the suppression of the Rhine mutiny than he did his son Drusus for his work in Pan-

---

[4] Tacitus, *Ann.*, I, 51. It was customary at this time to keep the auxiliaries together and to assign to them the defense of the flanks in battle or the vanguard and rear in marching order. Later, bodies of auxiliaries were attached to each legion. G. L. Cheesman, *The Auxilia of the Roman Imperial Army* (Oxford, 1914), 50-53, 103.

[5] Tacitus, *Ann.*, I, 52, 78.

[6] *Ibid.*, 55. Marsh, *Reign of Tiberius*, 70, among others, thinks the triumph unmerited. Germanicus was acclaimed *imperator* by his troops in 15 and 17 as a considerable number of inscriptions point out. *C.I.L.*, II, 1517, 2039, 2198; VI, 909; X¹, 460, 513, 1198, 1625, 4572; XIII, 1036.

nonia. Nevertheless, he impugns the sincerity of Tiberius' tribute to his nephew. "One cannot reason with him for whom deeds and words are not sufficient to judge a person, but who, instead, assumes inner thoughts without evidence." [7]

Germanicus prepared a major campaign for the summer of 15. As a preliminary to this projected expedition he led the army in a sudden attack on the Chatti, on the right bank of the Rhine, in the territory of Hesse-Nassau.[8] Roman hopes for a successful campaign were greatly augmented by the dissension that prevailed between Arminius and Segestes, two of the outstanding German leaders. Segestes had given evidence of his loyalty to Rome when he had warned Varus against the plans of Arminius that had culminated in the virtual annihilation of the Roman legions in the Teutoberg Wood. Personal enmities had further embittered the German chieftains, since Arminius had abducted and married Segestes' daughter.[9]

Germanicus entrusted command of four legions and 5,000 auxiliaries to the legate Caecina, apparently for use against the Cherusci and Marsi. The prince took the field with an equal number of legions and double the number of auxiliaries. He erected a fort at Mount Taunus (Hohe

---

[7] E. Wiesner, *Tiberius und Tacitus* (Krotoschin-Ostrowo, 1877), 15.

[8] Tacitus, *Ann.*, I, 55. The Chatti are described by Tacitus, *Germania*, XXX. They took part in many later uprisings against the Romans. See, Pauly, Wissowa, and Kroll (eds.), *Real-Encyklopädie*, III, 2199–2200.

[9] Tacitus, *Ann.*, I, 55. Arminius, the son of Sigimir, was born in 16 or 18 B.C. He served in the Roman army and was granted citizenship and equestrian rank, according to Velleius, *R.H.*, II, 118, who knew him personally. He probably assumed the name Arminius after his receipt of citizenship. Pauly, Wissowa, and Kroll (eds.), *Real-Encyklopädie*, II, 1192–94. Segestes had received citizenship from Augustus. Tacitus, *Ann.*, I, 58. He then took the name C. Julius Segestes. Velleius, *R.H.*, II, 118, 4, and Dio, *R.H.*, LVI, xix, 3, agree with Tacitus that he had tried to save Varus from imminent disaster by urging the Roman commander to arrest all the German chieftains. See, Pauly, Wissowa, and Kroll (eds.), *Real-Encyklopädie*, IIa, 1070–71.

between the Rhine and the Nedda), on the site of defensive works constructed by his father Drusus. He then proceeded into the Chattan country, leaving behind Lucius Apronius to build roads and bridges. This was a necessary precaution. An unusual summer drouth had left the streams shallow, and this facilitated the advance. Rains and flooded streams could be anticipated on the return march, however, and the vital importance of Apronius' works would then be manifest.[10]

The Chatti were taken by surprise and hostilities opened with a slaughter of noncombatants. The German fighting forces rallied and attempted to oppose the building of a bridge across the Eder. They were repulsed by the Roman archers and the missiles of the siege engines. When their subsequent efforts to negotiate peace were rebuffed, some surrendered, while the remainder scurried off into the forests. So thoroughly were they demoralized that no effort was made to ambush the Roman column on the return march. In the meantime, Caecina had done much to assure Roman success by forestalling efforts of the Cherusci and Marsi to come to the assistance of the Chatti.[11]

While on the way back to the Rhine the Roman army was overtaken by emissaries from Segestes, who implored

---

[10] Tacitus, *Ann.*, I, 56. Germanicus left from Mainz, while Caecina started from Xanten. Knoke, *Die Kriegzüge des Germanicus*, 48; Dahm, "Die Feldzüge des Germanicus," in *loc. cit.*, 47. The Cherusci were first mentioned by Caesar, *Gallic War*, VI, 10. Tacitus, *Germania*, XXXVI, locates them in close proximity to the Chatti and Chauci. Led by Arminius they played the major part in the defeat of Varus in A.D. 9. Velleius, *R.H.*, II, 117; Dio, *R.H.*, LVI, xviii. Their power virtually vanished after Arminius' death.

[11] Tacitus, *Ann.*, I, 56. The Chatti were taken by surprise, yet elsewhere Tacitus described them as the fiercest and most warlike of the Germans. *Germania*, XXX. See, Liebenam, "Zur Tradition über Germanicus," in *loc. cit.*, 793–99, for other inconsistencies in Tacitus' account of the German campaigns.

Roman protection against his own people, aroused against him by Arminius. His pro-Roman policies had met with disfavor, and the exhortations of his rival for hostilities against the Romans had prevailed. Germanicus decided to halt the return march to go to the aid of the suppliant.[12] Both Segestes and his daughter, Arminius' wife, were favorably received by the prince, who permitted the chieftain to settle on the Gallic side of the Rhine.[13]

Arminius' rage became frenzied when he learned that his wife was in Roman hands. He aroused the Cherusci by bitter invectives against Segestes and Germanicus. "A peerless father! a great commander! a courageous army whose united powers had carried off one wretched woman. Before his own sword three legions, three generals had fallen. For he practised war, not by the help of treason nor against pregnant women, but in open day and against men who carried arms." [14] The ambitions of Augustus and Tiberius had been frustrated by German valor. Why should his people now shrink to oppose a callow youth like Germanicus in command of a disloyal army? [15]

The Cherusci and a number of neighboring tribes responded to these appeals. Inguiomerus, Arminius' uncle, for whom the Romans had wholesome respect, joined the uprising and greatly increased the gravity of the situation. Germanicus sent Caecina with four legions through the territory held by the Bructeri to the Ems, allegedly to divide the enemy. He dispatched Pedo and the cavalry to

---

[12] Tacitus, *Ann.*, I, 57. It is difficult to explain Germanicus' decision to return to the Rhine. Kessler, *Die Tradition über Germanicus*, 35–36. If supplies were needed, how was it possible for him to turn about and fight a major campaign without apparently having received any?

[13] Tacitus, *Ann.*, I, 58. The son of Arminius and Thusnelda was named Thumelicus.

[14] Tacitus, *Ann.*, I, 59.

[15] *Ibid.*

THE GERMAN CAMPAIGNS

the Ems by a march along the Frisian frontier. The prince himself took four legions by ship through the "lakes" (Zuydersee). His infantry and cavalry ultimately were reunited on the Ems, probably at Rheine, and a junction likewise was made with Caecina's forces. The whole army, except a contingent of light-armed troops under Lucius Stertinius sent against the Bructeri, harried the territory between the Ems and the Lippe.[16]

These operations brought the army near the site of the disaster of Teutoberg Wood. Germanicus wished to visit the battlefield in order that proper honors might be paid to the fallen. Caecina was sent ahead to scout the trails through the forest and to construct bridges and causeways in the swampy terrain. The main body followed and ultimately reached the ruins of the camp that had been occupied by Varus just before his tragic defeat. Near by was a half-ruined wall and a shallow ditch where the remnants of the legions had attempted to make a stand after the overpowering assault of the barbarians. In the plain between the two sites were piles of bleaching bones, shattered javelins, and limbs of horses. Human skulls nailed to near-by trees enhanced the gruesomeness of the spot. In small groves close to the battleground were found altars before which the tribunes and centurions had been immolated. Survivors of the disaster pointed out where the prisoners had been hanged or buried alive and the standards desecrated.[17]

---

[16] *Ibid.*, 60. Knoke, *Die Kriegzüge des Germanicus*, 62; Dahm, "Die Feldzüge des Germanicus," in *loc. cit.*, 52. Virtually all the known references to Stertinius are in the *Annals*.

[17] Tacitus, *Ann.*, I, 61. Knoke, *Die Kriegzüge des Germanicus*, 71 ff., places the site at Iburg, near Osnabrück. His views are accepted by R. Tieffenbach, *Über die Ortlichkeit der Varusschlacht* (Berlin, 1891), and P. Baehr, *Die Ortlichkeit der Schlacht auf Idistaviso* (Halle, 1888). I am inclined to agree with Delbrück, *Gesch. der Kriegskunst*, Vol. I, Pt. I, 81–83, who places the site at Grotenburg, near Detmold. Dahm,

The bones of the slain were gathered and buried. Germanicus laid the first sod on the funeral mound and paid tribute to the memory of the dead. Grief among the soldiers, many of whom had lost friends or relatives in the battle, was mixed with their blazing anger against the Germans.[18] Upon receipt of report of the prince's actions, Tiberius expressed disapproval. Technical objection could be raised to Germanicus' participation in funerary rites, since he held the office of augur, and there was reason to fear that the horrible spectacle of the battlefield would unnerve the troops.[19]

Germanicus, with the cavalry serving as his advance guard, set out toward the Ems in pursuit of Arminius. Arminius ultimately attacked from ambush and threw the cavalry into confusion. Their flight, in turn, scattered the auxiliaries hastening to their support. The hard-pressed Romans were pushed toward the swamps, where they were at considerable disadvantage, since the enemy, un-

---

"Die Feldzüge des Germanicus," in *loc. cit.*, 54–55, also suggests a site near Detmold, as does H. Neubourg, *Die Ortlichkeit der Varusschlacht* (Detmold, 1887). T. Mommsen, "Die Ortlichkeit der Varusschlacht," *Gesammelte Schriften*, IV, 234–46, arguing from coin finds, presents a strong case for Barenau, northeast of Osnabrück. E. Meyer, *Untersuchen über die Schlacht im Teutoburga Wald* (Berlin, 1893), has injected another complication by holding that the battle occurred at the end of July or early in August, rather than in the early fall of A.D. 9. For review of the enormous literature on the subject, see, F. Knoke, *Gegenwärtiger Stand der Forschungen über die Römerkriege im nordwestlichen Deutschland* (Berlin, 1903), and C. Kuthmann, *Zur Schlacht im Teutoburger Wald und den Feldzügen des Germanicus* (Hanover, 1932). Most identifications now fall in the area from the middle Weser to the Ems, north of a line from Dümmer to the Ems.

[18] Tacitus, *Ann.*, I, 62. Glaser, "Bemerkungen zu den Annalen des Tacitus," in *loc. cit.*, 35–36, makes the interesting suggestion that Tacitus' description of the battlefield is modeled on Vergil, *Aeneid*, II, 27 ff.

[19] Tacitus, *Ann.*, I, 62. Liebenam, "Zur Tradition über Germanicus," in *loc. cit.*, 806, considers Germanicus blameworthy. Germanicus is designated as an augur in *C.I.L.*, II, 1517; III, 334; VI, 909; X^1, 460, 513, 1198, 4572; XII, 3942.

THE GERMAN CAMPAIGNS

encumbered by packs, were accustomed to fighting in such surroundings. Germanicus, nevertheless, succeeded in forming a line, and Arminius withdrew when he saw that the first assault had failed.[20]

When the army reached the Ems, Germanicus decided to take two legions back by ship, the same way they had come. The cavalry were ordered to march to the Rhine along the coast of the North Sea. Caecina and his four legions were ordered to return to the Rhine by a "well-known route"; the legate was admonished to exercise great care in crossing the "Long Bridges," the long, narrow causeway that had been built through the swamps by Lucius Domitius Ahenobarbus.[21] There is no adequate explanation as to the reason why Caecina was ordered to make the return march through this difficult terrain, with its marshes and streams.[22] The heavily wooded slopes flanking the line of march were occupied by Germans whose rapid movements through familiar country enabled them to offer battle on a site of their own choosing. Caecina, ordered to repair the "Long Bridges," decided to pitch a camp where the work of repair could proceed and proper vigilance could be exercised to fend off enemy attacks.

The labor of the legions made some progress despite the constant skirmishing and the efforts of the enemy to break through the Roman outposts. The position of the legions finally was made untenable, however, when the barbarians

[20] Tacitus, *Ann.*, I, 63. Germanicus did not lead back "the legions" but only two of them.
[21] Tacitus, *Ann.*, I, 63.
[22] Dahm, "Die Feldzüge des Germanicus," in *loc. cit.*, 65, believes that the strategy is inexplicable. Knoke, *Die Kriegzüge des Germanicus*, 236-73, holds that Caecina was expected to protect the left flank of Germanicus' army. This view is only tenable if his site of the "Long Bridges" northeast of Barenau is accepted. See, Kessler, *Die Tradition über Germanicus*, 38-39; Marsh, *Reign of Tiberius*, 72.

diverted the courses of several mountain streams so that the water flooded the ground where the soldiers were at work. Caecina decided to remove the wounded and the most heavily burdened troops, after which he planned to join battle with the Germans on a small level patch between the morass and the hills. The legions were arranged as they had been on the march back from the Marsi country the preceding year, that is, with the twenty-first and the fifth legions on the flanks, and the first and the twentieth in front and rear, respectively.[23]

Caecina did not need a dream, so graphically described by Tacitus,[24] to remind him of Varus' grim fate. At daybreak his worst forebodings seemed realized, for the legions on the flanks disobeyed orders and sought drier ground. When the baggage train was bogged down and the troops around it were thrown into disarray, Arminius gave the order to attack. During the first assault the horses were deliberately wounded by the barbarians to augment the confusion. Caecina's mount was struck down, and the legate narrowly escaped capture. Pillaging fortunately diverted the attention of the enemy, and the legions were able to throw up a makeshift rampart.[25]

A terrified horse broke from its tether and precipitated considerable confusion among the soldiers who rushed to secure it. The resultant clamor led to fears that the Germans were assaulting the camp, and there was a precipitant rush to escape by the gate farthest removed from the enemy. Caecina was unable to arrest the panic by command or entreaty; he finally threw himself in the gateway to bar the road while the tribunes and centurions quieted the fears of the soldiers.[26]

The legate explained that attempts to flee were fore-

[23] Tacitus, *Ann.*, I, 64.
[24] *Ibid.*, 65.
[25] *Ibid.*
[26] *Ibid.*, 66.

doomed to disaster. The legions had to remain within the ramparts until the Germans could be lured into an attack; then, a Roman sally could break through their lines, and the march to the Rhine could be resumed.[27] His stratagem was successful. Inguiomerus, in opposition to Arminius, successfully urged an immediate attack on the camp in the hope of securing more booty and a larger number of captives. At daybreak the Germans stormed the ramparts, which Caecina had caused to appear virtually undefended. The signal ultimately was given for the Romans to charge, and the enemy, taken by surprise, were scattered and hunted down until the approach of night forced cessation of the Roman operations.[28]

In the meantime, news arrived along the Rhine frontier that the legions had been caught in a trap and that the Germans were advancing on Gaul. So much fear was aroused that there was talk of destroying the bridge across the Rhine. Tacitus, who states that he relied on the account of the German wars written by Pliny the Elder, declares that Agrippina stationed herself at the bridge and prevented its demolition. When the legions ultimately arrived, she received them with her praise and thanks. If Tiberius were angered at the prominent part Germanicus' wife was playing in army affairs, he had abundant reason to be.[29]

Germanicus, too, encountered difficulties in the return of his legions. Two legions, the second and the fourteenth, were assigned to Publius Vitellius and ordered to march back by land. This decision was based on the desire to lighten the ships so that they could be navigated better in shallow waters. For a time Vitellius' march was unevent-

---

[27] *Ibid.*, 67. [28] *Ibid.*, 68.
[29] *Ibid.*, 69. See, Mommsen, "Die Familie des Germanicus," in *loc. cit.*, 286.

ful. Finally, however, a northerly gale, aggravated by the equinox, blew up.

The shore along which the column had been marching soon was inundated as the surf pounded in, and the legions were thrown into complete confusion. Vitellius finally managed to find high ground over which he led his demoralized troops to safety. After a miserable night "without necessaries, without fire, many of them naked or badly maimed" they pushed on to a river, probably the Hunse, where they were taken on board Germanicus' vessels. The incident surely affords grounds for questioning the strategic competence of the commander-in-chief. The troops had been successfully transported to the Ems on the eastward journey. It would seem that there was no compellent reason for the decision to transfer two legions to the shore. After a march of two days and nights, according to the Tacitean narrative, Vitellius' contingent again was taken on shipboard without difficulty.[30]

During the winter of 15–16 Germanicus refitted his army. The Gauls, Spain, and Italy offered weapons, horses, and gold to make up the losses his army had sustained, but the prince accepted only arms and horses. By personal solicitude for their welfare and disbursements from his private resources for the benefit of the needy, the commander improved the morale of the legions preparatory to the resumption of the campaign.

The major preparation for the ensuing campaign was the construction of a fleet of a thousand vessels under the direction of Silius and Caecina. The ships were built adaptable to the peculiar navigation conditions that would

---

[30] Tacitus, *Ann.*, I, 70. Vitellius, father of the future emperor, had taken the census in Gaul. *Ibid.*, II, 6. Later, he was one of the prosecutors of Piso. *Ibid.*, III, 10, 13. He held the praetorship but was ruined by the fall of Sejanus. *Ibid.*, V, 8. See also, Suetonius, *Vitellius*, II.

THE GERMAN CAMPAIGNS

be encountered in a voyage from the mouth of the Rhine to the Ems or Weser. The vessels, built for sailing or rowing, were short and broad and equipped with small poops and prows. Many of them were broad-bottomed to enable them to be operated effectively in shoal waters. Rudders were provided at each end to facilitate reversal of course, and decks were installed in some to carry the siege engines, horses, and supplies. The ships were assembled off the isle of Batavia, admirably suited to serve as a rendezvous and base for subsequent naval operations.[31]

While the ships were proceeding to the assigned rendezvous, Germanicus ordered Silius to raid the Chattan country with a light force. Heavy rains impeded his operations, however, so that little booty was secured, although a daughter of Arpus, the Chattan chieftain, was captured. Germanicus pressed on to the relief of a fort on the Lippe, probably Aliso,[32] established at the juncture of the Lippe and the Eliso. If by the Eliso is meant the Alme, the site would be near Paderborn; if the Ahse, it must have been near modern Hamm. No fighting ensued, for the barbarians abandoned their attack on the fort at the news of Germanicus' approach. The prince set up the altar to his father Drusus that had been thrown down by the Germans, and on the way back to the Rhine he established a number of strongholds.[33]

The major expedition then was begun. The ships sailed through the "Drusian Fosse," the widened channel of the Rhine and the canal between the Rhine and the Yssel, built by Drusus. The Yssel in turn gave access to the Zuydersee, which was successfully crossed to the Ems,

---

[31] Tacitus, *Ann.*, II, 6. Augustus exempted the Batavians from the payment of tribute because they furnished so many auxiliaries. Cheesman, *The Auxilia of the Roman Imperial Army*, 17.
[32] Cf., Kessler, *Die Tradition über Germanicus*, 44.
[33] Tacitus, *Ann.*, II, 7-8.

and thence the ships probably proceeded to the Weser.[34] The vessels anchored in the mouth of the river, and a number of days were spent in constructing a bridge. In the meantime, most of the legions and cavalry managed to cross the estuaries, apparently without awaiting completion of the bridge. A number of Batavians were drowned, however, while exhibiting their prowess as swimmers. Somewhat later, a minor revolt of the Angrivarii was crushed. Since these people lived on both sides of the Weser, and Tacitus speaks of this rebellion as occurring in the rear of the Roman troops, his statement that the ships anchored in the Ems is untenable unless one assumes that he neglected to refer to the passage of the army from the Ems to the Weser. The historian's dramatic account of a long-range conversation carried on between Arminius and his brother Flavus, presumably serving in the Roman army, must be dismissed without serious consideration. The participants in the colloquy must have had prodigious voices to enable them to understand each other from opposite banks of the Weser.[35]

[34] Tacitus says the ships sailed to the Ems. Nothing is said about a march or sail from the Ems to the Weser. The Angrivarii were crushed in the rear of the Roman army, apparently soon after the arrival of the fleet, and they lived on both sides of the Weser. I agree with Delbrück, *Gesch. der Kriegskunst*, Vol. II, Pt. I, 115–16, that the campaign is unintelligible unless we assume that Tacitus confused the rivers. See also, Kessler, *Die Tradition über Germanicus*, 49. Glaser, "Bemerkungen zu den Annalen des Tacitus," in *loc. cit.*, 37–39, suggests that Germanicus went from the Ems to the Weser by ship. Vitellius then led a contingent from the Ems to the Weser on foot, whereas Tacitus described this march as part of the return journey to the Rhine the preceding year. Glaser thinks that after the near disaster to his forces Vitellius joined Germanicus at the Weser. Dahm, "Die Feldzüge des Germanicus," in *loc. cit.*, 95, thinks Germanicus' army landed on the right bank of the Ems and proceeded through the territory held by the Chasauri and Angrivarii. For a summary of the many inconsistencies of the Tacitean account, see, Liebenam, "Zur Tradition über Germanicus," in *loc. cit.*, 793–99.

[35] Tacitus, *Ann.*, II, 9–10.

Germanicus considered it dangerous strategy to risk heavy losses to the legions by having them attempt to cross the river before the bridgeheads were adequately secured. Therefore, he ordered the cavalry to ford the stream to deliver attacks at widely scattered points. Chariovalda, leader of the Batavians, was drawn into an ambush by a feinted retreat of the Cherusci. The courageous leader was slain, but most of his warriors were extricated from their precarious position by the cavalry under Stertinius and Aemilius.[36]

Germanicus subsequently led the legions across the river without difficulty. He was informed by a German deserter that Arminius and other chieftains had concentrated their forces in the forest of Hercules, and reports of his scouts confirmed this information. According to the Tacitean account, the prince decided to probe the sentiment of his troops by going about the camp at night in disguise to hear in their conversations just what they thought of him. He "tasted his own popularity, while the men—serious or jesting, but unanimous—praised some the commander's lineage, others his looks, the most his patience and his courtesy." [37] A discordant note was introduced, however, when a German versed in the Latin tongue exhorted the legionaries to desert, promising wives, lands, and money to all who would accept the invitation. The troops indignantly spurned these overtures and vowed that in the expected battle they would win by valor the rewards promised for perfidy.[38]

Germanicus, enthusiastic over evidence of the high morale of his army, called an assembly of the troops. He drew attention to the equipment of the legionaries, which

---

[36] *Ibid.*, 11.   [37] *Ibid.*, 13. The incident is highly improbable.
[38] *Ibid.* The historian then reports Germanicus' dream, which must be dismissed as the invention of Tacitus or his source.

he regarded as well adapted to fighting in wooded country, and spoke disparagingly of the arms of the Germans. If the troops were weary of the campaign, he promised this to be the last battle; the march to the Elbe could be completed, and he had no ambition to go beyond it.[39]

Arminius, in turn, encouraged his followers by recalling the great defeat inflicted on Varus and casting aspersions on the legionaries so recently guilty of mutiny and much marked by the scars of fighting and the "wave and tempest-broken limbs." [40]

Battle was joined at Idisiaviso, described as a plain between the Weser and hills, with a forest in the rear. The main forces of the Germans were stationed in the plain and along the fringes of the forest, while the Cherusci were posted in the hills to sweep down upon the Romans in the plain. The Roman army advanced, with the auxiliaries and archers leading the way. After them came four legions which were followed by Germanicus with two praetorian cohorts and the cavalry. Next came the other four legions; and the light troops, mounted archers, and remainder of the auxiliaries were in the rear.[41]

The battle opened when the Cherusci prematurely charged from their position. Germanicus ordered his cavalry to attack the enemy flanks, while Stertinius was directed to make an encircling movement to strike the enemy in the rear. The prince himself held the main body of troops in readiness for a favorable moment to strike. His infantry then charged the enemy, while the cavalry threw their flanks and rear into disorder. The Germans

---

[39] Tacitus, *Ann.*, II, 14.   [40] *Ibid.*, 15.

[41] *Ibid.*, 16. The praetorian cohorts may have been sent to Germanicus after the suppression of the Pannonian mutiny and remained with him as a bodyguard in view of the danger of a recurrence of rebellion among his troops. P. Höfer, *Der Feldzug des Germanicus in J. 16 n. Chr.* (Leipzig, 1885), *passim*, argues unconvincingly that the battle occurred on the left bank of the Weser.

stationed along the fringes of the forest rushed into the plain, while those in the plain attempted to take cover in the woods. The Cherusci, who seem to have fallen back to their original positions, were dislodged, probably by the completion of Stertinius' encircling movement.

Arminius led an assault on the Roman archers, which was checked by auxiliaries. The German chieftain escaped, after smearing his face with blood to conceal his identity, although his flight may have been facilitated by Chauci in the Roman army. Inguiomerus also made his escape. The German casualties were heavy; the Romans continued to hunt down the enemy until nightfall, by which time the terrain for ten miles was said to have been littered with the bodies of the slain. The Romans, whose losses were comparatively small, raised a victory mound on the battlefield and saluted Tiberius as *imperator*.[42]

The Germans rallied and renewed the struggle. According to Tacitus, the sight of the Roman victory celebration enraged them so that they abandoned their plans to retreat to the Elbe.[43] It is far more likely that they renewed the battle because their defeat was not of such disastrous proportions as described by the historian. The barbarians, still under the leadership of Arminius and Inguiomerus, established themselves in a strong position. Roman efforts to dislodge them from a rampart which marked the boundary between the Angrivarii and the Cherusci [44] failed, and the nature of the terrain precluded the withdrawal of either army.[45]

A battle at close quarters ensued in which the Germans were at a disadvantage because of inability to employ their

---

[42] Tacitus, *Ann.*, II, 17–18. Germanicus as *dux* was emphasizing that the victory was really that of Tiberius, the *imperator* under whose auspices it had been won. Gagé, "La Victoria Augusti et les auspices de Tiberè," in *loc. cit.*, 5–6.

[43] Tacitus, *Ann.*, II, 19. [44] *Ibid.* [45] *Ibid.*, 20.

favorite tactics of impetuous charge. The Roman short swords and *pila* were better adapted to close combat than the long spears of the Germans. Although the German chieftains aroused their followers to deeds of valor both by exhortations and example, the Romans pushed through their ranks, and pitiless slaughter marked the end of the battle.[46] Shortly after the Roman victory the Angrivarii unconditionally surrendered.[47]

No precise description of the battle of Idisiaviso and its sequel can be given. The terrain is not accurately described, as the variance of modern "identifications" bears witness.[48] The tactics employed elude full understanding, particularly the scene of the Germans simultaneously rushing in and out of the forest. The Cherusci are said to have started the battle by their charge, yet subsequently they apparently were dislodged from their hill position by the forces commanded by Stertinius.

In July of 16 the prince began the return journey to the winter camp. Some of the legions were sent overland, while the remainder were transported by ship. The land march seems to have been uneventful, but heavy storms brought disaster to the fleet. Offshore gales drove some of the ships out to sea. When the force of the ebb tide was added to the strength of the wind, it was impossible to keep the remainder of the ships riding at anchor. Gigantic waves swamped some of the vessels; others were blown

---

[46] *Ibid.*, 21.   [47] *Ibid.*, 22.
[48] Dahm, "Die Feldzüge des Germanicus," in *loc. cit.*, 102, identifies a site near Minden. Knoke, *Die Kriegzüge des Germanicus*, 384–475, argues for a site near Eisbergen. For other identifications and references to the voluminous literature, see, Pauly, Wissowa, and Kroll (eds.), *Real-Encyklopädie*, IX, 903–904; H. Dexler, "Bericht über Tacitus für die Jahre 1913–1927," *Jahresbericht über die Fortschritte der klassischen Altertumswissenschaft*, CCXXIV (1927), 351–54. Delbrück, *Gesch. der Kriegskunst*, Vol. II, Pt. I, 118–19, 123–24, 128–32, expresses strong doubts that any actual battle occurred!

out to sea to be sunk or grounded on sunken shoals or the rocky shores of islands. Germanicus himself managed to reach the Chaucian coast. Here for several days he mourned the fate of his fleet and talked of suicide. With the abatement of the storms the surviving vessels, badly damaged, were gathered together, and relief was sent to men marooned on islands, although not all of these by any means were saved. The Angrivarii, who recently had made submission to Rome, exerted themselves to procure the liberation of survivors who had been picked up by the Germans and sent into the interior. Tacitus also alleges that a few survivors were returned from the coast of Britain.[49]

News of the disaster to the Roman fleet animated some of the German tribes with hopes for successful rebellion. Silius accordingly was sent against the Chatti, while the prince himself invaded the territory inhabited by the Marsi.[50] It will be noted that both these tribes, according to the Tacitean narrative, were crushed by earlier campaigns, yet further major expeditions against them were necessary. Nothing better illustrates the futility of the prince's policy of pushing eastward with unpacified peoples between the Rhine and the Ems, to say nothing of those only superficially conquered between the Ems and the Weser.

Tiberius was resolved to put an end to the dangerous adventures of his nephew. He recalled the prince to Rome

---

[49] Tacitus, *Ann.*, II, 24. See, Seneca, *Quaestiones Naturales*, V, v, 13. A. Stein, *Albinovanus Pedo* (Vienna, 1901), 11-13, presents a strong argument that Tacitus' account of the storm was based on an epic poem by Pedo, a fragment of which is preserved in Seneca, *Suasoriae*, I, 15. Germanicus was a beloved figure of Roman history, the storm was a highly dramatic theme, and, since Pedo the writer probably was the same man who commanded Germanicus' cavalry, Tacitus was fully justified in using him as a source.

[50] Tacitus, *Ann.*, II, 25.

to celebrate the triumph decreed to him, and attempted to minimize the sting of his refusal to permit Germanicus to remain in Germany for an additional year by providing that he hold the consulship for the year 17. The emperor, "who knew Germany like no other living man," [51] pointed out that experience had taught him that more could be accomplished in Germany by "policy" than by fighting. Left alone, the Germans would weaken themselves by internecine strife. If further fighting were requisite, Drusus could take command. Surely Germanicus would not begrudge him an opportunity to secure experience and fame. The emperor did not neglect to call attention, although without open reproof, to the "heavy loss by wind and wave" which Germanicus had sustained in the last campaign.[52] Tacitus was convinced that "jealousy was the motive which withdrew the prince from a glory already won." [53] Yet just what had Germanicus accomplished? His most enthusiastic admirer could hardly

[51] Dahm, "Die Feldzüge des Germanicus," in *loc. cit.*, 16. Germanicus had made no real gains; the Ems was out of the question as a frontier. *Ibid.*, 18-19, 136-37. See also, Knoke, *Die Kriegzüge des Germanicus*, 505-12; Dessau, *Gesch. der röm. Kaiserzeit*, Vol. II, Pt. I, 11; T. Frank, *Roman Imperialism* (New York, 1925), 354. Tacitus heartily approved imperialism, and generals like Germanicus, Agricola, and Corbulo, who allegedly fell as "victims" to jealous rulers, were his heroes. J. Vogt, *Tacitus als Politiker* (Stuttgart, 1924), 8-12. He favored conquest and imperialism, however, primarily to promote the virtue of the Roman aristocracy. R. Reitzenstein, "Tacitus und sein Werk," *Neue Wege zur Antike*, IV (1926), 165-67. Tacitus maintained that conquest was the mission of Rome. He was a strong believer in the virtues of military discipline and a great admirer of Germanicus. C. Marchesi, *Tacito* (Messina, 1924), 133-34, 141-42, 167. Yet in *Agricola*, XII, XIV, he emphasized the importance of dissension among barbarians as a factor in their conquest by Rome. Delbrück, *Gesch. der Kriegskunst*, Vol. II, Pt. I, 120, thinks that Germanicus' campaign of 16 was motivated by the belief, fostered by Segestes, that the appearance of the Romans would cause defection of the Cherusci from Arminius. Asbach, *Römisches Kaisertum und Verfassung bis auf Traian*, 14-15, sees in Germanicus' recall a blow to the old aristocracy.

[52] Tacitus, *Ann.*, II, 26.

[53] *Ibid.* See also, II, 73; C. Barbagallo, *Tiberio* (Rome, 1922), 26, 30.

THE GERMAN CAMPAIGNS 77

fail to see that attempts to establish a frontier at the Weser or the Elbe were foredoomed to failure, when even the country between the Rhine and the Ems was only tentatively pacified. Each of Germanicus' campaigns had been stalked by disaster. Caecina was ambushed, but why should he have been sent into the dangerous country of the "Long Bridges" in the first place? Repair of the roads would hardly have justified the risk involved, especially as no further campaigns were fought in this area. The prince lightened his ships to facilitate navigation, and heavy losses were sustained in the wreck of the fleet in the summer of 16. Auxiliaries might be recruited, but the loss of three legions at Teutoberg was considered by Augustus a well-nigh irreparable blow. Was there any justification for continuance of the campaigns with the attendant risk of another Teutoberg disaster? [54]

The wisdom of the emperor's reliance on internecine strife among the Germans to neutralize the danger to Rome's frontiers soon was demonstrated. The Suebi, under the rule of Marobodus, were attacked by Arminius and vainly appealed for Roman aid.[55] The Semonones

[54] "In the course of each expedition, the Roman army had hovered close to the danger of sharing the fate of the army of Varus. Only the prudent conduct of the officers, the discipline of the legions, and, at times, the over-anxiousness of the Germans for victory had saved the Romans." Liebenam, "Zur Tradition über Germanicus," in *loc. cit.*, 807. There was reason to fear disastrous defeat. Viertel, *Tiberius und Germanicus*, 10-11; Spengel, "Zur Gesch. des Kaisers Tiberius," in *loc. cit.*, 25-27; Kessler, *Die Tradition über Germanicus*, 100; Freytag, *Tiberius und Tacitus*, 91-92. Tacitus, *Ann.*, II, 88, says in eulogizing Arminius that he "threw down the challenge to the Roman nation, in battle with ambiguous results, in war without defeat." "No monument raised to the memory of Arminius will be as great and enduring as the words we find in the second book of the *Annals*." Marchesi, *Tacito*, 168.

[55] Tacitus, *Ann.*, II, 44. Marobodus' empire at one time included Bohemia, Moravia, Silesia, and territory between the Elbe and Weichsel in the north. Pauly, Wissowa, and Kroll (eds.), *Real-Encyklopädie*, XIV, 1907-1910.

and Lombards joined Arminius, whose main force was made up of Cherusci, but this was offset to some degree by the estrangement of Inguiomerus. A fierce battle ensued in which Marobodus was defeated and forced to retreat into the country held by the Marcomanni.[56]

Drusus had been sent into Illyria in 17, ostensibly because of the disturbed conditions that prevailed among the Germans.[57] The emperor also wanted to afford him an opportunity to gain military experience and to remove him from the pleasures of the capital, in which he indulged to excess.[58] There was little for the prince to do, for the Germans continued to fight each other. Catwalda, a chieftain of the Gotones who had been exiled by Marobodus, invaded the Marcomannian territory to avenge himself on his former conqueror, who in desperation was forced to find refuge in Italy.[59] Catwalda's triumph was short-lived, for he was defeated by the Hermunduri and the forces under Vibilius. Ultimately he found asylum in *Forum Julium* (Frejus), in Narbonensian Gaul, while his followers were settled along the left bank of the Danube, probably between the March and the Wag.[60]

Arminius was emboldened by his victory over Marobodus and the withdrawal of Germanicus' army, with the result that he tried to expand his authority and to secure recognition as king. He encountered serious opposition and finally was assassinated by his own relatives.[61]

Only one more German outbreak demanded attention during the remainder of Tiberius' reign. The Frisians, aroused by the onerous exaction of a tribute of oxhides

---

[56] Tacitus, *Ann.*, II, 46.
[57] *Ibid.*, 44.
[58] *Ibid.*, I, 76.
[59] *Ibid.*, II, 62–63.
[60] *Ibid.*, 63. L. Schmidt, "Das Regnum Vannianum," *Hermes*, XLVIII (1913), 293, locates their settlement between the March and the Eipel. Coin finds show that it was indubitably east of the March.
[61] Tacitus, *Ann.*, II, 88.

THE GERMAN CAMPAIGNS

that had been imposed by the elder Drusus, rebelled.[62] Lucius Apronius [63] marched against them from Lower Germany, and, although he failed to secure a decisive victory and suffered heavy losses, the uprising abated.[64]

Rome's military resources clearly were inadequate for the conquest of German territory from the Rhine to the Weser or Elbe. Years of intensive campaigning would have been requisite to ensure definitive subjugation of the tribes in that vast area, and the problem of maintaining it under Roman control would ultimately have been more difficult than the task of conquest. Adherence to the defensive policy of Augustus was fully justified, and, as Tiberius had foreseen, more was accomplished in diminishing danger to the Rhine frontier by permitting free play to strife among the various tribes than was achieved in the campaigns of 14–16. Aside from the risks immediately involved in these expeditions, the inevitable result was to encourage the union of the Germans.

[62] *Ibid.*, IV, 72.   [63] *Ibid.*, I, 56; III, 21.
[64] *Ibid.*, IV, 73. I am inclined to accept the view that the terms "Lower Germany" and "Upper Germany," in the reign of Tiberius, referred to military districts rather than provinces. See, Hirschfeld, "Die Verwaltung der Rheingrenze in den ersten drei Jahrhunderten der römischen Kaiserzeit," in *loc. cit.*, 373–74. Cf., Marquardt, *Römische Staatsverwaltung*, I, 120 ff.

Chapter IV

GERMANICUS IN THE EAST

There had been extensive criticism of the recall of Germanicus from Germany, and Tiberius' motives for this action had been impugned. The triumph granted to the returning hero doubtless had been motivated in some measure by the desire to allay this feeling. Germanicus, however, had no reason to regard his recall either as a demotion or as evidence of the loss of the emperor's confidence, for he was soon entrusted with a mission that promised to test his abilities to the full.

Augustus' policies in the East had two primary objectives. The first was the maintenance of the vassal states, particularly Armenia, under Roman control. The second was the preservation of ostensibly friendly relations with Parthia, inaugurated as a result of the negotiations that had culminated in restoration of the standards lost by Crassus in return for the extradition of Tiridates, a Parthian rebel.[1] As further evidence of friendly relations, Phraates IV had sent four of his sons to Rome in 9 B.C. to receive a Roman education and to serve as a guarantee of his pacific intentions.[2] In A.D. 7, after the deposition of the Parthian ruler, Oracles II, an embassy of nobles had requested Augustus to send Vonones, the eldest prince, to be their new ruler.[3] Vonones' reign was short and disastrous, for his subjects resented his arrogance and Roman

[1] Suetonius, *Augustus*, XXI; *Tib.*, IX.
[2] Tacitus, *Ann.*, II, 1.   [3] *Ibid.*, 2–3.

GERMANICUS IN THE EAST

manners, and an uprising in support of the usurper Artabanus soon forced the king to flee to Armenia.[4]

Armenian political affairs long had been in a ferment. Tiberius, as a legate of Augustus, had installed Tigranes III (20-19 B.C.) as king of the country in line with the policy of keeping the kingdom under Roman influence, and his conduct of the negotiations had been distinguished by tact and firmness.[5] Roman action again was necessary a few years later, and Gaius, Augustus' grandson, procured the elevation of Ariobarzanes. Gaius died in the East as a result of illness induced or aggravated by a wound suffered before Artogerassa.[6] Ariobarzanes, in turn, was overthrown, and virtual anarchy ensued in the Armenian kingdom. When Vonones arrived, a fugitive from Parthia, he accepted the invitations of a faction of the Armenian nobles to become their king. His elevation, of course, immediately led to hostile relations with Artabanus of Parthia.[7] In the opening years of Tiberius' reign, therefore, the foundations of Roman policy in the East were in jeopardy. In view of the events since the installation of Tigranes III, the maintenance of a pro-Roman ruler in Armenia promised to be difficult, if not impossible. The coronation of Vonones threatened to rupture the peace between Rome and Parthia, for in view of Augustus' policy which Tiberius was anxious to continue, Parthian

---

[4] *Ibid.* See, Gardthausen, *Augustus und seine Zeit*, Vol. I, Pt. III, 1141-45.

[5] Tacitus, *Ann.*, II, 3. Installation of Tigranes III was facilitated by the murder of Artaxias II (34-20 B.C.) by his subjects. Phraates IV of Parthia was peacefully inclined, in some measure because of the influence of Thea Musa, a former Italian slave girl, who had become his wife. Phraataces (2 B.C.-A.D. 2), however, was instrumental in overthrowing Tigranes III and the pro-Roman candidate, Artavasdes. These events necessitated the expedition of Gaius. P. P. Asdourian, *Die politischen Beziehungen zwischen Armenien und Rom von 190 v. Chr. bis 428 n. Chr.* (Venice, 1911), 66-71.

[6] Tacitus, *Ann.*, II, 4.   [7] *Ibid.*

interference in Armenia was to be avoided, even if such intervention was connected with the internal political situation in the Parthian kingdom.[8]

Vonones realized that he could not count on Roman support, and the opposition to his rule in Armenia, as well as the hostility of Parthia, forced him to flee to the Roman province of Syria, where he was held as a state prisoner. There was evidence that sentiment existed in Armenia for the coronation of Zeno, a Pontic prince, as the new king. From the Roman standpoint, the important consideration was to ensure the recognition of a king, who, because of his realization that he owed his throne to Roman support, would be pro-Roman in his policies, for "this constituted the best available insurance against war with Parthia." [9] The most important part of the mission which Tiberius now entrusted to his nephew was the delicate task of installing Zeno without endangering pacific relations with Parthia.

Diplomatic ability of the first order obviously was requisite for the full attainment of Rome's eastern policy. Germanicus, with the celebration of his triumph, had been recognized as the outstanding military leader of the times.[10] Tiberius and Gaius had performed similar missions in the East, and the tradition was therefore well established that the conduct of the necessary negotiations be entrusted to the heir apparent to the imperial throne. The importance of the objectives promised to minimize the criticism that Tiberius permitted jealousy to motivate him in his decision to recall Germanicus from command of the Rhine legions.[11]

[8] Marsh, *Reign of Tiberius*, 87.   [9] *Ibid.*, 82.
[10] Sievers, *Studien zur Gesch. der Röm. Kaiser: Tacitus und Tiberius*, 50.
[11] Marsh, *Reign of Tiberius*, 87. Transfer to the East, of course, removed Germanicus from the public eye. Abraham, *Tiberius und Sejan*,

The emperor had abundant cause for misgivings in assigning a major diplomatic task to his nephew. There is no reason to doubt that Germanicus' affability, as well as other favorable personal qualities, had endeared him to the Roman populace. He was immature, however, and nothing in his past career indicated that he possessed the resourcefulness and tact requisite for success in dealing with the intricate Partho-Armenian problem.[12] His conduct during the mutiny had not been particularly creditable, and on two occasions it is related that he had talked of suicide when confronted with critical situations.[13] In the progress of his campaigns he had failed to take skillful advantage of the enmities and dissensions that prevailed among the Germans.[14] Indeed, his ravaging of the territories penetrated by the legions had done much to consolidate German resistance.[15] His military expeditions showed that "for him, his youthful dreams of military renown and heroism counted for more than the obvious benefit of his country." [16] There was danger, therefore, that he would fail to carry out the emperor's instructions to avoid hostilities.

These considerations doubtless were responsible for Tiberius' decision to appoint Gnaeus Piso, an experienced provincial governor and a man of proved ability, to the governorship of Syria.[17] Creticus Silanus was removed from command in the province to make way for the new

---

10. It was a good thing for the prince's career, however, to make him known in the East and to familiarize him with conditions there. Motzo, "I commentari di Agrippina madre di Nerone," in *loc. cit.*, 45.

12. Marsh, *Reign of Tiberius*, 87.
13. Viertel, *Tiberius und Germanicus*, 14–15.
14. Liebenam, "Zur Tradition über Germanicus," in *loc. cit.*, 811.
15. Freytag, *Tiberius und Tacitus*, 91–92.
16. *Ibid.*, 131.
17. Tacitus, *Ann.*, II, 43. He had been talked of as a candidate for the throne. *Ibid.*, I, 13.

appointee.[18] Cordial relations prevailed between Germanicus and Silanus; indeed, the daughter of the latter had been betrothed to Nero, eldest son of Germanicus, although both were still infants.[19] There was every reason to foresee that co-operation between the Syrian governor and Germanicus would facilitate the successful performance of the eastern mission, and the recall of Silanus seemed to threaten to impair that co-operation.[20] It is possible, however, that the removal of Silanus was the result of the emperor's dissatisfaction with his action in keeping Vonones in his province, with the consequent danger of aggravating the displeasure of Artabanus of Parthia; yet Vonones was not released with the recall of the governor.[21]

The emperor had a number of motives for appointing Piso to the Syrian post. It was a sound precaution to have Germanicus under the vigilant eye of a man of mature judgment and widest experience, in view of the difficulties involved in the eastern problem.[22] The assignment of a mentor to an inexperienced prince was not unique. Sejanus, commander of the praetorian cohorts, had been sent with Drusus, son of the emperor, to suppress the mutiny of the Pannonian legions, and Sulpicus Quirinus had accompanied Gaius, grandson of Augustus, on his eastern

---

[18] *Ibid.*, II, 53.
[19] *Ibid.* See, Marsh, *Reign of Tiberius*, 88.
[20] Ferber, *Utrum metuerit Tiberius Germanicum*, 21. Tacitus' use of the pluperfect tense suggests that Silanus' removal was not connected with the appointment of Germanicus. Ritter, *Die taciteische Charakterzeichnung des Tiberius*, 25. The Syrian legate ordinarily served 3–5 years. E. S. Bouchier, *Syria as a Roman Province* (Oxford, 1916), 30.
[21] Viertel, *Tiberius und Germanicus*, 23–24. Liebenam, "Zur Tradition über Germanicus," in *loc. cit.*, 866, thinks Silanus may have been guilty of perfidy. Cf., A. von Gutschmid, *Geschichte Irans und seine Nachbarländer* (Tübingen, 1888), 119.
[22] Liebenam, "Zur Tradition über Germanicus," in *loc. cit.*, 867.

mission.[23] Tiberius, of course, had not forgotten the fact that the Rhine legions had offered the purple to Germanicus during the mutiny. Although the loyalty of Germanicus apparently had been above reproach on this occasion, Tiberius wished to guard against a possible recurrence of such an incident in the East.[24]

Gnaeus Piso was the son of L. Calpurnius Piso, a proud member of the old aristocracy. After the assassination of Caesar, the elder Piso had "subjected himself to a pointed and disdainful retirement, both in respect to the new Caesarinian nobility and towards the person of the prince." [25] The younger Piso had been the recipient of the favor of Augustus designed to win him over from his attitude of passive opposition to the imperial regime. His greatest honor had been his induction into the consulship as a colleague of Tiberius.[26] The conciliatory policy of the *princeps* somewhat allayed his bitterness, but his haughty pride remained unchastened; indeed, Augustus believed that he was bold enough to attempt to usurp the throne under propitious circumstances.[27]

Piso shared in full measure the arrogance of the old aristocracy and their disdain toward the imperial family.

---

[23] Spengel, "Zur Gesch. des Kaisers Tiberius," in *loc. cit.*, 41–45.

[24] Abraham, *Tiberius und Sejan*, 10.

[25] Casagrandi, "Il partito dell'opposizione repubblicana sotto Tiberio," in *loc. cit.*, 183–84.

[26] "An efficient co-operation of prince and Senate was only possible then if the bearers of the great names and proud traditions of the free state would be won for the emperor; for that reason Augustus exerted himself . . . to pledge them to his person and to his cause." E. Groag, "Zur Aemterlaufbahn der Nobiles in der Kaiserzeit," *Strena Buliciana* (Zagreb, 1924), 253. "It could not be immaterial to the emperors after what personages the years of their reigns were named. . . . The bestowal of the highest honorary office did not follow mere arbitrariness or whim." *Id.*, "Zum Konsulat in der Kaiserzeit," *Wiener Studien*, XLVII (1929), 144.

[27] Tacitus, *Ann.*, I, 13. See, Sievers, *Studien zur Gesch. der Röm. Kaiser: Tacitus und Tiberius*, 50–55.

"The surviving members of the nobility outwardly concluded peace with the principate, but with strong exclusiveness they maintained their nobility free from monarchial and courtly influence." [28] Piso's attitude toward Germanicus promised to be one of patronizing superiority.[29] He considered Germanicus an irresponsible youth, and believed that the eastern enterprise was destined to fail unless he saved the prince from the consequences of his incompetence and rashness.[30]

Piso probably received written instructions from Tiberius to govern his conduct in the East.[31] His directions as to the relationship that was to prevail between him and Germanicus were vague, and of necessity much was left to his discretion, for his policy would have to be determined in large measure by the actions of his nominal superior.[32] The Senate, in response to Tiberius' formal request, invested Germanicus with the *maius imperium* for the provinces east of the Adriatic,[33] and it must be remembered that he was the designated successor to the emperor

---

[28] M. Gelzer, "Die Nobilität der Kaiserzeit," *Hermes*, L (1915), 409. He believes that the nobles were those who were descended in the paternal or maternal line from pre-Caesarinian senators. His views are supported by E. Stein, "Zur Kontroverse über die röm. Nobilität der Kaiserzeit," *Hermes*, LII (1917), 564-71. For opposing views in regard to the imperial nobility, see, W. Otto, "Die Nobilität der Kaiserzeit," *Hermes*, LI (1916), 76, 83. Throughout the Julio-Claudian period the nobles were given important posts, including military commands. By the Adoptive period, however, it was the policy of the emperors to exclude them from military commands. Groag, "Zur Aemterlaufbahn der Nobiles in der Kaiserzeit," in *loc. cit.*, 253-56.

[29] Gelzer, "Die Nobilität der Kaiserzeit," in *loc. cit.*, 409.

[30] Freytag, *Tiberius und Tacitus*, 124; Viertel, *Tiberius und Germanicus*, 15. Sievers, *Studien zur Gesch. der Röm. Kaiser: Tacitus und Tiberius*, 51, thinks that Piso decided to check Germanicus on his own responsibility.

[31] Tacitus, *Ann.*, II, 43; III, 16.

[32] Freytag, *Tiberius und Tacitus*, 124.

[33] Tacitus, *Ann.*, II, 43. See, Gardthausen, *Augustus und seine Zeit*, Vol. I, Pt. III, 1133.

by provision of Augustus.[34] The authority of Germanicus, therefore, was ostensibly superior to the powers possessed by Piso as a provincial governor.[35]

On the other hand, Piso had received instructions directly from the emperor, which in all probability gave him reason to believe that he was to exercise supervision over the conduct of Germanicus.[36] This by no means is evidence that Tiberius wanted to hamper the activities of Germanicus so as to bring about his failure and the consequent damage to his prestige. Piso, however, needed no instructions to make him a carping, recalcitrant subordinate.[37]

In view of his age and the distinction of his earlier career, it is hardly credible that he would have accepted a mere provincial governorship—a post that he already had held—unless he understood that he was to exercise the more important function of controlling the actions and policies of the heir designate to the imperial throne.[38] The emperor could not have failed to understand that Piso was ill-suited by character and temperament to act in collaboration with anyone, particularly with a younger man whom he regarded as a parvenu. Even Tacitus credits Tiberius with success in selecting suitable appointees for administrative posts as evidence of his ability to evaluate men. The emperor, to be sure, could not have been expected to fore-

[34] *Infra*, 10, 26.
[35] Mommsen, *Staatsrecht*, I, 262. Schulz, "Das Wesen des römischen Kaisertums der ersten zwei Jahrhunderte," in *loc. cit.*, 60–61, thinks that the senatorial investment with the *imperium* is further evidence of Tiberius' wish to rule in a constitutional manner.
[36] Tacitus, *Ann.*, II, 43. See, Casagrandi, "Il partito dell'opposizione repubblicana sotto Tiberio," in *loc. cit.*, 192–93, 197; Ferber, *Utrum metuerit Tiberius Germanicum*, 43–44; Marsh, *Reign of Tiberius*, 87–88.
[37] Freytag, *Tiberius und Tacitus*, 124; Sievers, *Studien zur Gesch. der Röm. Kaiser: Tacitus und Tiberius*, 50–51.
[38] Viertel, *Tiberius und Germanicus*, 20–21.

see that the relationship between Germanicus and Piso would become so hostile as to jeopardize the whole eastern policy. Yet, knowing Piso as he doubtless did, his appointment of such a man to the Syrian governorship was a blunder of tragic proportions. The only alternative to such a verdict is to hold that he deliberately sacrificed the interests of the state in the hope of discrediting Germanicus.

Another factor that virtually precluded even a modicum of co-operation between Germanicus and Piso was the fact that both were accompanied to the East by their wives.[39] Agrippina, wife of Germanicus, prided herself on the fact she was a direct descendant of Augustus. She was "openly at odds with the empress mother, Livia, and very probably she was unfriendly to Tiberius himself." [40] Plancina, wife of Piso, as a member of the rich and aristocratic Planatian family of Tivoli, likewise had a reason to be proud of her lineage. Her father, Gnaeus Munatius Planca, had lost a brother as a victim of the proscriptions of the Second Triumvirate. He, on the other hand, had fled to Salerno in disguise, but he ultimately was betrayed to Marcus Antonius and put to death. Plancina and her sister were reared by their mother and an uncle who had become a convert to the cause of Octavian.[41] Imperious and ambitious, Plancina was only too ready to show her jealousy of Agrippina and to thwart her at every turn.[42] In view of the characters and personalities of these two leading female participants in the eastern affair, secret

---

[39] *Ibid.*, 19.
[40] Marsh, *Reign of Tiberius*, 77; Lang, *Beiträge zur Gesch. des Kaisers Tiberius*, 55–56; Gagé, "Divus Augustus," in *loc. cit.*, 17–18.
[41] Casagrandi, "Il partito dell'opposizione repubblicana sotto Tiberio," in *loc. cit.*, 188.
[42] Viertel, *Tiberius und Germanicus*, 19.

instructions from Livia to Plancina were hardly necessary to produce trouble.⁴³

Germanicus left for the East in the fall of 17. He visited Drusus, son of Tiberius with whom he was on cordial terms, in Illyria. He proceeded to Nicopolis, where he assumed the consulship for the year 18 as a colleague of Tiberius.⁴⁴ His voyage on both the Adriatic and Ionian seas had been stormy, and he spent a few days in a visit to the site of the battle of Actium, while his vessels were refitted.⁴⁵ He subsequently went on to Athens, where his democratic bearing and indubitable charm of manner made a favorable impression, as evinced by the compliments paid him by the Athenian populace.⁴⁶

From Athens he went to Euboea. He joined Agrippina, who had preceded him on the journey because of her pregnancy, at Samos.⁴⁷ The voyage seems to have been resumed almost immediately, which may indicate that the birth of Livilla occurred prior to Germanicus' arrival.⁴⁸

The couple and their entourage then crossed Thrace

⁴³ Tacitus, *Ann.*, I, 43. See, Abraham, *Tiberius und Sejan*, 11; Willrich, *Livia*, 23.

⁴⁴ Tacitus, *Ann.*, II, 53. J. J. Savage, "Germanicus and Aeneas," *Classical Journal*, XXXIV (1939), 237-38, compares Tacitus' account of Germanicus' voyage with the *Aeneid*, I, 81-123. Germanicus' consulships are widely noted in the inscriptions, as, for example, *C.I.L.*, II, 1517, 2039, 2198, 3103, 3104; III, 334; IV$^{1-2}$, 1885, 5432; V, 4308; VI, 909; IX, 962; X¹, 513, 1198, 1625, 4572; XI, 1166; XIII, 1036.

⁴⁵ Tacitus, *Ann.*, II, 53. See, *I.G.R.R.*, III, 715; IV, 11, 326, 327, 979.

⁴⁶ Tacitus, *Ann.*, II, 53. The base of a statue, dedicated to Germanicus and commemorating his visit to Athens, is extant. P. Graindor, "Athènes de Tiberè à Trajan," *Université Égyptienne, Recueil de travaux publiés par la faculté des lettres*, VIII (Cairo, 1931), 6. Germanicus' conduct was open to criticism on the grounds that he courted the flattery of the Athenians. Viertel, *Tiberius und Germanicus*, 17; Ferber, *Utrum metuerit Tiberius Germanicum*, 28-29.

⁴⁷ Mommsen, "Die Familie des Germanicus," in *loc. cit.*, 280.

⁴⁸ Livilla later was known as Julia. Tacitus, *Ann.*, II, 53, says her birth occurred on Lesbos. Cf., Mommsen, "Die Familie des Germanicus," in *loc. cit.*, 280.

and tarried for a time at Perinthus and Byzantium.[49] Their journey continued into Asia Minor, where Germanicus relieved the sufferings of the provincials, which had been attributable to internecine strife. Germanicus visited Troy and examined its ruins with interest.[50] At Colophon he consulted the famous oracle of the Clarian Apollo.[51]

In the meantime, Piso set out to assume his Syrian post. In contrast to the leisurely travel of Germanicus, he made all possible haste.[52] Upon his arrival in Athens, he greeted the citizenry with a tirade in which he made scathing references to their past allegiance to Mithridates of Pontus and Marcus Antonius.[53] It is hardly likely that the ire of Piso had been aroused by failure of the Athenians to accord him a reception comparable with that of Germanicus. According to the account of Tacitus, his attitude was truculent at his entrance into the city, and he knew that he was not entitled to the honors paid to a member of the ruling house of the empire.[54] He probably intended his actions as a rebuke to Germanicus who, he believed, apparently with some justice, had courted adulation.[55] His asperity may have been sharpened by a private grievance arising from the refusal of the Athenian authorities to release a convicted forger at his behest.[56]

By sailing along a short course through the Cyclades, Piso succeeded in overtaking Germanicus at Rhodes. As his ships neared the dangerous Rhodian coast, a violent storm suddenly arose and drove them toward the rocks. The crews of Germanicus' vessels, however, lent timely aid, and the imminent disaster was averted.[57] Tacitus

---

[49] Ferber, *Utrum metuerit Tiberius Germanicum*, 28-29, calls attention to the strategic importance of the places visited by Germanicus as a suspicious circumstance.
[50] Tacitus, *Ann.*, II, 54.
[51] *Ibid.*
[52] *Ibid.*
[53] *Ibid.*
[54] Viertel, *Tiberius und Germanicus*, 17.
[55] *Ibid.*
[56] Tacitus, *Ann.*, II, 55.
[57] *Ibid.*

GERMANICUS IN THE EAST

claims that Germanicus already had learned of Piso's conduct at Athens and cites the Rhodian incident as evidence of Germanicus' magnanimity.[58] It was hardly possible for Germanicus to have received news from Athens so promptly; the historian probably made this statement to enhance the dramatic effect of the rescue.[59] After reluctantly tarrying a single day at Rhodes, Piso hurried on to Syria, apparently anxious to arrive in the province before Germanicus.[60]

Upon his arrival in Syria he took prompt measures to secure the loyalty and devotion of the legions. Largesses were distributed, and a number of centurions were dismissed and replaced by his own adherents.[61] Piso received salutation as "Father of the Legions," a title which with much greater propriety should have been bestowed on Germanicus.[62] Plancina also took steps to ingratiate herself with the soldiery and allegedly derided both Germanicus and Agrippina.[63] Such actions could not have failed to produce the belief that the governor and his wife could count on the support of the emperor in the event that Germanicus brought matters to an open issue.[64]

Germanicus apparently took no cognizance of the actions of Piso, but immediately proceeded into Armenia. Sentiment for the recognition of Zeno, son of King Polemo of Pontus, already had been manifested, "for the prince, an imitator from earliest infancy of Armenian institutions and dress, had endeared himself equally to the higher and the lower orders by his affection for the chase, the banquet, and the other favorite pastimes of barbarians." [65] Parthia evinced no objections to his choice,[66] and

---

[58] *Ibid.*   [59] Viertel, *Tiberius und Germanicus*, 17–18.
[60] Tacitus, *Ann.*, II, 55.   [61] *Ibid.*   [62] *Ibid.*   [63] *Ibid.*
[64] *Ibid.;* Viertel, *Tiberius und Germanicus*, 20.
[65] Tacitus, *Ann.*, II, 56.
[66] See, Dessau, *Gesch. der röm. Kaiserzeit*, Vol. II, Pt. I, 17.

Germanicus accordingly placed the regal diadem on his head at Artaxata. The new king received the homage of his subjects and took the royal name of Artaxias III (A.D. 18–34) as a concession to Armenian nationalistic sentiment.[67] Cappadocia then was made a Roman province, with Quintus Veranius as temporary governor,[68] and an immediate result was the alleviation of the tax burdens on the Cappadocian populace.[69] Commagene was placed under the administration of a Roman propraetor.[70]

Germanicus had ordered Piso or his son to lead the legions into Armenia, but the governor had not obeyed.[71] Germanicus apparently wanted the legions to make a military demonstration in support of Zeno.[72] At first sight, it would appear that Piso had been guilty of flagrant insubordination.[73] Yet, as we have seen, his instructions must

[67] Tacitus, *Ann.*, II, 56; Asdourian, *Die pol. Beziehungen zw. Armenien und Rom*, 80. Attainment of the Roman objective was facilitated by the existence of a delicate balance between the pro-Roman and pro-Parthian parties in Armenia. Many of the Armenian feudal lords were sincere proponents of Roman culture. Germanicus' settlement of Armenian affairs endured until A.D. 34, when Artabanus of Parthia installed Arsaces I. Tiberius backed the candidacy of Mithridates, but the issue was still in doubt at the end of his reign. Asdourian, *Die pol. Beziehungen zw. Armenien und Rom*, 73–74, 81–82.

[68] Tacitus, *Ann.*, II, 56.

[69] *Ibid*. The extravagance of cities, particularly in the East, was a major cause of financial difficulties and the consequent high taxation. F. F. Abbott and A. C. Johnson, *Municipal Administration in the Roman Empire* (Princeton, 1926), 81, 149.

[70] Tacitus, *Ann.*, II, 56. Commagene on the upper Euphrates was of great strategic value in the event of hostilities with Parthia. Bouchier, *Syria as a Roman Province*, 32. A Palmyran emissary was probably employed in the conduct of these negotiations, as recorded in an inscription found in 1930. J. Cantineau, "Textes Palmyreniens du Temple de Bel," *Syria*, XII (1931), 167. Coins were issued commemorating the annexation of Commagene. Mattingly, *Coins of the Roman Empire*, I, cxli.

[71] Tacitus, *Ann.*, II, 57.

[72] Viertel, *Tiberius und Germanicus*, 27.

[73] Casagrandi, "Il partito dell'opposizione repubblicana sotto Tiberio," in *loc. cit.*, 197; Ferber, *Utrum metuerit Tiberius Germanicum*, 28; Mommsen, *Staatsrecht*, I, 262, n.4.

have given him considerable latitude. He may have thought that a demonstration in force in favor of Zeno would involve the pointless risk of antagonizing Parthia and "if this was [his] view of the situation he probably was well within the instructions of Tiberius in refusing to place at the disposal of Germanicus a force for which the prince had no legitimate use."⁷⁴ Both Piso and Germanicus were unfamiliar with the terrain through which the legions would have had to march. Although Piso had been enthusiastically received by the Syrian legions, their signs of loyalty had been evoked in response to efforts to earn their affection, which he considered it necessary to make. He had not been at his post sufficiently long to assure himself that their discipline and mettle would stand the test of an expedition to a point far from their base, even though the chance of hostilities was remote.⁷⁵ Piso apparently favored the restoration of Vonones to the Armenian throne, or at least the policy of keeping him under Roman protection as a diplomatic weapon to be employed against Parthia.⁷⁶ Germanicus' installation of Zeno may have appeared to Piso as a tacit recognition of Parthia's right to intervene in Armenia, for the flight of Vonones into Syria certainly had been mainly the result of the hostility of Artabanus.⁷⁷ It is hard to see, however, how Rome could have continued even the appearance of fostering the claims of Vonones without the danger of embittering Parthia, a contingency which Tiberius certainly wished

⁷⁴ Marsh, *Reign of Tiberius*, 90–91.
⁷⁵ Viertel, *Tiberius und Germanicus*, 20–27.
⁷⁶ Tacitus, *Ann.*, II, 58.
⁷⁷ Willenbücher, *Tiberius und die Verschwörung Sejans*, 13. Kuntz, *Tiberius and the Roman Constitution*, 50–52, thinks that the strife between Germanicus and Piso was the result of their different attitudes toward the constitutional program of the emperor. She holds that Piso represented the imperialism of the senatorial aristocracy. Viertel, *Tiberius und Germanicus*, 33, thinks that this was the crux of the whole affair.

to avoid. In any event, conviction rather than deliberate insubordination probably determined Piso's refusal to send the troops.[78]

Germanicus made an effort to bring about a reconciliation with Piso when they met at Cyrrus (Khoros), the winter quarters of the legions.[79] This would seem to indicate that Germanicus did not consider Piso's action in withholding the troops as an act of overt insubordination.[80] The friends of the prince, however, endeavored to excite his anger against the governor, who certainly made no effort to reciprocate the conciliatory gestures of Germanicus, but openly dissented from his views in the conferences of the officers.[81]

Subsequent events widened the breach. At a banquet at Nabat, Germanicus and Agrippina received gold crowns as gifts from the Parthian monarch. Piso and Plancina were given crowns of lesser value, which they disdainfully refused to accept.[82] It is hardly likely that Piso would have publicly exhibited jealousy because of the greater value of the gifts tendered to Germanicus and Agrippina. His action may have been intended to rebuke the prince for accepting gifts which might lead to the charge of bribery.[83] But if such was his object, he placed ludicrous importance on the whole affair.

Germanicus soon had an opportunity to retaliate. Vonones, it will be recalled, still was in Syria as a state prisoner. Artabanus, the Parthian ruler, now requested that the exile be transferred to Cilicia and imprisoned.

---

[78] Viertel, *Tiberius und Germanicus*, 18–20, points out that Tiberius would not have condoned military insubordination under any circumstances.
[79] Tacitus, *Ann.*, II, 57.
[80] Marsh, *Reign of Tiberius*, 91; Freytag, *Tiberius und Tacitus*, 128.
[81] Tacitus, *Ann.*, II, 57. See, Viertel, *Tiberius und Germanicus*, 28.
[82] Tacitus, *Ann.*, II, 57.
[83] Viertel, *Tiberius und Germanicus*, 29.

Germanicus immediately complied with this request.[84] His decision was primarily motivated by diplomatic considerations, for Vonones certainly no longer figured in Rome's eastern plans. Nevertheless, he knew that Vonones was the recipient of the patronage of Piso and Plancina, who therefore considered his removal a personal affront.[85]

Despite the recalcitrance of Piso, which had reached the point of unconcealed enmity, Germanicus had capably discharged his eastern mission. The emperor was completely satisfied; "he showed more pleasure at having kept the peace by diplomacy than if he had concluded a war by a series of stricken fields." [86] The Senate decreed an ovation for him, and arches bearing the images of Tiberius and Germanicus were erected on each side of the temple of Mars the Avenger.[87] It was doubtless the conviction that his work was done—and well done—that impelled Germanicus to make his memorable journey to Egypt.

The Egyptian trip probably was prompted by no more sinister motives than curiosity and enjoyment of travel to strange places.[88] Nevertheless, the visit was a major blunder. In Egypt, Augustus and his successor were regarded as the heirs of the Ptolemies. The administration was different from that of the provinces, for Egypt was considered the private property of the emperor and was governed by a prefect appointed from the ranks of the *equites*.

---

[84] Tacitus, *Ann.*, II, 58. He later was killed trying to flee to Armenia. *Ibid.*, 68.

[85] Viertel, *Tiberius und Germanicus*, 31, thinks that purely personal considerations were responsible for Germanicus' decision. He rightly points out that Germanicus made no response to Artabanus' request for a personal interview.

[86] Tacitus, *Ann.*, II, 64; Dessau, *Gesch. der röm. Kaiserzeit*, Vol. II, Pt. I, 17.

[87] Tacitus, *Ann.*, II, 64.

[88] *Ibid.*, 59; Suetonius, *Tib.*, LII. A. Stein, *Untersuchen zur Geschichte und Verwaltung Aegyptens unter Roemischer Herrschaft* (Stuttgart, 1915), 107.

Men of senatorial rank were forbidden to visit the country without the emperor's permission, for, because of the vital importance of Egyptian grain to Italy, "any usurpation in Egypt meant nothing less than danger of famine to the capital of the world." [89] Germanicus could not have been ignorant of this regulation.[90] In view of the precedent set by Augustus, he could hardly have believed that his *maius imperium* included Egypt. His differences with Piso certainly had been serious enough to induce a more prudent man to take every precaution to guard against treachery.[91]

The conduct of the prince in Egypt was indiscreet, to say the least. He curried the favor of the Alexandrian populace by affected simplicity and Greek dress. In view of the high prices of grain that prevailed because of imminent famine, he opened the granaries at Neopolis and distributed grain to the populace.[92] He did not open the imperial granary, however, and his action in no wise caused a dearth of grain in Rome in the winter of 19, for the grain he distributed was from the harvest of 18, of which the portion destined for Italy already had been shipped.[93] Still,

---

[89] E. Hohl-Rostock, "Ein Römischer Prinz in Ägypten," *Preuszische Jahrbücher*, CLXXXII (1920), 347, 350. In Egypt there "existed from the beginning the political order of the future: the uncurtailed power of the ruler, the firm position of the dynasty, the insurance of absolute rule by the public forms of the imperial cult." J. Vogt, *Römische Politik in Ägypten* (Leipzig, 1924), 6. See also, O. Hirschfeld, *Die Kaiserlichen Verwaltungsbeamten bis auf Diocletian*, 2nd ed. (Berlin, 1905), 343–61.

[90] C. Cichorius, "Die Ägyptischen Erlasse des Germanicus," *Römische Studien* (Berlin, 1922), 376, thinks that Tiberius would have given permission if a request had been made.

[91] Viertel, *Tiberius und Germanicus*, 35. Sievers, *Studien zur Gesch. der Röm. Kaiser: Tacitus und Tiberius*, 52, claims that this shows that Germanicus did not fear Piso.

[92] Tacitus, *Ann.*, II, 59; Cichorius, "Die Ägyptischen Erlasse des Germanicus," in *loc. cit.*, 375–88.

[93] U. Wilcken, "Zum Germanicus-Papyrus," *Hermes*, LXIII (1928), 48–65.

he had exceeded his authority, even though his action may have been justified on humanitarian grounds.[94] The grateful populace did not stint in according him honors, while he was unwise in parading too openly as the heir to the throne.[95] Tiberius learned of the Egyptian activities of his nephew, probably from a report of Caius Galerius, the prefect, and responded with a sharp rebuke.[96] But Germanicus had gone up the Nile to visit sites of historic interest, and so he did not learn of the emperor's displeasure until his return.

In the meantime, Piso utilized the absence of the prince to good advantage by countermanding his orders and endeavoring to undermine his influence in Syria.[97] Doubtless he realized that Germanicus had compromised himself by his actions in Egypt. It is likely that he learned of the emperor's reprimand of the prince, and, exaggerating its significance, believed that he could move against him with impunity.[98]

[94] Hohl-Rostock, "Ein Römischer Prinz in Ägypten," in *loc. cit.*, 351.
[95] *Ibid.*, 359. See, R. H. Bevan, "The Deification of Kings in the Greek Cities," *English Historical Review*, XVI (1901), 632 ff. The prince renounced the rights of purveyance which he could have demanded. U. von Wilamowitz-Moellendorff and F. Zucker, "Zwei Edikte des Germanicus auf einem Papyrus des Berliner Museum," *Sitzungsberichte der Königlich Preussischen Akademie der Wissenschaften* (1911), II, 794, 800, 803. He virtually ignored the local officials, but his refusal to permit salutations of divinity was probably intended to disarm criticism in Rome. *Ibid.*, 817, 819.
[96] Tacitus, *Ann.*, II, 59. For identification of the Egyptian prefect, see, L. Cantarelli, "Un prefetto di Egitto," *Studi Romani e Bizantini* (Rome, 1915), 216–17. Spengel, "Zur Geschichte des Kaisers Tiberius," in *loc. cit.*, 18, says that "like a father earnestly concerned about the rearing of his son Tiberius did not spare him a strong reprimand if he considered it necessary." The reprimand, however, was stronger than paternal chiding, even though there is no evidence that the emperor regarded the prince's conduct as "not far removed from that of a pretender to the throne," as Liebenam, "Zur Tradition über Germanicus," in *loc. cit.*, 870, declares.
[97] Tacitus, *Ann.*, II, 69.
[98] Ferber, *Utrum metuerit Tiberius Germanicum*, 42–43, thinks Piso understood that he was expected by the emperor to ruin Germanicus.

Germanicus was informed of Piso's actions on his way back to Syria, and bitter recriminations were exchanged between him and the governor upon his arrival in the province.[99] Piso then announced his intention to quit his province.[100] The news that Germanicus was seriously ill, however, caused him to reconsider his decision to leave, and he remained in Antioch. When it was reported that the prince's condition had taken a turn for the better, he ordered lictors to stop the public fulfillment of vows which had been offered to the gods by the populace of the city to promote the recovery of Germanicus.[101]

Germanicus soon suffered a relapse, while Piso proceeded to Seleuceia, where he apparently awaited the outcome of the prince's malady. He kept in close touch with the progress of his superior's illness, and Tacitus narrates that his emissaries "were accused of keeping a too inquisitive watch upon the ravages of the disease." [102] It was also alleged that "explorations in the floor and walls brought to light the remains of human bodies, spells, curses, leaden tablets engraved with the name of Germanicus, charred and blood-smeared ashes, and others of the implements of witchcraft by which it is believed the living soul can be devoted to the powers of the grave." [103] If such discoveries were made, it is likely that they were made by slaves "who found what they knew they were expected to find." [104]

By this time Germanicus was convinced that Piso was

---

[99] Tacitus, *Ann.*, II, 69.
[100] *Ibid.* Viertel, *Tiberius und Germanicus*, 38, maintains that Germanicus ordered him to leave at this time, rather than later, as Tacitus, *Ann.*, II, 70, narrates.
[101] Tacitus, *Ann.*, II, 69.   [102] *Ibid.*   [103] *Ibid.*
[104] Marsh, *Reign of Tiberius*, 95. Ferber, *Utrum metuerit Tiberius Germanicum*, 31, suggests that the ubiquitous friends of Germanicus concealed those objects to arouse the prince's superstitious fears and fan the hatred between him and Piso.

plotting against his life. Tacitus claims that he said, "If this threshold were besieged, if he must surrender his breath under the eye of his enemies, what must the future hold in store for his unhappy wife—for his infant children? Poison was considered too dilatory: Piso was growing urgent—imperative—to be left alone with his province and his legions." [105] Thereupon the prince renounced his friendship with Piso [106] and presumably ordered him to leave the province.[107] Piso set sail, but proceeded leisurely, apparently in order to be able to return speedily if the prince should die.

It should be noted that Germanicus is reported to have said that "poison was considered too dilatory." This seems to indicate that he had learned of a poison plot against him which had failed to materialize, or that an actual attempt had been made to poison him and had proved abortive.

After another brief rally, Germanicus' condition rapidly became worse, and, realizing that he was dying, he summoned his wife and friends to his bedside and allegedly said:

If I were dying by the course of nature, I should have a justified grievance against Heaven itself for snatching me from parents, children, and country, by a premature end in the prime of life. Now, cut off as I am by the villainy of Piso and Plancina, I leave my last prayers in the keeping of your breasts: report to my father and brother the agonies that rent me, the treasons that encompassed me, before I finished the most pitiable of lives by the vilest of deaths. . . . You will have your opportunity to complain before the senate and to invoke the law. The prime duty of friends is not to

[105] Tacitus, *Ann.*, II, 70.
[106] A strange procedure to say the least. Why, in view of all that allegedly happened between them, should Germanicus now renounce friendship with Piso? See, Liebenam, "Zur Tradition über Germanicus," in *loc. cit.*, 871.
[107] Freytag, *Tiberius und Tacitus*, 129, thinks Germanicus had no right to order Piso to leave.

follow their dead with passive laments, but to remember his wishes and carry out his commands. Strangers themselves will bewail Germanicus: *you* will avenge him—if you loved me and not my fortune.[108]

Then he turned to Agrippina and implored her "by the memory of himself, and for the sake of their common children, to strip herself of pride, to stoop her spirit before the rage of fortune, and never—if she returned to the capital—to irritate those stronger than herself by a competition for power." [109]

Funerary rites were celebrated at Antioch in a simple manner. The body before cremation was exposed in the forum of the city. "Whether it bore marks of poisoning was disputable: for the indications were variously read, as pity and preconceived suspicion swayed the spectator to the side of Germanicus, or his predilections to that of Piso." [110] Tacitus does not commit himself as to the poisoning charge which was circulated. It might also be noted that, according to his account, Piso had at least some sympathizers in the Syrian metropolis.

Suetonius also alludes to charges of poisoning. He declares:

There was some suspicion that he [Germanicus] was poisoned; for besides the dark spots which appeared all over his body and the froth which flowed from his mouth, after he had been reduced to ashes his heart was found entire among his bones; and it is supposed to be a characteristic of that organ when steeped in poison it cannot be destroyed by fire.[111]

[108] Tacitus, *Ann.*, II, 71. In Asia the friends (*Amici*), or personal entourage of the governor, constituted an advisory council. V. Chapot, *La province Romaine proconsulaire d'Asie* (Paris, 1904), 292.
[109] Tacitus, *Ann.*, II, 72. Here is an obvious hint of possible danger from the emperor but also a frank recognition of Agrippina's character as a factor that might cause trouble.
[110] Tacitus, *Ann.*, II, 73.
[111] Suetonius, *Caligula*, I. Ferber, *Utrum metuerit Tiberius Ger-*

GERMANICUS IN THE EAST

Dio's account includes elements found in the narratives of both Tacitus and Suetonius. He declares:

> His death occurred at Antioch as the result of a plot formed by Piso and Plancina. For bones of men that had been buried in the house where he dwelt and sheets of lead containing curses together with his name were found while he was yet alive; and that poison was the means of his carrying off was revealed by the condition of his body, which was brought into the Forum and exhibited to all who were present.[112]

Charges that the prince had been poisoned certainly were circulated. Germanicus himself, if the account of Tacitus is correct, believed that he had fallen victim to the plotting of Piso and Plancina.[113] He did not believe that the emperor was responsible, for he charged his friends to "Report to my father and brother the agonies that rent me, the treasons that encompassed me. . . ."[114] If Piso had wished to poison the prince, it would seem that he would have attempted to win his confidence; yet his actions as described by Tacitus could have no other result than to arouse his anger and suspicion.[115] Germanicus himself, while holding Piso and Plancina responsible for his death, does not seem to have believed that he had been poisoned.[116] Action on the poisoning charges was inevitable. Germanicus allegedly had spoken to his friends of "opportunity to complain before the Senate and to

---

manicum, 34, holds that Tacitus was not trying to calumniate Tiberius or he would have included the heart story. Germanicus probably died on October 10, A.D. 19. *C.I.L.*, I², 249; XIV, 244.

[112] Dio, *R.H.*, LVII, xviii, 9–10. See also, Josephus, *Antiquities of the Jews*, XVIII, 54.
[113] Tacitus, *Ann.*, II, 71.
[114] *Ibid.* See, Dessau, *Gesch. der röm. Kaiserzeit*, Vol. II, Pt. I, 27–28.
[115] Freytag, *Tiberius und Tacitus*, 127.
[116] Tacitus, *Ann.*, II, 70. Casagrandi, "Il partito dell'opposizione repubblicana sotto Tiberio," in *loc. cit.*, 198, thinks strain caused Germanicus' death.

invoke the law." [117] Friends who were present at the deathbed had sworn to avenge him.[118] Agrippina could be expected to strengthen the demands for an investigation upon her return to Rome. Trial of Piso clearly was foreshadowed; his actions following the death of the prince sealed his doom.

[117] Tacitus, *Ann.*, II, 71.   [118] *Ibid.*

Chapter V

THE TRIAL OF PISO

Piso's conduct after the death of Germanicus was most indiscreet. When he learned of the prince's fate while at Cos, he gave way to unrestrained rejoicing. Plancina's sister recently had died, but despite this bereavement, her delight at the demise of Germanicus was so great that she joined in her husband's demonstrations.[1] Piso now decided to return to Syria to resume his position as governor, which he had legally forfeited when he had departed ostensibly for Rome. His son vainly tried to dissuade him, pointing out that this rash act could be considered treasonable, since force undoubtedly would be needed to win the province from the friends of Germanicus, who had installed Sentius as governor.[2]

Piso had reason to believe that he was within his rights in returning to the province. He held his *imperium* directly from the emperor, with the approval of the Senate. While he had been subordinate to Germanicus, he might have reasoned that the *imperium* bestowed on him was still in effect and was superior to that possessed by Sentius.[3] Desertion of a provincial command was, of course, legally tantamount to forfeiture of the *imperium*. Piso, however, had left his province in response to exceptional conditions and circumstances. While he seems to have left ostensibly on his own volition, relations between him

---

[1] Tacitus, *Ann.*, II, 75; Viertel, *Tiberius und Germanicus*, 52–53.
[2] Tacitus, *Ann.*, II, 76–78.
[3] It might be argued that the *imperium* of Sentius went back to Germanicus. Ferber, *Utrum metuerit Tiberius Germanicum*, 34–40.

and Germanicus had become so strained that pressure doubtless had been brought to bear to force him to this step; indeed, there is some reason to believe that Germanicus had ordered him to leave. He had originally been installed to oversee the conduct of the young prince. It might have seemed to him that there was every reason for him to be at his post, since the friends of Germanicus had assumed control apparently without authorization from the emperor.[4]

After Piso had dispatched a letter to Tiberius notifying him of his intention to return to Syria, Domitius, an intimate friend of the former goverrner, was sent with a warship to prepare the way.[5] Piso soon followed. En route his ship passed the vessels escorting Agrippina, widow of Germanicus, to Rome. Recriminations were exchanged by the commanders of the respective ships. The commander of Agrippina's flotilla angrily ordered Piso to return to Rome. He allegedly replied that he would not return to the capital unless legally summoned by the praetor in charge of poisoning cases.[6] It cannot be argued that this episode shows that Piso had poisoned Germanicus and was therefore expecting prosecution on the charge. Doubtless he knew of the rumors circulated against him even before he left the province, and he knew that Agrippina certainly would capitalize on these allegations. Indeed, it would seem that, if Piso had had a guilty conscience, he would have hurried back to Rome as fast as possible to give his version of his relations with Germanicus before the arrival of Agrippina.

Domitius, in the meantime, had landed in Syria, and Sentius, the *de facto* governor, prepared to resist the in-

---

[4] Piso well may have thought that he was doing the right thing. *Ibid.*, 35-36.
[5] Tacitus, *Ann.*, II, 78.   [6] *Ibid.*, 79.

vasion.⁷ Piso, upon his arrival in Cilicia, took possession of a small fortress and sought to secure the favor of the Syrian legions and the aid of Cilician princelets by negotiation. He argued that he had been unjustly deprived of his province by Sentius solely as a result of personal animosity, in direct defiance of the authority conferred on him by the emperor himself. He reminded the legions that he had been saluted as the "Father of the Legions" and tried to win them to his cause.⁸

Sentius, in command of stronger forces, resolved to take the offensive. He attacked Piso in his fortress and forced him to sue for peace. Favorable terms were granted, for Piso was given a safe conduct and supplied with ships to convey him to Rome.⁹ He was now in a precarious position. His actions had made him vulnerable to charges of treason, since he had attempted to seize the Syrian province by force. Agrippina had preceded him to Rome, hence he could anticipate that popular hostility would be raised to a fever heat against him. Only the emperor could save him, but could Tiberius condone his attempt to seize the province, especially in view of the attitude of the populace?

Great excitement prevailed in Rome as the citizenry urged the lavish grant of honors to the memory of Germanicus and vehemently clamored for the punishment of Piso.¹⁰ Tiberius ordered a medallion to be struck in honor of the late prince and permitted his statue to be placed in the hall of fame for orators and writers, although he refused to accede to the demand that Germanicus' statue should be larger and more ornate than those of the others honored by inclusion in the hall.¹¹ The birth of twins to

---

[7] *Ibid.* See, Marsh, *Reign of Tiberius*, 99.
[8] Tacitus, *Ann.*, II, 80. He especially relied on the sixth legion. *Ibid.*, 79, 81.
[9] *Ibid.*, 81.   [10] *Ibid.*, 82.   [11] *Ibid.*, 83.

Drusus and Livilla, however, in some measure diverted the attention of the populace from these demonstrations of public sorrow.[12]

The arrival of Agrippina at Brundisium with the ashes of her late husband furnished fresh sensations, as mourning friends and admirers greeted her with lamentations and accompanied her to Rome.[13] Tiberius did not come to meet her, but state dignitaries were present as a sign of respect.[14] It was charged that the emperor was secretly overjoyed at the death of his nephew.[15] He and Livia refrained from appearing in public during the funerary services, and Tacitus charges that their absence was attributable to their knowledge that they could not conceal their real feelings.[16] Yet at the funeral of his own son, Tiberius had resolutely concealed his grief even from Sejanus, his favored minister. Certainly such a dissembling man as Tacitus portrays could have realistically counterfeited grief had he so desired. The absence of the emperor probably was attributable to his conviction that some restraint should be exercised in view of the evident tendency of the populace to go to extremes in mourning the death of the popular prince. He quite properly reminded the people that the state was eternal, and that the time had come for reversion to the ordinary interests and activities of daily life.[17] Nevertheless, his absence from the funeral was a mistake. It was bound to be misinterpreted, and it had the effect of sustaining the excitement, the very thing the emperor wished to allay.

Cessation of mourning did not end the public clamor,

---

[12] *Ibid.*, 84. [13] *Ibid.*, III, 1. [14] *Ibid.*, 2. [15] *Ibid.*
[16] *Ibid.*, 3. Ferber, *Utrum metuerit Tiberius Germanicum*, 39, thinks the emperor really rejoiced. See, Stahr, *Tiberius*, 96-97.
[17] Tacitus, *Ann.*, III, 4, 46. The emperor may have wished to avoid a scene with Agrippina. Ritter, *Die taciteische Charakterzeichnung des Tiberius*, 28.

THE TRIAL OF PISO

for there was considerable eagerness to prepare for the prosecution of Piso. Sentius, who had been installed as governor of Syria, sent Martene, reputedly versed in the poisoning arts of the East, to Rome, ostensibly to strengthen the poisoning charge. She was known to have been an intimate friend of Plancina, and therefore such evidence as she may have been prepared to submit would have been correspondingly more damaging to Piso.[18] She suddenly died, however, almost immediately after her arrival at Brundisium. No marks of violence were found on her body, but poison allegedly was discovered secreted in her hair.[19] Her death certainly seemed opportune for Piso, but the death of an aged woman after a long, arduous sea voyage cannot be regarded as suspicious in the absence of corroborative evidence.[20]

Piso delayed his return to Rome with the natural purpose of gaining time for the bitter hostility against him to subside. He sent his son to Tiberius to appraise the situation in the capital and to endeavor to temper the emperor's anger. Tiberius received him with the courtesy due to one of his station, but gave no encouragement in regard to the fundamental purpose of his visit.[21] On his leisurely progress to Rome, Piso visited Drusus, son of the emperor, in Dalmatia and endeavored to secure his favor. Drusus, who had been on the best of terms with Germanicus and who had greatly mourned his death, graciously received Piso and gave him to understand that he was suspending judgment in regard to the charges pending against him. It is possible that he had been ad-

---

[18] Tacitus, *Ann.*, III, 7.
[19] *Ibid.*
[20] Ferber, *Utrum metuerit Tiberius Germanicum*, 41, holds that friends of Germanicus killed Martene to strengthen suspicion against Piso!
[21] Tacitus, *Ann.*, III, 8.

vised by his father to refrain from any unequivocal statement.²²

Upon his eventual arrival in Rome, Piso manifested no signs of fear or contrition. He entertained friends and relatives with a festive dinner in his home almost immediately after his arrival.²³ His purpose probably was to create the impression that his conscience was untroubled and that he was confident of the outcome of the anticipated proceedings against him. Nevertheless, in view of the prevalent bitterness, his conduct exhibited his usual lack of discretion.

In the meantime, three friends of Germanicus, Q. Veranius, Q. Servaeus, and P. Vitellius, prepared to prosecute the erstwhile governor. Fulcinius Trio, a well-known lawyer and prosecutor, also busied himself with the case, apparently at the behest of Agrippina.²⁴ Fulcinius failed in his first attempt to initiate proceedings, but he subsequently gained the concession of authorization to impugn Piso's whole career.²⁵

Tiberius agreed to preside over the trial.²⁶ This probably meant that he extended his own tribunician inviolability to members of the imperial family, and it was therefore proper for him to take charge, at least in so far as the allegation of poisoning was at issue.²⁷ Piso did not demur,

---

[22] *Ibid.* The conduct of Drusus was most tactful. Freytag, *Tiberius und Tacitus*, 137.

[23] Tacitus, *Ann.*, III, 9.

[24] *Ibid.*, 10–11.

[25] *Ibid.* Kessler, *Die Tradition über Germanicus*, 79, 84, maintains that Tacitus made use of documentary evidence on Piso's trial. T. Mommsen, "Das Verhältnis des Tacitus zu den Acten des Senats," *Gesammelte Schriften*, VII, 263, believes that the speeches of the accusing rhetors were one of Tacitus' main sources. See, *Ann.*, III, 13; IV, 10, 40.

[26] Tacitus, *Ann.*, III, 10. See, *ibid.*, III, 17, 68; IV, 19, 34; Dio, *R.H.*, LVII, xviii, 10.

[27] E. Ciaceri, "L'imperatore Tiberio e i processi di lesa maestà," *Processi politici e relazioni internazionali* (Rome, 1918), 272.

THE TRIAL OF PISO

for, finally appreciating how strong sentiment was against him, he believed that he could secure a fairer trial under Tiberius' direction.[28]

The defendant was prosecuted under the Sullan law of *lex sicariis* which dealt with capital offenses,[29] and the third chapter of which dealt with murders committed elsewhere than at Rome or in Italy.[30] This merely served to initiate proceedings, however, for after the beginning of the trial an adjournment was given to enable the prosecution to formulate additional charges.[31]

Tiberius then withdrew from the case and remanded it to the Senate for trial.[32] He probably considered the poisoning charge unworthy of serious consideration. Piso's most serious offense was his attack on Syria, which was treason in the eyes of the law. Yet the emperor's personal interests were involved, for Piso, it was charged, had rejoiced at the news of Germanicus' death. Since both the interests of the state and those of his family were involved, he believed that prosecution by the Senate would make more clear the attitude of strict and impartial justice which he wanted to assume during the course of the trial. This interpretation seems to be borne out by the opening address which, according to Tacitus, he made when the Senate trial began. Tiberius declared that, "If [this] case is one of a subordinate who, after ignoring the limits of his commission and the deference owed to his superior, has exulted over that superior's death and my own sorrow, I shall renounce his friendship, banish him from my house, and redress my grievances as a man without invoking my powers as a sovereign." [33]

The emperor further clarified the questions at issue be-

---

[28] Tacitus, *Ann.*, III, 10.   [29] *Ibid.*
[30] J. L. Strachan-Davidson, *Problems of the Roman Criminal Law*, 2 vols. (London, 1912), II, 149.
[31] Tacitus, *Ann.*, III, 13.   [32] *Ibid.*, 10.   [33] *Ibid.*, 12.

fore the Senate. The Fathers were called upon to decide if "Piso's treatment of the armies [made] for disorder and sedition? Did he employ corrupt means to win the favour of the private soldiers? Did he levy war in order to possess himself of the province? . . . For what was the object in stripping the corpse naked and exposing it to the degrading contact of the vulgar gaze? Or in diffusing the report—and among the foreigners—that he fell a victim of poison, if that is an issue still uncertain and in need of scrutiny?"[34] While further consideration of the poison charge was not precluded, the emperor certainly indicated that the expediency of proceeding on this matter was questionable. Each of the three charges, stirring up civil war, treason, and blasphemy against the house of Augustus, was punishable by death, and the acquittal of Piso was, therefore, a remote possibility.[35] The emperor closed his address to the Fathers with the plea that they should refrain from convicting the defendant simply because he was personally interested in the case.[36]

A two-day adjournment then was declared for the formulation of the charges.[37] Piso was unable to secure competent counsel and was forced to be content with

[34] *Ibid.*
[35] Viertel, *Tiberius und Germanicus*, 52–53.
[36] Tacitus, *Ann.*, III, 12. The Senate served as a high court when Cicero prosecuted Catiline. See, Hammond, *The Augustan Principate*, 170–71. In Tiberius' reign the Senate began regularly to take cognizance of cases involving its own members, provincial governors, client princes, and defendants accused of treason. D. McFayden, *The Rise of the Princeps' Jurisdiction Within the City of Rome*, in *Washington University Studies*, Humanistic Series, Vol. X, Pt. II (1923), 181–264. The Senate was a court of appeal in cases involving senatorial provinces and a joint participant with the emperor in criminal cases in which technically it advised the *princeps*. T. Mommsen, *Römisches Strafrecht* (Leipzig, 1899), 255. See, Gardthausen, *Augustus und seine Zeit*, Vol. II, 331, n.22. C. Jullian, *Les transformations politiques de l'Italie sous les empereurs romains* (Paris, 1883), 51, holds that Piso's trial was extralegal, but his arguments are by no means convincing.
[37] Tacitus, *Ann.*, III, 13.

the mediocre services of Manius Lepidus, Lucius Piso, and Livineius Regulus.[38]

With the resumption of proceedings, Fulcinius Trio opened the case by accusing Piso of maladministration in Spain, in accordance with the permission he had secured to enlarge the scope of the trial by denouncing Piso's conduct prior to the Syrian affair. Vitellius followed by accusing the defendant of relaxing discipline and corrupting the troops, making much of the point that Piso had been saluted as the "Father of the Legions." He continued by directly charging the accused with poisoning Germanicus and with blasphemy. He concluded by properly emphasizing Piso's armed attack on Syria, the strongest indictment in the case against him.[39]

The defense faltered on all counts save the poisoning charge, which was dropped on the ground that it could not be proved. "It was, indeed, none too plausibly sustained by the accusers, who argued that, at a dinner given by Germanicus, Piso (who was seated above him) introduced the dose into his food. Certainly, it seemed folly to assume that he could have ventured the act. . . ."[40] Piso offered to have his slaves put to the torture to refute the poisoning charge, and the failure to resort to this expedient further indicates the weakness of the charge.[41]

The Senate then asked that the correspondence concerning Syria be produced, but both Tiberius and Piso refused to accede to this request.[42] This correspondence must have contained compromising material, else the re-

---

[38] *Ibid.*, 11. F. B. Marsh, "Roman Parties in the Reign of Tiberius," *American Historical Review*, XXX (1926), 238, believes that Piso expected the support of the Tiberian party against the partisans of Germanicus, but they shrank from a conflict.
[39] Tacitus, *Ann.*, III, 13.   [40] *Ibid.*, 14.
[41] W. W. Flint, "The Delatores in the Reign of Tiberius," *Classical Journal*, VIII (1912), 39.
[42] Tacitus, *Ann.*, III, 14.

fusal to accede to the senatorial request is inexplicable. On the other hand, Tiberius can hardly be presumed to have been foolish enough to put confidential instructions in writing which he could conveniently have given to Piso orally prior to his departure for the East.[43] It is unlikely that Piso would have withheld evidence that would have shown that he had acted in the East in accordance with orders received from the emperor, virtually his only hope to escape condemnation, unless he did so in return for assurance that the emperor would interfere to prevent his conviction. The emperor's actions in the case up to this point had indicated that such intervention was not to be expected, and he had made evident his intention to have the case tried strictly on its merits. Suetonius claims that Piso "would have produced his instructions had not Tiberius caused them to be taken from him when Piso privately showed them."[44] Tacitus, well informed as to the course of the trial, knew nothing of this version. It is intrinsically improbable that Piso would have failed to take the best care of documents upon which his life might depend. He allegedly had shown them to his friends, and they, of course, would have been in a position to testify as to the existence and tenor of the documents if they had ever existed.

Upon conclusion of the first day of the trial, Piso was removed to his home in a litter. There was danger of mob violence against him, and he accordingly was accompanied by an escort furnished from the ranks of the prae-

[43] Viertel, *Tiberius und Germanicus*, 56.
[44] Suetonius, *Tib.*, LII. F. B. Marsh, "A Modern Historical Myth. A Defense of Tacitus," *Classical Weekly*, XIX (1925–1926), 135–38, argues that Piso had received instructions from the emperor to prevent Germanicus from securing a hold on the Syrian legions comparable with his former position in the Rhine legions. He thinks Piso far exceeded his instructions.

torians.⁴⁵ When the trial began, Plancina stated that she would remain loyal to her husband and share his fortune. The good offices of Livia were employed in her behalf, however, with the result that she was pardoned for her part in the eastern affair.⁴⁶

A number of motives influenced the emperor in arriving at his decision to pardon Plancina. His action, of course, was pleasing to Livia. At the same time, it was perhaps intended as a rebuff to Agrippina, who had given every indication that she was going to make the most out of the alleged murder of her husband, to gain the sympathy and support of the Roman populace. Plancina's guilt in sharing Piso's joy at the death of Germanicus was primarily an offense against the imperial house, although it could be interpreted as a crime against the state. On the other hand, it was reported that she, like her husband, had attempted to win the support of the Syrian legions; but if this were the case, no such charge was made during the course of Piso's trial. It is also possible that Tiberius was still angry because of the part Agrippina had played among the Rhine legions when, according to the Tacitean account, she intervened to forestall imminent disaster.⁴⁷ The emperor may have believed that the conduct of Plancina in regard to the legions had been no more objectionable than that of Agrippina, and accordingly had refrained from pressing accusations on this point.

After her pardon Plancina made no effort to help her husband, and this apparent desertion profoundly depressed him. On the second day of his trial the charges

---

⁴⁵ Tacitus, *Ann.*, III, 14, 16.
⁴⁶ *Ibid.*, 15. Sievers, *Studien zur Gesch. der röm. Kaiser: Tacitus und Tiberius*, 61, thinks that charges against her should have been pressed. She committed suicide in 33 after charges of an unknown nature were lodged against her. Tacitus, *Ann.*, VI, 26.
⁴⁷ See, *infra*, 67.

were repeated against him, and the senators obviously were hostile. All hope of imperial intervention was lost, for the emperor sat completely detached from the proceedings in the Senate chamber.[48] Piso had every reason to despair. Upon the conclusion of the session he again went to his home. After making his usually careful toilet, he penned a note; and after his wife left the bedchamber, barred the door. He was found the next morning with his throat cut and his sword by his side.[49] The note, according to Tacitus, stated that he had been "broken by a confederacy of [his] enemies and the hatred inspired by their accusations, since the world has no room for the truth and innocence."[50]

There is no need to seek mystery in the death of Piso. The note alone virtually proves that he was a suicide. Time and again persons whose conviction on a capital charge seemed assured took their own lives "for thus by their wills they secured their estates to their children, and burial for their bodies. A conviction would forfeit both."[51]

Piso also had tried to shield his sons. In the note which he left he stated that his son Marcus had advised him against attempting to resume control of the Syrian province, and that his other son also was guiltless.[52] He naturally expected that his suicide would allay the public indignation and thus strengthen the chance that his sons would be treated justly. His hopes were fulfilled, for Tiberius absolved them from guilt in the attack on Syria.[53] The exculpation of Plancina was made formal and official by a hurried trial that resulted in her acquittal; in all likelihood these proceedings were concerned only with

---

[48] Tacitus, *Ann.*, III, 16.   [49] *Ibid*.   [50] *Ibid*.
[51] Flint, "The Delatores in the Reign of Tiberius," in *loc. cit.*, 42.
[52] Tacitus, *Ann.*, III, 16.   [53] *Ibid.*, 17.

her alleged attempts to influence the legions, since this point had not been dealt with before.

Tiberius was satisfied with the outcome of the trial, for he recommended that three of the prosecutors be raised to the priesthood, whereas the fourth, Fulcinius Trio, was promised his support in a coming election.[54] It would be difficult to criticize the emperor's conduct during the entire affair.[55] There was ample precedent for his assumption of the direction of the trial in its initial stage, for he could hold that since the alleged murder of Germanicus involved the offense of treason, that charge could be taken from the cognizance of the praetorian court. The extension of his tribunician inviolability to cover members of the imperial family likewise was well established by precedent. According to the Tacitean account, a source unfavorable to the emperor, he made no effort to put pressure on the Senate. Piso was unquestionably guilty of an attack on Syria. He may have believed that his action was justified, but the emperor certainly could not condone the attack on a province by a member of the old aristocracy. With the conclusion of the trial the party of Agrippina stood in bolder relief, for she doubtless was infuriated by the acquittal of Plancina. The growing power of Sejanus, prefect of the Praetorian Guard, was destined to bring to a head the latent opposition to the emperor.

[54] *Ibid.*, 19.
[55] Ciaceri, "L'imperatore Tiberio e i processi di lesa maesta," in *loc. cit.*, 286–87. See, Kuntz, *Tiberius and the Roman Constitution*, 57.

Chapter VI

SEJANUS

Lucius Aelius Sejanus was born in Volsinii, in Etruria, between 4 and 1 B.C. He was the son of Seius Strabo, prefect of Egypt, and Cosconia Gallitta of the Lentulus family.[1] On his paternal side he was descended from a family of rich equestrians, and on his mother's side from a family of the old nobility.[2] He was adopted by Aelius Gallus, and his only brother, L. Seius Tubero, attained consular rank. Early in his career he attached himself to Gaius, grandson of Augustus, and traveled with the prince to the East. It was rumored at this time that he had unwillingly become a favorite of the rich debauchee, Marcus Gabius Apicius.[3]

Soon after his return from the East, Sejanus was associated with his father, Seius Strabo, who had become commander of the praetorian cohorts. In A.D. 16-17, Strabo was appointed prefect of Egypt, and with his father's

---

[1] The mother of Sejanus was the sister-in-law of Junius Blaesus, who commanded in the war in Africa against Tacfarinas. C. Cichorius, "Zur Familiengeschichte Seians," *Hermes*, XXXIX (1904), 468.

[2] Tacitus, *Ann.*, IV, 1. "The picture of a parvenu that one is able to draw so easily from the Tacitean account is hindered by the facts that Sejanus, through his mother and his grandmother [Terentia], was not only related to the families of the higher nobility but was included in the inner circle of the imperial house." Cichorius, "Zur Familiengeschichte Seians," in *loc. cit.*, 471. See, A. Stein, *Der Römische Ritterstand* (Munich, 1927), 350-52.

[3] Tacitus, *Ann.*, IV, 1. For the consulship of L. Seius Tubero, see, Velleius, *R.H.*, II, 127; Stein, *Der Römische Ritterstand*, 302. The fact that Sejanus accompanied Gaius to the East indicates that he had the full confidence of Augustus. Stahr, *Tiberius*, 185.

SEJANUS

promotion Sejanus became sole commander of the Praetorian Guard. While still in joint command with his father, he had accompanied Drusus on the expedition to suppress the mutiny of the Pannonian legions.[4] This is the first instance where there is evidence that Tiberius had begun to put considerable trust in him.

Sejanus as sole commander of the praetorian cohorts instituted several significant changes in that organization. He concentrated the troops into one camp, which made possible better discipline, more efficient dispatch of orders, and a better morale for the troops. The camp was placed on the outskirts of the city, away from urban distractions. Its location discouraged the soldiers from mixing with the populace, and thus minimized the danger that their loyalty to the emperor might be weakened if he should need them to quell disorders in the capital.[5] Yet, "What factor, indeed, could prevent a body of nine cohorts, one thousand infantry and two hundred cavalry in all, dedicated to the

---

[4] Tacitus, *Ann.*, I, 24. See, Freytag, *Tiberius und Tacitus*, 178; Sievers, *Studien zur Gesch. der röm. Kaiser: Tacitus und Tiberius*, 63.

[5] Tacitus, *Ann.*, IV, 2. The origin of the guard can be traced back to the picked troops that protected the generals in the field. Maecenas was reputed to have been the first praetorian prefect. No special office was created for him; Dio is probably correct in stating that prefects were first appointed to the specific office in A.D. 2. C. Maroni, "Uno sguardo ai fasti dei prefetti al pretorio," *Rivista di Storia Antica*, IV (1899), 339-40. The guard constituted a powerful weapon for the emperor, but it was also a two-edged sword that might be used against him. Abraham, *Tiberius und Sejan*, 15. Drusus, son of the emperor, opposed the policy of concentration. Tacitus, *Ann.*, IV, 7. The establishment of the permanent camp was in large measure the response of Tiberius to the intrigues of Agrippina and her partisans. Asbach, *Römisches Kaisertum und Verfassung bis auf Traian*, 14. "The result was that the foundation of physical force which underlay the principate, even under Augustus, was now uncovered. It could no longer be represented, in the presence of such a force, that the authority of the *princeps* rested solely upon the unfettered consent of the people." McFayden, *History of the Title Imperator*, 62. Herzog, *Gesch. und System der Röm. Staatsverfassung*, Vol. II, Pt. I, 248, holds that the guard was the real foundation of Tiberius' power.

defense of one individual, from becoming conscious of its own strength."⁶

The power of Sejanus gradually increased. As a knight his position was quite compatible with his social station, but the command of the guard was in addition a strategic vantage point for one who was ambitious to attain higher honors. Even before the death of Germanicus in A.D. 19, the prefect was a powerful figure by reason of the emperor's friendship for him. He probably was already seeking a marital alliance for himself which would raise him above the ranks of the *equites,* for his daughter was betrothed to the son of the future emperor Claudius (41–54).⁷ His power was manifested in imperial appointments when he was instrumental in securing the position of proconsul of Africa for his relative Blaesus.⁸

Tiberius was beginning to consider Sejanus well-nigh indispensable, for he rendered "notable services, and the unselfishness with which he seemed to live and work only for the emperor, coupled with the real talent for governing he possessed . . . impressed him who so seldom had seen an honorable man." ⁹

---

⁶ Maroni, "Uno sguardo ai fasti dei prefetti al pretorio," in *loc. cit.,* 342. See also, Willenbücher, *Tiberius und die Verschwörung des Sejans,* 3. The scorpion was the distinguishing insignia of the guard, and there is reason to believe that a special type of cuirass, reaching to the hips and worn with a leather kilt, also was used exclusively by them. A. Blanchet, "Les armes Romaines," *Journal des Savants,* XXV (1927), 10–11.

⁷ Tacitus, *Ann.,* III, 29. Stahr, *Tiberius,* 196, maintains that the betrothal aroused the ambitions of the prefect. Willenbücher, *Tiberius und die Verschwörung des Sejans,* 3, 5–6, 12, even connects Sejanus with Piso's hostility toward Germanicus.

⁸ Tacitus, *Ann.,* III, 35, 72. For account of African War, see, *infra,* 182–90; L. Cantarelli, "Tacfarinata," *Atene e Roma,* IV (1901), 11.

⁹ Freytag, *Tiberius und Tacitus,* 216–17. "No sentimental memories of the old Roman Republic deterred him from rendering such services for the emperor as he required. . . . But he did not only know how to obey and to carry out the orders he received with understanding, but, self-reliant, he also knew how to carry out these policies so as to strengthen the imperial power." Abraham, *Tiberius und Sejan,* 15.

Sejanus had been elevated to the position of praetor before Germanicus' death, but soon after the prince's demise he became the confidential adviser and general administrative assistant of the emperor as well. He was "strong, ruthless, and daring; with these qualities he possessed a penetrating understanding and especially the ability to turn circumstances to his own account." [10] As the commander of the Praetorian Guard he succeeded in winning the respect of the soldiers by his able administration and careful attention to details. There is no question that he was working diligently and loyally for the emperor, whose affections he secured by talents which were bound to please so methodical a man as Tiberius.

The high esteem in which he was held by the emperor was evidenced by the fact that no objection was made to the erection of statues in his honor.[11] He was probably the only living person whom Tiberius so honored. In the Forum the effigies of the prefect were honored along with the eagles and altars of the legions, and the emperor named him "the 'partner of his toils' not only in conversation but before the Fathers and the people." [12] He had reached the pinnacle of success; but with success, greater ambition doubtless was incited in his mind, and weaknesses of character began to become apparent.[13] At this time, however, his good qualities indubitably outweighed the defects in his character. It was only when he became familiar with the intrigues within the imperial family, that he decided to place himself in the vanguard of the opposition to the faction that was supporting Agrippina, widow of Ger-

---

[10] Freytag, *Tiberius und Tacitus*, 178.
[11] Tacitus, *Ann.*, III, 72; Dio, *R.H.*, LVII, xxi, 3-4. Levy, *Quo modo Tiberius se gesserit*, 78, points out that Sejanus' lack of aristocratic background promised to make him a reliable confidential adviser. He compares Tiberius' relations with Sejanus with Augustus' dependence on Agrippa.
[12] Tacitus, *Ann.*, IV, 2.   [13] *Ibid.*, 1.

manicus, and from that time on he was more than the friend and chief administrative assistant of the emperor—he was the leader of a political faction.[14]

It was soon recognized in Rome that Sejanus could reward friends and punish enemies. "The leading citizens, including the consuls themselves, regularly resorted to his house at dawn, and communicated to him not only all the private requests that any of them wished to make of Tiberius, but also the public business which required to be taken up. In a word, no business of this sort was transacted henceforth without his knowledge."[15] Tiberius knew how much power had come into Sejanus' hands, but also realized that if he abused this power, his downfall could easily be encompassed since he was a member neither of the imperial family nor of the old aristocracy.[16]

Drusus, son of the emperor, was by nature proud. His character seems to have been weakened by the undeserved honors and unearned military distinctions which his father had bestowed on him. The emperor had considered him unequal to the task of settling the eastern problems,[17] and the incompetence of the prince doubtless was partially responsible for Tiberius' dependence on Sejanus.[18] As a member of the Julio-Claudian house and heir apparent to the throne after the death of Germanicus, it was natural that Drusus should bitterly resent the growing power of Sejanus and feel that his place in his father's affections had been usurped by the prefect.[19] The thought

[14] G. Ferrero, "The Women of the Caesars: Tiberius and Agrippina," *Century Illustrated Magazine*, LXXXII (1911), 618.

[15] Dio, *R.H.*, LVII, xix, 7.

[16] It would have been foolish for the emperor to try to make it appear that he *and the Roman people* had chosen Sejanus to help rule the state, as Velleius, *R.H.*, CXXVII, declares.

[17] Tacitus, *Ann.*, II, 43.   [18] Velleius, *R.H.*, CXXVII.

[19] Tacitus, *Ann.*, IV, 3. In most of the inscriptions Drusus is named Drusus Caesar, son of Tiberius Augustus, grandson of the deified

rankled that while he was away on the frontier, Sejanus was in Rome enjoying the bounty and winning the augmented confidence of the emperor. Drusus already felt bitter toward Sejanus when an altercation occurred which reached a climax when he struck the favorite. Sejanus certainly was implacably resolved to avenge the insult, but there seems to have been little possibility that he had conceived aspirations to the throne.[20]

If Drusus should succeed his father, Sejanus' career would end; indeed, he would be fortunate to escape with his life. If, on the other hand, Sejanus could bring about the death or ruin of the prince, the children of Germanicus were in line for the succession. The emperor already had indicated that this was his intention, for Drusus had adopted the children of the late prince, presumably at his father's direction.[21] Sejanus could anticipate nothing better than a possible regency.[22]

Augustus. He is also named Drusus Julius, son of Tiberius, *C.I.L.*, V, 2151, 6416; or Drusus Julius Caesar, *ibid.*, II, 1553. He held the consulship in 15 and 18, the second time as a colleague of his father. *Ibid.*, I¹, 761, 762, 763; II, 2049, 2338, 5048; IV¹⁻², 5214; V, 4954, 5121; VI, 910; IX, 35; X¹, 4573, 4617, 4638; XII, 147, 1847; XIII, 1036. He received the tribunician power in A.D. 21. *Ibid.*, II, 2040, 2338; VI, 910; IX, 35. He celebrated a triumph in June, A.D. 21. *Ibid.*, XIV, 244.

[20] Tacitus, *Ann.*, IV, 3. K. Scott, "Drusus Nicknamed 'Castor,'" *Classical Philology*, XXV (1930), 161, says, "The people may have said, 'Drusus wants to be considered one of the Dioscuri, Drusus Castor as his father was, patron of the knights!' Very well! He certainly would make a fine Castor and protector for the equites, if one may judge from the blows he had given one of their body. They were, I think, having a laugh at Drusus as a sorry patron of the knights and at the same time at the identification of the rulers with Gods." Germanicus and the younger Drusus, however, were closely associated with Castor and Pollux. See, *id.*, "The Dioscuri and the Imperial Cult," *ibid.*, XXV (1930), 379 ff.

[21] Marsh, *Reign of Tiberius*, 163.

[22] *Ibid.*, 166. For an extreme view of the allegedly sinister intentions of Sejanus, see, Ihne, *Zur Ehrenrettung des Kaisers Tiberius*, 71-72. He declares that "Sejanus planned from the beginning nothing less than the ruin of the whole house of the emperor and the winning of the imperial crown for himself."

Livilla, wife of Drusus, would seem to have little to gain by the death of her spouse. If Drusus survived Tiberius, there was every likelihood that she would be empress. It is possible that her fears had been incited by Drusus' adoption of the children of Germanicus and Agrippina, which she had reason to interpret as a move to set aside her children's claims.[23] Then, too, passion had driven her into the arms of Sejanus, and it was probably this illicit relationship that made her willing to encompass Drusus' death.[24] If Sejanus were involved in the plot, however, he was motivated not by ambition but by the desire for revenge and the fear of retaliatory action by the prince if he should succeed his father.[25]

The plot allegedly was carried out by Sejanus, Livilla, Eudemus, a physician, and Lygdus, who, it was charged, actually administered the fatal potion. Eudemus was necessary for the success of the conspiracy since, as a physician, he had access to the prince's bedside and could allay suspicion by pronouncing the illness a natural one. Sejanus apparently had deceived Livilla by promise of marriage, and to allay her misgivings as to the sincerity of his protestations, he divorced his wife, Apicata.[26]

Drusus died in 23 after a lingering illness, and no suspicions were aroused. It was not until eight years later (31) that the plot that allegedly had cost the life of the prince was revealed by Apicata, after the death of Sejanus.[27] Where did she get her information? It is inconceivable that Livilla and Sejanus would have made her privy to any scheme they might have concocted to murder the emperor's only son. Her charges were simply the act

---

[23] Willenbücher, *Tiberius und die Verschwörung des Sejans*, 24.
[24] Tacitus, *Ann.*, IV, 3; Dio, *R.H.*, LVIII, xi, 6.
[25] Marsh, *Reign of Tiberius*, 164.
[26] Tacitus, *Ann.*, IV, 3. See, Suetonius, *Tib.*, LXI–LXII.
[27] Tacitus, *Ann.*, IV, 8, 11.

SEJANUS

of a woman who had every right to feel vindictive. Her former husband, Sejanus, had just been put to death after the emperor had denounced him by letter to the Senate. Their two children had been executed, although there was virtually no reason to connect them with their father's deeds or plans.[28] As a prelude to her own suicide,[29] she at least had the satisfaction of hurling charges which she knew would hurt Tiberius. He could hardly fail to be remorseful at the thought that his own son had died at the hands of the favorite whom he, and he alone, had raised to power.[30] Then, too, as a wife who had been spurned by her husband, she had the additional satisfaction of ruining Livilla, the woman for whom her spouse had divorced her. The evidence of Apicata, therefore, cannot be regarded as proof that Drusus' life had been sacrificed to the plottings of Sejanus and Livilla. Eudemus and Lygdus allegedly confessed their parts in the crime at Capri. These confessions, however, were made under torture and are to be discounted.[31] Livilla, it was reported, had been spared by the emperor, but her mother, Antonia, ordered that she be starved to death.[32] In view of the excitement that prevailed after the fall of Sejanus, almost any rumor would have been believed that reflected still greater infamy on the fallen favorite. Such a punishment, if actually meted out to Livilla, would have been sufficiently accounted for by the charge that she had been in adulterous relations with Sejanus, and in any event it does not constitute proof that Drusus died the victim of a poison plot.

During his son's illness Tiberius maintained his custom-

---

[28] *Ibid.*, 9.   [29] Dio, *R.H.*, LVIII, xi, 6.
[30] Ferrero, "Tiberius and Agrippina," in *loc. cit.*, 622.
[31] Suetonius, *Tib.*, LXI–LXII. Dio, *R.H.*, LVII, xxii, 4, cites no evidence to bolster his statement that some "who had encompassed Drusus' death" were punished immediately after the prince's demise.
[32] Dio, *R.H.*, LVIII, xi, 7.

ary austere calm and continued the performance of his governmental duties. Even after the death of the prince, the emperor with fortitude reminded the mourning consuls of the demands of duty and dignity. He delivered before the Senate a panegyric to his son's memory, and Nero, son of Germanicus, was permitted to deliver a eulogy in the Forum. At the same time Tiberius entrusted the care of Nero and Drusus, sons of Germanicus, to the Senate.[33]

Before the death of Germanicus there had existed a Germanican party in Rome consisting of the lesser nobles and many members of the old republican families. With the death of Germanicus this group had rallied to Agrippina's leadership, but the prospective succession nonetheless had devolved on Drusus. Agrippina's party thereupon began to foster Nero as a candidate for the succession, and when Drusus died, these efforts naturally were greatly stimulated. As senators and others who were in sympathy with the party of Agrippina wept for the deceased prince, they "exulted in secret over the new fortunes of the house of Germanicus." [34]

Agrippina was a worthy antagonist for Sejanus. She was passionate, vehement, and reckless, and "abused both the relationship which protected her and the pity which her misfortune had aroused." She taunted Tiberius openly

[33] *Ibid.*, LVII, xxii, 4. Tiberius thought that Drusus had "died of disease due to his bad habits. . . ." Suetonius, *Tib.*, LXII. Mattingly, *Coins of the Roman Empire*, I, cxli, suggests that drachms struck at Caesarea in Cappadocia in 33-34, and 34-35, which bear the likeness of Drusus, were issued preparatory to Vitellius' campaign against Parthia. The coins likewise commemorated the discovery of the real cause of Drusus' death. Nero, in the inscriptions, is named Nero Caesar, *C.I.L.*, III, 2808; VI, 913; or Nero Julius, *ibid.*, V, 23, 853, 6416. Drusus Caesar was a pontiff in A.D. 33. *Ibid.*, III, 380. He also was given the Julian name. *Ibid.*, V, 6416a.

[34] Tacitus, *Ann.*, IV, 12. See, Willenbücher, *Tiberius und die Verschwörung des Sejans*, 17.

for his alleged complicity in the death of her husband by words and actions "which impressed the public even more strongly than open accusations could have done." [35] Innuendo was far more effective than open charges, which could have easily been refuted.

The year 23 can be considered as a pivotal one, not only because of the fresh hopes incited in the minds of Agrippina and her following by Drusus' death, but also because of its effects on the plans of Sejanus.[36] Before this time the favorite had served Tiberius loyally and well, and, as we have seen, there is no conclusive evidence that he had been involved in a plot to murder Drusus. Now, he had reason to fear a reconciliation between the party of Agrippina and the emperor, for Tiberius had made the sons of Germanicus presumptive heirs to the throne, and had ignored the children of Drusus and Livilla. Sejanus, then, in order to safeguard his own position, assumed leadership of the anti-Agrippinian party as subsequent events seem to prove.

The chastity of Agrippina was impenetrable, although Tiberius later accused her of illicit relations with Asinius Gallus. Nevertheless, Sejanus was not to be thwarted, for he enlisted the aid of Livia and Livilla, who set afoot pernicious gossip to arouse the smoldering spirit of Agrippina.[37] In view of her character, Agrippina needed little prodding, and she and her supporters already were probably trying to hasten the accession of Nero.

The first intimation that the pro-Agrippina party was trying to force the issue of Nero's claims to the throne came when vows were offered to Tiberius, which were

---

[35] Ferrero, "Tiberius and Agrippina," in *loc. cit.*, 615.
[36] R. S. Rogers, "The Conspiracy of Agrippina," *Transactions and Proceedings of the American Philological Association*, LXII (1931), 151.
[37] Tacitus, *Ann.*, IV, 12.

also granted to Nero and Drusus, sons of Agrippina. Tiberius reprimanded the pontiffs for permitting vows to be made to mere youths and asked them if they had been induced to commit this indiscretion by Agrippina.[38] The incident certainly had the effect of causing the parties to stand out in bolder relief.[39]

Measures were taken to check this party strife. The immediate objective was to deprive the pro-Agrippina party of the services of its effective leaders, Gaius Silius and Titius Sabinus.[40] Silius was a distinguished commander, and his wife Sosia was an intimate friend of Agrippina. In 21 Silius had suppressed the Sacrovir revolt, but his reputation had been tarnished by charges that he had been guilty of extortionate practices. His military reputation made him an asset to Agrippina; perhaps it was even believed that in the event of open rebellion against the emperor he could recruit and command an army.

Probably at the instigation of Sejanus, Silius was accused by Varro, one of the consuls. The plea of the defendant for postponement of the trial was denied, and the emperor held that it was perfectly proper for the

[38] *Ibid.*, 17.
[39] *Ibid.* Herzog, *Gesch. und System der Röm. Staatsverfassung*, Vol. II, Pt. I, 258, argues that they were not parties but groups with special interests. There is no evidence that they had popular support. I. Gentile, *L'imperatore Tiberio secondo la moderna critica storica* (Milan, 1887), 44-45, thinks sentiment of the Senate was preponderantly monarchist. But many senators wanted a change of rulers, since they resented the rise of officials like Sejanus, and desired restoration of their subsidies and opportunities to enrich themselves in the provinces. F. Abraham, *Velleius und die Parteien in Rom unter Tiberius* (Berlin, 1885), 4-5, 11-12, points out that the party in support of the emperor included a group of close adherents of Livia, partisans of Sejanus, sentimental republicans, and those who, although opposed to governmental officials, had no hostility toward the emperor himself. Velleius, he holds, was close to Tiberius, but he was not affiliated with the partisans of Livia or the strong supporters of Sejanus. *Ibid.*, 13-14.
[40] Rogers, "The Conspiracy of Agrippina," in *loc. cit.*, 152.

consul to arraign Silius since the state was in danger.[41] The boasts of the defendant and the plot to install Nero were known to Sejanus, and he doubtless made the most of what at best could have advanced little beyond the stage of rash talk. The defendant, realizing that his alleged extortions during the suppression of the Sacrovir revolt would tell against him, despaired of acquittal and committed suicide. His wife was exiled, and his property was confiscated for the benefit of the emperor's treasury.[42]

The favorite was also largely instrumental in initiating the prosecution of Cremutius Cordus, who committed suicide to forestall condemnation. He was charged in 25 with having praised Brutus and Cassius in a history he had written, and formal accusation was lodged against him by adherents to Sejanus. According to Tacitus, he presented an able defense, but, when he realized that the emperor was against him, he decided to starve himself to death. The offensive history was publicly burned.[43] Objectionable history writing was not a "new and unheard of crime." The history of Titus Labienus was publicly burned in the reign of Augustus, as was that of Cassius Severus, who was exiled to Crete. The real offense of Cordus was not his praise of the republican leaders but the fact that he seemed to justify the assassination of Caesar. The personal enmity of Sejanus was a major factor in his prosecution.[44]

In 27 Titius Sabinus was tried for *maiestas*.[45] He was an illustrious member of the equestrian order and he had been devoted to Germanicus and his widow. Prosecution was

[41] Tacitus, *Ann.*, IV, 19. See, *infra*, 198–99, 203.
[42] *Ibid.*   [43] Tacitus, *Ann.*, IV, 34–35.
[44] G. M. Columba, "Il processo di Cremuzeo Cordo," *Atene e Roma*, IV (1901), 361–81. Dio, *R.H.*, LVII, xxiv, 3, states that Cordus had cast aspersions on the Senate and the Roman people.
[45] Rogers, "Conspiracy of Agrippina," in *loc. cit.*, 144.

planned as early as 24, but it was not until the defendant was entrapped into incriminating himself that proceedings actually were instituted. Latinius Latiaris, Porcius Cato, Petilius Rufus, and Marcus Opsius, all ex-praetors who were ambitious for elevation to the consulship, came forward as accusers. Latiaris, an intimate friend of Sabinus, encouraged him to rail against Sejanus and the emperor, while the three others, who subsequently joined in the accusation, were hidden in a garret of the house, where they could hear all that was said. Sabinus was condemned to death, and when the sentence was pronounced, he allegedly cried that "these were the ceremonies that inaugurated the year, these the victims that bled to propitiate Sejanus."[46] His body was thrown into the Tiber. The emperor commended the execution and intimated that he believed that Agrippina and Nero were conspiring against him.[47]

Sejanus now had rid the opposition party of two outstanding leaders, but there still remained Asinius Gallus and Lucius Arruntius, both of whom were influential in the Senate.[48] It is to be assumed that, in view of his influence with the emperor, he made every effort to prevent members of the pro-Agrippina faction from being appointed to office.

A turning point in the career of Sejanus came with his request for the hand of Livilla, widow of Drusus, with whom he had enjoyed illicit relations facilitated by his alleged promises to marry her.[49] She probably pressed him to carry out his agreement, and it is extremely unlikely that he failed to realize that the marriage would greatly increase his prestige, although one need not regard his suit

---

[46] Tacitus, *Ann.*, IV, 70.   [47] *Ibid.*
[48] Rogers, "Lucius Arruntius," in *loc. cit.*, 36.
[49] Tacitus, *Ann.*, IV, 39.

as evidence of aspirations for the throne.⁵⁰ The prefect submitted his request to the emperor in writing. He stated that "He had never asked for baubles of office . . . and yet he had reached the supreme goal—he had been counted worthy of an alliance with the Caesar." He also touched on the delicate subject of the "animosities of Agrippina." ⁵¹

Tiberius' reply to Sejanus was a model of circumlocution. After praising Sejanus he stated that public opinion had to be considered, and he feared that Livilla's marriage would accentuate the division in the state. "For, Sejanus," he continued, "you delude yourself, if you imagine you can keep your present rank, or that Livilla who has been wedded successively to Gaius Caesar and Drusus will be complaisant enough to grow old at the side of a Roman Knight." The emperor continued by pointing out that complaint would arise if Sejanus were raised above the magistrates. "One point only I shall make clear," he continued, "no station, however exalted, would be unearned by your qualities and your devotion to myself; and when the occasion comes, either in the Senate or before the public, I shall not be silent." ⁵²

The request had been handled by the emperor in such a fashion as to indicate to Sejanus that he was opposed to the union. On the other hand, the rebuff was obviously

---

⁵⁰ G. Ferrero, "The Women of the Caesars: The Daughters of Agrippina," *Century Illustrated Magazine*, LXXXII (1911), 401, 412. Cf., Abraham, *Tiberius und Sejan*, 16.

⁵¹ Tacitus, *Ann.*, IV, 39. Willenbücher, *Tiberius und die Verschwörung des Sejans*, 37, thinks that Livilla was forcing Sejanus' hand by insistence that he marry her.

⁵² Tacitus, *Ann.*, IV, 40. Sejanus' father had married a woman of a senatorial family, and there were a number of other intermarriages between the classes in the early empire. See, Stein, *Der Römische Ritterstand*, 349–52. The real reason for Tiberius' refusal was his natural unwillingness to ally his powerful minister with the senatorial aristocracy.

tempered by the hint of greater honors to be bestowed on the favorite. Sejanus showed no disposition to press the matter further; indeed, he may have regarded the emperor's answer as a rebuke to his ambition to rise above his social station. There seemed reason to believe that Tiberius thought an alliance between Sejanus and Livilla would infuriate Agrippina and destroy all hope of reconciling her to him.[53]

Sejanus' unsuccessful suit for the hand of Livilla probably impelled Agrippina to consider the prospect of marriage.[54] Tiberius visited her while she was ill, and she took the opportunity to ask him to arrange for her marriage, but the emperor refused to commit himself. As in the case of Sejanus he fully realized the political implications of the prospective marital union. The husband Agrippina had in mind was probably Asinius Gallus; some time after her death Tiberius charged that she had been in adulterous relations with him.[55] The emperor hardly could have been expected to approve Agrippina's marriage to a man whom Augustus had considered ambitious enough to attempt to secure the rule of the empire, and, aside from this, any husband would immediately become a leader of the opposition party which the emperor was deter-

---

[53] Marsh, *Reign of Tiberius*, 177. "This reply is significant because it proves to us that Tiberius, who is accused of harboring a fierce hatred against the sons of Germanicus and Agrippina, was still seeking, two years after the death of Drusus, to appease both factions." Ferrero, "Tiberius and Agrippina," in *loc. cit.*, 618.

[54] Tacitus, *Ann.*, IV, 53. This is the famous chapter in which Tacitus directly refers to his use of the commentaries of Agrippina the Younger. Motzo, "I commentari di Agrippina madre di Nerone," in *loc. cit.*, 19–20. C. A. Knabe, *De Fontibus Historiae Imperatorum Julianorum* (Halle, 1864), 18–20, went so far as to argue that Tacitus' treatment of Germanicus, Piso, Sejanus, and Agrippina was based primarily on this source.

[55] "It seems to me unlikely that Tiberius would voice so sensational a charge if it had no foundation in fact." Rogers, "Conspiracy of Agrippina," in *loc. cit.*, 155.

mined to check if efforts for reconciliation proved abortive.⁵⁶

Agrippina's conduct toward the emperor now became intolerable; we have no reason to doubt that she virtually defied him, for the incidents are reported by Tacitus, who is notoriously partial to her. One incident occurred during the trial of Claudia Pulchra for adultery. The defendant, who had been arraigned by Domitius Afer, was Agrippina's cousin. Agrippina hastened to intercede for her. She rushed in upon Tiberius while he was worshiping before the image of Augustus and cried that "It was not for the same man to offer victims to the deified Augustus and to persecute his posterity." ⁵⁷ Tiberius kept his temper and calmly answered that Agrippina was not necessarily "A woman injured if she lacked a throne." ⁵⁸ The exchange was enlightening. Agrippina had taken care to taunt the emperor with the fact of her blood relationship with Augustus. Tiberius' answer indicated that he fully understood that Agrippina's real grievance was her belief that she should rule in person or through her sons. Despite Agrippina's intervention, Claudia was condemned.⁵⁹

Agrippina continued to aggravate the emperor despite the rebuffs she sustained on the occasion of her marital request and her appeal for Claudia. On one of the few occasions when she dined at the emperor's table, she ostentatiously refused to accept an apple from Tiberius' own hands. The suggestion that she feared that she would be poisoned was unmistakable. Turning to his mother the emperor declared that "he had resolved on slightly rigor-

---

⁵⁶ Cf., Ferrero, "Tiberius and Agrippina," in *loc. cit.*, 618-19.
⁵⁷ Tacitus, *Ann.*, IV, 52.
⁵⁸ *Ibid.* "Do you think a wrong is done you, dear daughter, if you are not empress?" Suetonius, *Tib.*, LIII.
⁵⁹ Tacitus, *Ann.*, IV, 52.

ous measures against a lady who accused him of murder by poison." [60] Tacitus ascribes the incident to Sejanus, who, he declares, sent "agents to warn her, under color of friendship, that poison was ready for her; she would do well to avoid the dinners of her father-in-law." [61] This seems to be an unfounded elaboration of the story. Would Agrippina have hearkened to warnings emanating from a foe, even if Sejanus should have been so diabolically cunning as to arrange the whole affair? Ever since her return from the East with the ashes of Germanicus, Agrippina had made capital of the rumors, which her partisans professed to believe, that the emperor had been implicated in the poisoning of her husband. She was throwing this charge in his face; we need look no further than to the rash, arrogant nature of Agrippina to find an explanation of her insulting action.

Sejanus profited by the folly of Agrippina. He had worked against her and her partisans since the death of Drusus. The emperor, however, had attempted to conciliate her, and this was probably one of the reasons that impelled him to refuse Sejanus' request for the marriage with Livilla. Certainly the conduct of Agrippina must have convinced the emperor of the futility of conciliation.[62] Such was the situation when the emperor decided to withdraw from Rome and take up residence on the island of Capri.

[60] *Ibid.*, 54.   [61] *Ibid.*
[62] See, Dessau, *Gesch. der röm. Kaiserzeit,* Vol. II, Pt. I, 21–22.

CHAPTER VII

THE RETIREMENT TO CAPRI AND THE FALL OF SEJANUS

In 26 Tiberius left Rome to dedicate a temple in Campania and a similiar edifice erected in honor of Augustus at Nola. During the course of the journey he stopped to dine with Sejanus at a spot "known as the Grotto, built in a natural cavern between the Gulf of Amyclae and the mountains of Fundi." The roof of the cavern suddenly gave way. The emperor's servants fled for their lives, but "Sejanus alone hung over the Caesar with bent knee, face and hands, and opposed himself to the falling stones." [1] Here was dramatic proof of Sejanus' loyalty to the emperor, who naturally held him in even higher esteem. If the favorite were plotting against the emperor, he would hardly have risked his life to protect him.[2] Tiberius completed the dedicatory ceremonies as planned and then withdrew to the island of Capri. The isle was a natural fortress, and it was close enough to Rome to enable the emperor to keep in touch with events in the capital.[3]

Tiberius' withdrawal was primarily attributable to his advanced age and his natural desire to have surcease from the arduous duties which his presence in Rome entailed.

---

[1] Tacitus, *Ann.*, IV, 59. The grotto was near Tarracina. Pauly, Wissowa, and Kroll (eds.), *Real-Encyklopädie*, X, 509.
[2] Spengel, "Zur Gesch. des Kaisers Tiberius," in *loc. cit.*, 49.
[3] Tacitus, *Ann.*, IV, 67; VI, 21. For description of the ruins of the emperor's villas and a fine series of plates, see, M. Boutterin, "La villa de Tiberè à Capri," *Monumenta Antiques,* Supp. VI (1914), 9 *et passim.* Hirschfeld, *Die Kaiserlichen Verwaltungsbeamten,* 471, holds that his removal to Capri meant the end of the Augustan constitution.

Then, too, his disgust at the calumnies and scurrilities that allegedly had been circulated against him by Votienus Montanus [4] may have made him more amenable to the persuasion of Sejanus, as he "little by little . . . began to denounce the drudgeries of the capital, the jostling crowds, the endless streams of suitors." [5] It will be recalled that he had stipulated that his assumption of the throne be made contingent upon future senatorial permission to retire.[6] Even earlier during his career he had retired from public life to live as a virtual exile at Rhodes. His disgust at the conduct of Agrippina and the intrigues of her supporters likewise influenced his decision.[7] It is hardly likely that Sejanus alone persuaded the emperor to withdraw,[8] but he certainly was aware that the step would increase his own power and, therefore, probably encouraged the momentous decision. Tacitus' suggestion that the emperor "was driven into exile by the imperious temper of his mother, whose partnership in his power he could not tolerate, while it was impossible to cut adrift one from whom he held that power in fee" [9] is only tenable if one accepts the view that Livia's title of Augusta in reality indicated her position as joint ruler.[10]

In the meantime, the party of Agrippina had not been idle. Sejanus clearly stood in the way of the attainment of their ambitions to install Nero on the throne, and there

---

[4] Tacitus, *Ann.*, IV, 42.
[5] *Ibid.*, 41. Sievers, *Studien zur Gesch. der Röm. Kaiser: Tacitus und Tiberius*, 70, thinks that the emperor had reason to be fearful when he retired.
[6] *Infra*, 33–34.
[7] Willenbücher, *Tiberius und die Verschwörung des Sejans*, 27.
[8] Tacitus, *Ann.*, IV, 57.
[9] *Ibid.* Dio, *R.H.*, LVII, xii, 6, also ascribes the emperor's withdrawal to his desire to emancipate himself from Livia's influence.
[10] Rostovtzeff, "L'empereur Tiberè et le culte impérial," in *loc. cit.*, 24. Suetonius, *Tib.*, LI, says the emperor decided to go to Capri after Livia read old letters of Augustus that sharply criticized him.

THE RETIREMENT TO CAPRI 135

was some indication that the power of the party already was weakening.[11] Agrippina and her partisans therefore decided upon a bold policy and pushed their plans to procure the accession of Nero. They claimed that "It was this the nation desired and the armies yearned for, and Sejanus, who now trampled alike on the patience of an old man and the tameness of a young one would not risk a counterstroke." [12]

Nero needed little urging to push himself forward. His arrogant conduct and indiscreet statements left little doubt of his complicity in the schemes to procure his elevation.[13] His movements and plans were reported to Sejanus through Julia, daughter of Livilla and the late Drusus. Sejanus set Drusus, son of Germanicus, against his brother by pointing out that Nero's accession would mean that his claims to the throne would be ignored. He also incited jealousy between the brothers by stressing Agrippina's partiality for her eldest son.[14] The Agrippinian party needed the co-operation of Drusus, who apparently failed to realize that he was being duped by Sejanus and used by him as a tool to thwart the attainment of the ambitions of Agrippina and Nero.

Sejanus, ostensibly as the representative of the emperor in the capital city, assumed the attitude of a prosecutor rather than a political rival of the Agrippinian party. Soldiers were ordered to report the movements and correspondence of the leaders of the party and to detail "their activities open and secret with the exactitude of annalists." [15] Efforts were made to persuade Agrippina to take refuge with the legions in Germany or to make an unequivocally rebellious move in the Forum. Agrippina and

---

[11] Ferrero, "Tiberius and Agrippina," in *loc. cit.*, 619.
[12] Tacitus, *Ann.*, IV, 59.   [13] *Ibid.*, 60.
[14] *Ibid.*   [15] *Ibid.*, 67.

Nero refused to fall into the trap, and they were wise to refrain from an overt act of insurrection.[16]

Tiberius' letter of praise to the Senate following the condemnation of Sabinus indicated that he was aware that Agrippina and Nero and their partisans were a menace to his security.[17] Asinius Gallus, an intimate friend of Agrippina and, according to rumor, her paramour, now proposed that the emperor should commit his fears to the Senate so that proper measures could be taken to safeguard the state.[18] Tiberius refused to accede to this request. Tacitus charges that "Of all of his virtues as he regarded them there was none which Tiberius held in such esteem as his power of dissimulation; whence the chagrin with which he received this attempt to reveal what he chose to suppress." [19] The emperor doubtless had good reasons for refusing to inaugurate senatorial action at this time. It is hardly likely that he had conclusive evidence against Agrippina and Nero, and he therefore believed that the proposal of Gallus was an effort to force his hand and divulge his intentions prematurely. Sejanus is reported to have mollified the emperor, "not from love of Gallus, but in order to await the issue of the emperor's hesitations." [20] He, too, realized the peril of proceeding against Agrippina and her partisans before the evidence against them was irrefutable and the strength of the opposition had been accurately gauged.

Sejanus' power naturally was growing with the emperor's absence from the capital. Tiberius refrained from visits to Rome, whereas Sejanus frequently journeyed to Capri, with the natural result that it was believed that he was authorized to speak and act for the absent emperor.

---

[16] *Ibid.*   [17] *Infra*, ooo.   [18] Tacitus, *Ann.*, IV, 71.
[19] *Ibid.*; Rogers, "Conspiracy of Agrippina," in *loc. cit.*, 156–57.
[20] Tacitus, *Ann.*, IV, 71.

THE RETIREMENT TO CAPRI 137

Efforts of the senators to secure an audience with Tiberius failed;[21] indeed, it became increasingly difficult for them to approach Sejanus, upon whose friendship many of them felt dependent.[22]

Uneasiness in the capital increased after Livia's death in 29. Tiberius, according to Tacitus, refrained from visiting his mother during her fatal illness. Public honors to her memory were minimized, although her funeral was public. Gaius, her great-grandson, delivered the eulogy, and she was entombed in the mausoleum of Augustus.[23] "Tiberius, however, without altering the amenities of his life, excused himself by letter, on the score of important affairs, for neglecting to pay the last respects to his mother, and, with a semblance of modesty, curtailed the lavish tributes decreed to her memory by the Senate."[24] The emperor had restrained the Senate in the award of honors to his mother at the time of his accession, and there can be little doubt that he had discouraged her in her efforts to interfere in the affairs of government. His absence from the funeral may well have been in line with his policy, for he may have feared that the funeral would offer an opportunity for the Agrippinian party to organize a demonstration against him.[25]

Not long after Livia's death a letter arrived from the emperor, who was at Capri, charging Nero with unnatural vices and Agrippina with overbearing conduct. Tacitus intimates that Livia hitherto had restrained the em-

---

[21] *Ibid.*, 74.   [22] *Ibid.*
[23] *Ibid.* Dio, *R.H.*, LVIII, ii, 6, states that the emperor refused to build a memorial arch voted to Livia. Kornemann, "Neues von Kaiser Tiberius," in *loc. cit.*, 343, thinks that the emperor was not really free until after his mother's death.
[24] Tacitus, *Ann.*, V, 1–2; Dio, *R.H.*, LVIII, ii. Willrich, *Livia*, 40–41, does not think that the differences between Tiberius and his mother were really serious.
[25] Willenbücher, *Tiberius und die Verschwörung des Sejans*, 30–31.

peror "since deference to his mother was ingrained in Tiberius, nor did Sejanus venture to claim precedence over the authority of a parent. But now, as though freed from the curb, they broke out unrestrained, and a letter denouncing Agrippina and Nero was forwarded to Rome; the popular impression being that it was delivered much earlier and suppressed by the old empress, since it was publicly read not long after her death." [26] In view of the historian's insistence on Livia's enmity toward Germanicus and Agrippina, this statement must be dismissed without serious consideration.

The Senate was somewhat at a loss as to how to proceed in view of the absence of any charges of treasonable actions by Agrippina and Nero. Cotta Messalinus, a well-known supporter of the emperor, moved that proceedings should begin. Junius Rusticus, an adherent of Agrippina, successfully urged delay. He warned that "a touch could turn the scale in the gravest of matters: it was possible that some day the extinction of the house of Germanicus might prove the old man's [Tiberius] penitence." [27] Thus, there was strong opposition in the Senate to any direct move by the emperor against Agrippina and her son, at least in the absence of more specific charges. While the Senate was deliberating concerning the disposition of Tiberius' letter, a crowd surrounded the curia.

[26] Tacitus, *Ann.*, V, 3. N. Cortellini, "A proposito di alcune date incerte dell'ultimo decennio del regno di Tiberio," *Rivista di Storia Antica*, III (1898), I, 20, holds that Agrippina and Nero were banished at the end of 29 or the beginning of 30. The Tacitean account cannot be reconciled with Suetonius, *Caligula*, X. *Ibid.*, 21. Rivalry between Livia and Agrippina was natural, for "neither was inferior to the other in ambition or fierceness of spirit." Barini, "La tradition superstite ed alcuni giudizi di moderni su Livia," in *loc. cit.*, 31.

[27] Tacitus, *Ann.*, V, 4. Cotta was prosecuted on a number of charges in 32 and convicted, but he successfully appealed to the emperor. See, R. S. Rogers, "Der Prozess des Cotta Messalinus," *Hermes*, LXVIII (1933), 122–23.

THE RETIREMENT TO CAPRI   139

Carrying images of Agrippina and Nero, the demonstrators clamored that the letter of denunciation was spurious and that "it was contrary to the emperor's wish that destruction was plotted against the house of Germanicus." [28] Anonymous attacks on Sejanus also were circulated. It would seem from the Tacitean account of the affair that the demonstration was not an evidence of popular hostility against the emperor but an attack on Sejanus, and that efforts were made to exculpate Tiberius from responsibility for the charges against Agrippina and Nero.[29]

Tiberius probably had no report of the incident other than that furnished by Sejanus. Resolved to ruin the Agrippinian party, it would have been natural for the favorite to magnify the political implications of the demonstration. "The Senate had spurned the sorrow of its emperor, the people had forsworn its allegiance. Already disloyal harangues, disloyal decrees of the Fathers were listened to and perused: what remained but to take the sword and in the persons whose effigies they had followed as their ensigns to choose their generals and their princes?" [30]

Tiberius acted promptly after receipt of the report of the Senate's failure to respond to his first communication. He announced that he had taken the case against Agrippina and Nero under his own jurisdiction and issued an edict rebuking the populace for the demonstration.[31] The Senate "proceeded, not indeed to decree the last penalties

---

[28] Tacitus, *Ann.*, V, 4.
[29] Abraham, *Tiberius und Sejan*, 17, thinks that Tiberius' power was challenged by the demonstration.
[30] Tacitus, *Ann.*, V, 4. Lang, *Beiträge zur Gesch. des Kaisers Tiberius*, 55-56, argues that Tiberius' patience with Agrippina and his designation of Drusus and Nero as his heirs, as well as his treatment of Gaius (Caligula), show conclusively that he had no desire to ruin Agrippina and her family.
[31] Tacitus, *Ann.*, V, 5.

(that course was forbidden) but to assert their readiness for vengeance, from which they were debarred by compulsion of the sovereign."[32] The senators apparently were ready to make amends by proceeding against Agrippina and Nero, but the case had been taken out of their hands. The emperor exiled Agrippina to Pandateria under a military guard. Nero was exiled to Pontia, where he died or committed suicide in 31.[33] Tacitus' account in the extant portion of Book V breaks off with Chapter V; Suetonius claims that Agrippina was cruelly treated by order of the emperor until she finally starved herself to death.[34]

Sejanus had succeeded in breaking the power of the Agrippinian party. "He had dared to do what Tiberius had never succeeded in doing; he had destroyed the center of opposition which gathered about Agrippina in the house of Germanicus."[35] This by no means proves that he was planning to usurp the throne or to ensure his succession.[36] Drusus and Gaius, sons of Germanicus and Agrippina, still were uncompromised with the emperor, who would naturally look toward them in considering the succession issue. Tiberius probably had been led by

---

[32] *Ibid.;* Suetonius, *Tib.*, LIII. Tacitus' account probably was based on the commentaries of Agrippina the Younger. Motzo, "I commentari di Agrippina madre di Nerone," in *loc. cit.*, 48 ff.

[33] Suetonius, *Tib.*, LIII–LIV.

[34] *Ibid.* Gaius (Caligula) brought his mother's bones to Rome after his accession. *C.I.L.*, VI, 886. Dio, *R.H.*, LVII, xxii, 4, states that Agrippina and Nero were put to death because they rejoiced at the death of Drusus.

[35] Ferrero, "Tiberius and Agrippina," in *loc. cit.*, 621.

[36] Marsh, *Reign of Tiberius*, 186, and Willenbücher, *Tiberius und die Verschwörung des Sejans*, 33, think Sejanus may have provoked the uprising to convince Tiberius of the necessity for action. "Sejanus, in order to bring about the fulfillment of his ambitious plans, resorted to any means to throw the family of Germanicus into a sinister light before the emperor." Cortellini, "A proposito di alcune date," in *loc. cit.*, 19.

THE RETIREMENT TO CAPRI

Sejanus to exaggerate the danger of the alleged conspiracy fomented by Agrippina and her partisans. Doubtless there had been plenty of indiscreet talk, and Agrippina had not refrained from studied affronts. The demonstration by some of the populace of the capital in behalf of Agrippina and Nero, however, could hardly be interpreted as a hostile move against Tiberius. The Senate had decided against taking action in response to the emperor's first request, but evidence of his displeasure had been followed by immediate compliance and efforts to placate him. If there were an appreciable number of Agrippina's supporters in the Senate, they did not dare to oppose the emperor on an issue of vital importance to their cause. The banishment of Agrippina and Nero evoked no manifestation of popular hostility and, above all, no signs of discontent among the legions. The conspiracy of the Agrippinian factions could not have proceeded much beyond the stage of rash talk and wishful thinking.

The following year (30), Asinius Gallus, another leader of the Agrippinian party, was condemned. Although he had begun to pay court to Sejanus, either to advance his own interests or to thwart the favorite by simulated friendship,[37] Tiberius charged him with envy of Sejanus and ordered his imprisonment. He died in prison in 33.[38] The real cause for his condemnation, of course, was his involvement in the intrigues of the Agrippinians.[39]

Drusus, the second son of Agrippina, was pronounced a public enemy the same year and tried before the Senate. Prosecuted by Casius, he was convicted and sentenced to imprisonment. He ultimately committed suicide or was

---
[37] Dio, *R.H.*, LVIII, iii, 1-2.
[38] Tacitus, *Ann.*, VI, 23; Rogers, "Lucius Arruntius," in *loc. cit.*, 32, 34.
[39] Tacitus, *Ann.*, VI, 23.

starved to death by his jailers.⁴⁰ He had opposed the plans of the Agrippinians after his jealousy had been skillfully aroused by Sejanus. It is possible, however, that adherents of Agrippina and Nero, who retained their courage even after the disastrous blows which their cause had suffered, had turned to Drusus as a last desperate resort, and he may have been foolish enough to compromise himself sufficiently to enable charges to be brought against him with a measure of plausibility.

Sejanus now was at the height of his power.⁴¹ The important leaders of the opposition party had been ruined, and three members of the Julio-Claudian house had been exiled, largely as a result of his efforts. There was still a major obstacle in the way if the minister aspired to the succession. Gaius, the third son of Agrippina, was living with Tiberius at Capri—a strong indication that the emperor intended to designate him as his successor. On the other hand, Sejanus was on the point of realizing his cherished ambition for a marital alliance with the ruling family, for the emperor had sanctioned his betrothal to Julia, the daughter of Drusus.⁴² He had been invested with praetorian authority and anticipated the bestowal of proconsular powers. Receipt of these honors would mean that only the grant of tribunician powers would be necessary to make him the colleague of the emperor. By this time, then, he had reason to hope for the succession, or at least for installation as Gaius' colleague.

He needed the support of the legions, however, for if he could not count on control of the provinces, his com-

---

⁴⁰ Cortellini, "A proposito di alcune date," in *loc. cit.*, 21, maintains that he was put to death shortly before Gaius was made a pontiff in 31.
⁴¹ Tacitus, *Ann.*, IV, 74.
⁴² *Ibid.*, III, 29; VI, 8. Possibly Julia Livilla, the widow of Drusus, and the original object of Sejanus' marital ambitions.

mand of the Praetorian Guard would not suffice to assure his recognition as emperor if his plans to secure the throne met with success. Many of the military commanders were of the old republican aristocratic families,[43] and it obviously would be difficult, if not impossible, to enlist their support. By a series of marital alliances and absentee appointments, however, Sejanus succeeded in strengthening his position in this respect.[44] It may well have seemed to the populace of the capital that "Sejanus was too great a person by reason both of his excessive haughtiness and of his vast power, that to put it briefly, he himself seemed to be the emperor and Tiberius a kind of island potentate." [45]

He was given a free hand in completing the destruction of the Agrippinian party. He procured the accusation of Fufius Geminus on charges of treason. The defendant had been a favorite of Livia as well as of Agrippina largely because of his physical attractiveness. He and his wife committed suicide in the Senate chamber after he had read his will bequeathing his property to his children and to the emperor.[46]

Tiberius may have begun to realize that Sejanus was too powerful, but he continued to bestow honors upon him, possibly to conceal his suspicions until he was ready

---

[43] Groag, "Zur Aemterlaufbahn der Nobiles in der Kaiserzeit," in *loc. cit.*, 253–58.

[44] In 29 Lentulus Gaetulicus was appointed legate of Upper Germany; his daughter was betrothed to a son of Sejanus. In Lower Germany, the father-in-law of Gaetulicus, L. Apronius, was given command; his son was a friend of Sejanus. Moesia, Macedonia, and Achaea were controlled by Poppaeus Sabinus, whose daughter was married to an intimate of Sejanus, T. Ollius. Absentee legates had been appointed for Syria and Spain. Marsh, *Reign of Tiberius*, 190–91; Cichorius, "Zur Familiengeschichte Seians," in *loc. cit.*, 70; Rogers, "Lucius Arruntius," in *loc. cit.*, 37.

[45] Dio, *R.H.*, LVIII, v, 1.   [46] *Ibid.*

to strike. In 31 Sejanus was made consul as a colleague of the emperor, who also honored him with the salutation of "Sharer of My Cares." He was addressed by Tiberius in letters to the Senate in the intimate terms of "My Sejanus," and statues were dedicated to him as well as to the *princeps*. On the occasion of the departure of Sejanus from Capri, the emperor had acted as if "a part of his own body and soul were being wrenched away from him." [47] The favorite also was given reason to believe that his benefactor intended to return to Rome in the near future.

The emperor then began to use the weapon of suspense to disconcert the man who had risen so high by his favor. Tiberius sent dispatches to Rome complaining that his health was so bad as to threaten imminent death, and he followed these missives by communications in which he stated that he was so well that he was preparing to leave for Rome. One letter honored Sejanus and his friends, while another mildly criticized the favorite and denounced his intimates.[48] The emperor was preparing for the ultimate overthrow of the powerful minister, and his tergiversation gained precious time to carry the plan to fruition. Continued evidences of favor to Sejanus avoided the danger that he would take alarm and resort to the desperate expedient of revolt with the potential support of the Praetorian Guard while the emperor was virtually defenseless at Capri.[49]

[47] *Ibid.* Asbach, *Römisches Kaisertum und Verfassung bis auf Traian*, 17, points out that the consulship of Sejanus was a crowning blow to the old aristocracy. A bronze coin honors Sejanus as Tiberius' consular colleague. H. Cohen, *Descriptions historique des monnaies*, 3 vols. (Paris, 1880), I, 198.

[48] Dio, *R.H.*, LVIII, vi.

[49] Tiberius had no weapon but his cleverness. Freytag, *Tiberius und Tacitus*, 247.

In line with this "fast and loose" policy Tiberius elevated Sejanus and Gaius to the pontificate and bestowed proconsular powers on the former.[50] Proconsular powers really did little if anything to strengthen the position of Sejanus, for his command of the Praetorian Guard already had given him military command. On the other hand, the ordination of Gaius marked his first appearance as a rival of Sejanus for the favor of the emperor, who thus gave added indication that he intended to designate his young grandnephew as his successor. The emperor's policy in respect to Gaius was a popular measure; it might even have been regarded by the Agrippinians as a conciliatory gesture.

Since Sejanus had identified himself so closely with the ruin of the house of Germanicus, the emperor's policy in respect to Gaius was a rebuff to the prefect in the same measure that it could be interpreted as an effort to appease the Agrippinians. The powerful minister, however, now suffered an indubitably severe blow. Tiberius suddenly resigned his consulship and forced Sejanus, his colleague, to do likewise. To be sure, there were hints of greater honors in store for the favorite, but when he asked permission to visit the emperor at Capri for a fuller explanation of this latest measure, the request was refused on the grounds that the emperor planned an early return to Rome.[51]

If Sejanus had lost the consulship, he still controlled the subservient Senate; but he soon lost even this support. When he brought charges against Lucius Arruntius, absentee legate of Hispania Citerior, Tiberius quashed the

[50] Dio, *R.H.*, LVIII, vii, 4.
[51] *Ibid.* These measures clearly indicate that the emperor was resolved to overthrow his minister. Willenbücher, *Tiberius und die Verschwörung des Sejans*, 38.

indictment and accorded immunity to absentee legates from such prosecutions in Rome.⁵² This episode was of the greatest significance. "To Tiberius at Capri it must have been evident that if his praetorian prefect could compass the overthrow of Arruntius, he was master of Rome —To the Senate it meant the salvation of one of its most eminent members. To Tiberius it meant the grateful support of the Senate if and when it should be necessary to take further measures against Sejanus." ⁵³

Tiberius continued to harry the minister. In a letter to the Senate concerning the death of Nero, he referred to Sejanus without the customary titles and honors.⁵⁴ Shortly afterward he forbade sacrifices to any human being, and this action was interpreted as a blow aimed at Sejanus' vanity.⁵⁵

Sejanus now realized that the emperor probably was undermining him. He had forfeited the support of the Senate by his abortive prosecution of Arruntius, and there was every likelihood that Tiberius soon would formally designate Gaius as his successor with no provision for the minister to serve as regent or colleague. Only revolt could secure the throne, but it would have been sheer folly for him to resort to the desperate expedient of rebellion while there was still chance that he would receive indispensable tribunician powers from the Senate at the direction of the emperor. On other occasions during the past months his misgivings had been allayed by renewed evidence of the emperor's confidence; there was as yet no reason for him to despair.

At this juncture an informer, Satrius Secundus,⁵⁶ probably told Antonia that Sejanus was plotting rebellion and

---

⁵² Dio, *R.H.*, LVIII, viii, 3.
⁵³ Rogers, "Lucius Arruntius," in *loc. cit.*, 31.
⁵⁴ Dio, *R.H.*, LVIII, viii, 3-4.   ⁵⁵ *Ibid.*   ⁵⁶ Tacitus, *Ann.*, VI, 47.

THE RETIREMENT TO CAPRI

usurpation of the throne.[57] Antonia, Tiberius' sister-in-law, had always been on good terms with the emperor. "No one exercised so much influence as she over the diffident and self-centered spirit of the emperor. Whoever wished to obtain a favor from him could do no better than to intrust his cause to Antonia."[58] When she learned of the alleged plot, she dispatched a messenger to Tiberius with its details.[59] Tiberius' position was a strong one, for he had the support of the Senate because of his quashing of the indictment against Arruntius; moreover, his bestowal of honors on Gaius had gained the approval of the populace.

Naevius Sertorius Macro, a trusted bodyguard of Tiberius, then was sent from Capri by night with a letter to the Senate to be read the following morning. Memmius Regulus, one of the consuls, was informed of Macro's mission and given secret instructions.[60] Graecinius Laco, commander of the night watch, also was made a party to the emperor's plan. At dawn Macro ascended the Palatine and encountered Sejanus, who was on his way to a Senate session in the Temple of Apollo. He informed the minister that he was about to receive the coveted tribunician power in response to a letter which he brought from the emperor. Sejanus, overjoyed at the news of this decisive concession from Tiberius, hastened into the Senate chamber. Macro dismissed the praetorians who had accompanied Sejanus and stationed Laco and the night watch around the temple. He then hurried off to the praetorian camp to forestall any uprising in support of Sejanus, whose ruin he knew was imminent.[61]

---

[57] Ferrero, "The Daughters of Agrippina," in *loc. cit.*, 400–401.
[58] *Ibid.*, 412.
[59] Josephus, *Antiquities*, XVIII, 6; Abraham, *Tiberius und Sejan*, 17.
[60] Dio, *R.H.*, LVIII, ix.
[61] *Ibid.* Macro's wife, Ennia, was a granddaughter of Thrasyllus, one

In the meantime, the consul, Memmius Regulus, began to read the emperor's letter to the senators, many of whom apparently shared Sejanus' belief that the missive would order the bestowal of additional honors upon the favorite. The letter began with the customary amenities. From the recital of petty matters the content changed to mild strictures on the conduct of Sejanus; these, in turn, were followed by sharp criticisms of the minister. Two senators who had been his intimates then were specifically denounced and ordered placed under arrest. Finally, as a spectacular climax, Sejanus' arrest was ordered.[62] While the tone of the letter became more and more critical of Sejanus, many senators who had crowded about him at the beginning of the session drew away. Upon the conclusion of the reading of the letter, Regulus ordered the stupefied minister to come forward; Sejanus was so dazed by the damning denunciation that he did not immediately respond. When he finally arose from his seat in the chamber, he was taken into custody by Laco, to the accompaniment of the jeers of the senators, and was led away to prison.[63] On the way to prison the fallen minister was treated with scorn and violence. The populace showered him with reproaches for the lives he allegedly had taken, and destroyed statues that had been erected in his honor.[64]

The same day the senators reassembled in the Temple of Concord, reassured by the enmity demonstrated by the populace toward Sejanus and the failure of the prae-

---

of the emperor's few intimates. This would account in some measure for the trust that Tiberius placed in Macro. C. Cichorius, "Der Astrologe Thrasyllos und sein Haus," *Römische Studien* (Berlin, 1922), 390–98. The watch (*vigiles*) was organized in A.D. 6. First mention of the *prefectus vigilium* is in the reign of Tiberius. *C.I.L.*, XIV, 3947. Laco subsequently became a Gallic procurator and ultimately received consular insignia. P. K. Baillie Reynolds, *The Vigiles of Imperial Rome* (Oxford, 1926), 7, 14, 27–28, 31–32.

[62] Dio, *R.H.*, LVIII, ix–xi.   [63] *Ibid.*   [64] *Ibid.*

torians to rise in his behalf. They thereupon condemned the former favorite to be strangled and cast down the Gemonian stairs. The rabble abused the body after the execution, until it was thrown into the Tiber three days later.[65] "But on what charge was he condemned? Who informed against him? What was the evidence, who the witnesses who made good the case? Nothing of the sort; a great and wordy letter came from Capri." [66]

Tiberius had been uneasy concerning the outcome of Macro's mission. He had given orders that Drusus, who was still in prison, should be set free, and, if occasion demanded, made commander-in-chief of the armed forces. He had even ordered ships to be held in readiness to take him to the legions and had arranged an elaborate signal system between the isle of Capri and the mainland so he might know immediately the outcome of his move against Sejanus.[67]

The children of Sejanus shared their father's fate. Son and daughter both were imprisoned, strangled, and thrown down the Gemonian stairs. Apicata, wife of Sejanus, was not condemned, but after learning of the death of her children, she divulged the alleged poisoning of Tiberius' son, Drusus, and committed suicide. The estate of the fallen minister was confiscated by the emperor.[68]

The city remained in an uproar, for many persons had been injured by Sejanus or his henchmen and naturally clamored for vengeance. The praetorians, angered be-

---

[65] Seneca, *On the Tranquillity of the Mind*. He was put to death on October 18. *C.I.L.*, VI, 2028c.

[66] Juvenal, *Satires*, X.

[67] Dio, *R.H.*, LVIII, xiii. See, J. A. Kingman, "Isle of Capri, an Imperial Residence and Probable Wireless Station of Ancient Rome," *National Geographic Magazine*, XXXVI (1919), 230.

[68] The daughter was violated by the executioner before she was strangled. It was illegal to execute a virgin in prison. R. Lugand, "Le viol rituel les Romains," *Revue Archéologique*, XXXII (1930), 37-38. See, Tacitus, *Ann.*, V, 9; Dio, *R.H.*, LVIII, xi, 5-6.

cause they had apparently been suspected of supporting Sejanus' schemes in view of the fact that the night watch had been employed to arrest him, burned and plundered in various parts of the city.[69] The Senate feared the retribution of the emperor, but the more courageous Fathers rallied and blamed their misfortunes and past conduct on Sejanus. Decree after decree was issued to defame the name of Sejanus, while Tiberius and his faithful servitors, Laco and Macro, were honored.[70]

A period of delation, which involved accusation, counteraccusation, and condemnation, now ensued. Among those who gave information concerning alleged machinations of Sejanus were some of his former adherents. Under such circumstances convictions were easily secured, for the accusers could profess to know Sejanus' intimate secrets.[71] Some of the accused defended themselves, but others committed suicide so that their children might inherit their property.[72] Tiberius placed the delation trials in the hands of the Senate and accepted confiscated estates. The number of prosecutions was not large, however, in view of the fact that the emperor apparently was convinced of the actual existence of a conspiracy.[73]

Among the first to be brought to trial was Sextius Paconianus who was accused of aiding and abetting Sejanus in a plot against Gaius (Caligula). He saved his life by informing against Latinius Latiaris.[74] Cotta Messalinus was prosecuted on the allegation that he had insulted Gaius and Tiberius, but the emperor quashed the indict-

[69] Dio, *R.H.*, LVIII, xii, 2.
[70] *Ibid.* See, *C.I.L.*, III, 12036; XI, 4170, for commemorations of Sejanus' fall.
[71] Dio, *R.H.*, LVIII, xii, 2-4.
[72] Flint, "The Delatores in the Reign of Tiberius," in *loc. cit.*, 42.
[73] Schott, *Die Kriminaljustiz unter den Kaiser Tiberius*, 13.
[74] Tacitus, *Ann.*, VI, 3.

THE RETIREMENT TO CAPRI 151

ment.[75] Tiberius, on the other hand, ordered Cestius to denounce Quintus Servaeus and Minucius Thermus as "ringleaders in crime." [76] When the defendants were found guilty, they turned informers. When Publius Vitellius was accused of offering the keys of the treasury together with the army fund to the cause of revolution, he became frightened and committed suicide.[77] Fulcinius Trio, a lawyer and professional delator, accused Memmius Regulus, his consular colleague, of remissness in the prosecution of Sejanus' accomplices. Regulus countered by threatening an investigation of Trio's part in the conspiracy.[78] Senators tried to mediate between the consuls, but they remained hostile until the end of their terms.[79]

In the trial of Marcus Terentius the defendant pleaded: "I shall confess that not only was I a friend of Sejanus, but that I strove for his friendship; . . . the closer a man's intimacy with Sejanus, the stronger his claim to the emperor's friendship. . . . For we courted, not Sejanus of Vulsinii, but the member of those Claudian and Julian houses into which his alliances had won him entry; . . . let the dividing line be drawn true; let treason against the realm, projected assassination of the sovereign, meet their punishment; but when friendship and its duties are in question, if we terminate them at the same moment as you, we are vindicated, Caesar, along with yourself." [80] This brave defense resulted in the acquittal of the defendant and the punishment of his accusers.

---

[75] *Ibid.*, VI, 5. He allegedly had cast doubt on the manhood of Gaius. It also was charged that he had boasted that he had been instrumental in the withholding of divine honors from Livia and that Tiberius would take care of him in financial litigation in which he was involved. Rogers, "Der Prozess des Cotta Messalinus," in *loc. cit.*, 122.
[76] Tacitus, *Ann.*, VI, 7. [77] *Ibid.*, V, 8.
[78] *Ibid.*, 11. [79] Four years later Trio committed suicide.
[80] Tacitus, *Ann.*, VI, 8. Lentulus Gaetulicus took the same line of defense. *Ibid.*, 30.

Shortly after the case of Terentius was disposed of, Sextus Vistilius was denounced by the emperor for impugning the morals of Gaius. He committed suicide when his efforts to secure pardon were rebuffed. The mother of Fufius Geminus, who already had incurred the displeasure of Tiberius, was executed, as well as Junius Marinus, who, it was charged, had aided Sejanus.[81] A public execution of others held in prison on charges of complicity in Sejanus' schemes followed. Although Tacitus speaks of a "huge hecatomb of victims . . . scattered or piled in mounds," it is more likely that this is the same incident described by Suetonius, who declared that only twenty suspects were put to death in a single day.[82]

T. Ollius also was prosecuted and fell "a victim to the friendship of Sejanus." Lentulus Gaetulicus, commander of the legions in Upper Germany, was accused because he had promised his daughter in marriage to Sejanus' son. He was not condemned, however, but remained unscathed "and high in favor." [83]

In 33 Agrippina probably starved herself to death, and Drusus also was permitted to starve. The deaths of Agrippina and her son convinced the populace that Sejanus had not been responsible for the emperor's prosecutions of them, for both had been maltreated after the minister's death.[84] Gaius, the sole survivor of the Germanican house, remained with Tiberius as heir apparent to the throne.

The question whether Sejanus really had conspired against the emperor is difficult to decide. The charge that he had consummated a successful poison plot against Drusus, son of the emperor, seems incredible on the basis of existent evidence. Doubtless he played a leading role

---

[81] *Ibid.*, 9–10.   [82] *Ibid.*, 19; Suetonius, *Tib.*, LXI.
[83] Tacitus, *Ann.*, VI, 30.   [84] *Ibid.*, 23, 25; Suetonius, *Tib.*, LIII–LIV.

in the struggle against the Agrippinians that led to the exile of Agrippina and Nero. It cannot be conclusively proved, however, that he was motivated by an ambition to seize the throne or to procure the succession. It is quite possible that he was sincerely convinced that he was serving the vital interests of Tiberius in frustrating the schemes of Agrippina and her partisans, but the conduct of the leaders of this faction had been so indiscreet that, in all likelihood, retaliatory action by Tiberius would have been forthcoming sooner or later without the intervention of the favorite.

It is difficult to maintain that Tiberius decided to overthrow his hitherto trusted minister when he became convinced that he had procured the ruin of the house of Germanicus.[85] Agrippina and Nero were not released after the fall of Sejanus. There is no evidence of any amelioration of their lot; indeed, if anything, they suffered more after the fall of the minister. Although Tiberius was warned by Antonia that Sejanus was plotting against him, it is doubtful if he needed any warning. He had become convinced that Sejanus was too powerful. The succession of Gaius would be threatened by the presence of so powerful a figure close to the throne, and his plan to designate Gaius as his successor left no alternative to the ruin of the minister. The security of the dynasty demanded it.

The emperor never returned to Rome after Sejanus' fall.[86] In 32 he came to his gardens along the Tiber, but went back to Capri without entering the city.[87] Apparently his unwillingness to resume residence in the capital

---

[85] Suetonius, *Tib.*, LXI; Marsh, *Reign of Tiberius*, 308-10.
[86] Tacitus, *Ann.*, VI, 15; Suetonius, *Tib.*, LXXII.
[87] Tacitus, *Ann.*, VI, 10; Suetonius, *Tib.*, LXXII.

was partially dictated by fear of revolt or assassination, otherwise it is difficult to account for the proposals made before the Senate with the avowed object of affording him greater security. A motion proposed by Togonus Gallus suggested that twenty senators be chosen by lot to act as his bodyguard.[88] The emperor raised a number of objections to the plan, but it is quite possible that the real reason for his opposition was the fear that he might fall a victim to armed senatorial conspirators as did Julius Caesar.[89]

The emperor further pointed out that he could still rely on the Praetorian Guard,[90] but he denounced the proposal of Junius Gallio that the praetorians should be granted the right to share the first fourteen rows in the theater with the *equites*. He apparently interpreted this suggestion as an implied criticism of his dependence upon the praetorians. The originator of the motion was expelled from the Senate, and, after a short exile, placed under surveillance in Rome.[91] Tiberius finally disposed of schemes to provide for his safety by requesting the Senate to permit a retinue, headed by Macro, to escort him when he came into the Senate chamber.[92] Such authorization, indeed, was voted by the Senate, but as the emperor continued to absent himself from the capital, the procedure never was utilized.

In 33 the emperor came within four miles of the city to arrange for the marriages of the daughters of Germanicus. Drusilla was married to Lucius Cassius, and Julia was given to Marcus Vinicius.[93] No elaborate public ceremonies or festivities attended the nuptials, apparently at the emperor's insistence. About the same time, Gaius, the

[88] Tacitus, *Ann.*, VI, 2.   [89] Dio, *R.H.*, LVIII, xvii, 3-4.
[90] *Ibid.*   [91] Tacitus, *Ann.*, VI, 3.
[92] *Ibid.*, 15; Dio, *R.H.*, LVIII, xviii, 5-6.
[93] Tacitus, *Ann.*, VI, 15; Dio, *R.H.*, LVIII, xxi, 1-2.

THE RETIREMENT TO CAPRI 155

future emperor, was made quaestor in line with the apparent plan to ensure his succession to the throne.[94]

The following year the twentieth anniversary of the reign was celebrated by the incumbent consuls in Rome, while the emperor tarried at Tusculum. The officiating consuls were executed later in the year, apparently upon conviction on charges of *maiestas*,[95] the justification of which it is impossible to determine. Shortly afterward, the emperor moved to Antium, where in 35 he arranged for the marriage of Gaius to Claudia, daughter of Marcus Silanus.[96]

Deeds of lust and cruelty, according to the ancient authorities, besmirched the emperor's declining years. Lust, drunkenness, and unnatural vices, detailed almost with relish by Suetonius, allegedly revealed his true character, so long concealed by hypocrisy and dissimulation.[97] Few historians today are prepared to believe that a man, admittedly austere, moderate, and conscientious, who during his long reign had been solicitous for the preservation of public morality, devoted the last years of his old age to debauch, assuming that he retained the physical stamina to indulge in such excesses. Study of the administration of Italy and the provinces during these years reveals no flagging of the emperor's efforts to ensure effective government,[98] and this factor, so at variance with the charges of the historians, makes it virtually impossible to accept the lurid accounts.

After a lingering illness the emperor died at the age of

---

[94] Dio, *R.H.*, LVIII, xxiii, 1–2.   [95] *Ibid.*, xxiv, 1–2.
[96] Tacitus, *Ann.*, VI, 20; Dio, *R.H.*, LVIII, xxv, 2.
[97] Tacitus, *Ann.*, VI, 1; Suetonius, *Tib.*, XLIII–XLV; Dio, *R.H.*, LVIII, xvii.
[98] H. Mattingly, *The Imperial Civil Service of Rome* (Cambridge, 1910), 33, cites no evidence besides that of the ancient writers to support his contention that provincial administration deteriorated after Tiberius' retirement to Capri.

78 at Misenum. In view of his age it was hardly necessary for Macro and Gaius to expedite his death,[99] although the sinister rumors which had attended his entire reign were not wanting when death brought the surcease from care which he had yearned for, even at the time of his elevation to the throne.

It is difficult, if not impossible, to derive a reasonably plausible impression of the emperor's character from the writings of the ancient historians. Suetonius depicts a self-reliant man of independent judgment,[100] whose sterling traits, earlier evinced in the camp,[101] subsequently were manifested on the throne in administrative ability and devotion to the public weal.[102] Courteous to the Senate,[103] as well as solicitous for the maintenance of its dignity,[104] he permitted freedom of speech [105] and interposed no objections when measures he personally opposed were passed.[106] He was just,[107] pacific,[108] and patient,[109] and his frugality [110] never impelled him to parsimony in expenditures for public benefit.[111] Modest [112] and austere,[113] he disliked flattery [114] and exercised his powers as far as feasible for the moral reformation of the populace.[115]

Yet, according to Suetonius, many of these good qualities were mere hypocritical shams.[116] Niggardliness [117] culminated in avarice, while the interests of the state were neglected after the withdrawal to Capri.[118] The emperor

---

[99] Dio, *R.H.*, LVIII, xxviii, 2–4; Tacitus, *Ann.*, VI, 50.
[100] Suetonius, *Tib.*, XVIII.
[101] *Ibid.*, XVII–XIX.
[102] *Ibid.*, XXXII.
[103] *Ibid.*, XXIX.
[104] *Ibid.*, XXX–XXXII.
[105] *Ibid.*, XXVIII.
[106] *Ibid.*, XXXI.
[107] *Ibid.*, XXXIII.
[108] *Ibid.*, XXXVII.
[109] *Ibid.*, XXVIII.
[110] *Ibid.*, XXXIV.
[111] *Ibid.*, XLVIII.
[112] *Ibid.*, XXVI, XXXII.
[113] *Ibid.*, XXI.
[114] *Ibid.*, XXVII.
[115] *Ibid.*, XXXIII, XXXV.
[116] *Ibid.*, XIV, XXV.
[117] *Ibid.*, XLVI–XLVII.
[118] *Ibid.*, XLI.

was cruel,[119] particularly to Germanicus and his family,[120] and fears for his personal safety were justified by popular odium.[121] The rapid degeneration of his character ultimately engendered the orgies with which he sullied his last years.[122]

Dio likewise presents the remarkable portrait of an emperor of vicious character conscientiously governing the state with outstanding competence and justice. He allegedly embarked on no major policy without consultation with the Senate. Freedom of discussion was upheld, even when the Fathers opposed him, and he was ready to acquiesce in adverse decisions. He was zealous in defense of justice and respectful in his demeanor toward the magistrates.[123] His reluctance to assume honors was expressed by forthright renunciation of a number of distinctions that were tendered him.[124] Dissimulation and hypocrisy, however, were deliberately chosen means for the attainment of his ends, which served to hide a character that actually was capricious, cruel, and sensual.[125]

Tacitus begins his account of the reign with a sinister note—the murder of Agrippa Posthumus.[126] The curtain rises on what the reader is led to believe will be a somber drama of cruelty and horror. Conclusive evidence of Tiberius' responsibility for the removal of a potential rival is not adduced; indeed, the historian abstains from unequivocal accusation.[127] The desired effect is secured, and the unwary are prepared to accept "the first crime of the new reign" as a cue to its subsequent nature. The composite picture is that of an interloper, artfully, perhaps criminally elevated to the throne by the wiles of his

---

[119] *Ibid.*, LIV, LVII, LIX, LX, LXI, LXII.   [120] *Ibid.*
[121] *Ibid.*, LXIII.   [122] *Ibid.*, XLIII–XLIV.
[123] Dio, *R.H.*, LVII, vii–xiii.   [124] *Ibid.*, LVII, viii, 1.
[125] *Ibid.*, LVII, iii, 5–7; vii, 4; xix, 1–3; LVIII, iii, xxii.
[126] Tacitus, *Ann.*, I, 6.   [127] *Infra*, 14–17.

mother,[128] posing as the designated candidate of the Senate.[129] The emperor is acutely aware of Livia's role in procuring his succession, and his jealous resentment mounts as he is confronted with evidences of her popularity, until his conduct during her last illness is indicative of hatred.[130]

Hypocrisy was Tiberius' most glaring weakness of character, if we judge from the number of allusions to this trait in Tacitus' account of the reign.[131] This charge is most convenient for Tacitus, since it enables him repeatedly to ascribe worthy conduct to dissimulation. Devoid of sincerity, the emperor, we are told, was morbidly suspicious,[132] and Germanicus, Agrippina, and their children, to say nothing of lesser persons, fell victims to the cruelties of a prince whose unfounded suspicions they had been so unfortunate as to arouse. This suspicious nature impelled the emperor to devious, underhand methods,[133] while his affected moderation failed to conceal his conceit.[134]

He was greedy, indeed rapacious, and the gravity of these vices was augmented by his natural cruelty.[135] Grudges were cherished for years [136] and ultimately avenged without forbearance or pity, which were foreign to his character.[137] Even when he acted justly, he could not refrain from harshness,[138] and his application of the *maiestas* law went beyond the demands of justice to afford expression of his churlishness, jealousy, and cruelty.[139]

---

[128] Tacitus, *Ann.*, VI, 46. [129] *Ibid.*, I, 5, 7.
[130] *Ibid.*, 14; III, 64; V, 2.
[131] *Ibid.*, I, 4, 11, 33; II, 28; III, 16, 22; IV, 4, 31; VI, 1.
[132] *Ibid.*, I, 13, 69; II, 5, 26; IV, 67; VI, 46.
[133] *Ibid.*, II, 66. [134] *Ibid.*, I, 8; II, 84.
[135] *Ibid.*, IV, 57; VI, 1, 19. [136] *Ibid.*, IV, 29.
[137] *Ibid.*, III, 15, 51, 67. [138] *Ibid.*, I, 75.
[139] *Infra*, 137.

THE RETIREMENT TO CAPRI

Sejanus preyed upon his morbid fears and further agitated a mind poisoned by suspicion, until the fall of the minister inaugurated the bloody reprisals that culminated in a veritable reign of terror.[140] As the dissimulation and hypocrisy behind which the emperor so long had concealed his true nature were stripped away, lust, hitherto bridled, conjoined with cruelty and led to horrid deeds.[141] There was no change in the emperor's character. His life after his elevation to the throne was essentially the gradual revelation of his actual nature.

Despite this severe indictment, Tacitus would have us believe that the emperor was an able and conscientious ruler who evinced unimpeachable integrity in his conduct of public business.[142] He was fair and impartial, particularly in his attitude toward Germanicus and Drusus,[143] generous in recognizing the achievements of other men,[144] and appreciative of the services of his subordinates.[145] His diplomacy, although resolute and skillful, was dedicated to the preservation of peace.[146] Although economical,[147] he was not greedy,[148] and he was ever ready to expend his resources for constructive purposes and the alleviation of distress.[149]

He hated flattery and preferred to eschew meaningless titles of adulation.[150] A sense of humor was not absent from his personality,[151] and on occasion he published anonymous letters that sharply criticized him.[152] Not

---

[140] Tacitus, *Ann.*, VI, 19, 24, 39, 40, 50.
[141] *Ibid.*, IV, 57, 67; VI, 1.   [142] *Ibid.*, II, 38; III, 69; VI, 5.
[143] *Ibid.*, II, 29, 33, 34, 35, 48, 52, 83; III, 37, 50, 51, 54, 55, 56, 69, 70, 76; V, 7; VI, 30.
[144] *Ibid.*, I, 55; II, 52, 64.   [145] *Ibid.*, I, 80.
[146] *Ibid.*, II, 64; IV, 32.   [147] *Ibid.*, I, 78; III, 52.
[148] *Ibid.*, I, 75; II, 48; III, 18.
[149] *Ibid.*, I, 75; II, 42, 47, 48; IV, 13, 64, 65.
[150] *Ibid.*, I, 8, 72.   [151] *Ibid.*, VI, 2.
[152] *Ibid.*, I, 72.

only was he free from vice, but simplicity, sobriety, and appreciation of learning were fundamental qualities of his character.[153]

Such is the contradictory Tacitean account that for centuries has served as the classic portrait of Tiberius' character.[154] Close examination shows that most of the strictures are attributable to the historian's attempts to discover the motives for the emperor's acts. Time and again favorable impressions created by the depiction of laudable deeds and conscientious attention to the business of state are effaced or beclouded by impugning the motives for such actions. When sinister effects are not imparted by alleged motivations, Tacitus frequently resorts to the repetition of rumors, which, however, he is usually careful not to endorse without reservation.[155]

In the main, Tacitus' attempts to blacken the reputation of Tiberius are the result of his bias against the principate.[156] The historian started his literary career as a monarchist and ended it, at least emotionally, a republican.[157] In the *Dialogue on Orators* he approved the principate as a form of government, on the ground that it at least eliminated the license and disorder that cast a somber shadow on the last years of the Republic.[158] In the reign of Domitian, however, his own career suffered a temporary set-

---

[153] *Ibid.*, 75; II, 48.
[154] C. C. Mierow, "Two Roman Emperors," *Classical Journal*, XXXVI (1941), 260–66. The balancing of good and bad characteristics is probably the result of the rhetorical tradition. J. Schmaus, *Charakterbilder römischer Kaiser aus der Zeit des Prinzipats (31 v. Chr.–284 n. Chr.)* (Bamberg, 1919), 10–19.
[155] Mierow, "Two Roman Emperors," in *loc. cit.*, 267–73. G. Boissier, *Tacite* (Paris, 1903), Bk. II, iii, believes that Tacitus sincerely sought to learn the truth.
[156] Mierow, "Two Roman Emperors," in *loc. cit.*, 267–68; Vogt, "Tacitus als Politiker," in *loc. cit.*, 14–17.
[157] F. Klinger, "Tacitus," *Die Antike*, VII (1932), 152.
[158] Vogt, "Tacitus als Politiker," in *loc. cit.*, 5.

THE RETIREMENT TO CAPRI 161

back.[159] This disappointment, coupled with the fall from favor of his father-in-law, Agricola, caused him to adopt a more skeptical attitude toward the imperial government,[160] and in the *Annals* he became an outright critic of the principate. Augustus was portrayed virtually as an usurper, while the Senate was described as a futile and hopeless survival of the Republican era.[161]

It is difficult to ascribe the historian's pessimism to Stoicism.[162] Traditions in regard to the sinister nature of Tiberius' reign were hardly in existence at the time he wrote.[163] In all his works there was a cumulative tendency to bemoan the unhappy state of the world,[164] and he came

---

[159] P. Fabia, "La carrière senatoriale de Tacite," *Journal des Savants*, XXIV (1926), 195–96. For an account of the *cursus honorum* in the empire, based on inscriptional evidence, see, L. Cantarelli, "La famiglia e il cursus honorum," *Bullettino della Commissione Archeologica Communale di Roma*, 2nd Series, XII (1884), 81–92.

[160] Vogt, "Tacitus als Politiker," in *loc. cit.*, 7; A. Stein, "Tacitus als Geschichtsquelle," *Neue Jahrbücher für das klassische Altertum Geschichte und Deutsche Literatur*, XXXVI (1915), 363–64.

[161] Vogt, "Tacitus als Politiker," in *loc. cit.*, 14–17.

[162] Marchesi, *Tacito*, 135. Tacitus, Lucan, and Juvenal "write as though they were living in the worst of all possible worlds. . . . It may be reasonably said that the combination of pessimism with a capacity for savage epigram is not a promising equipment for the historian." J. S. Reid, "Tacitus as a Historian," *Journal of Roman Studies*, XI (1921), 191.

[163] Jerome, *Some Aspects of Roman History*, Chap. XVI, presents strong evidence to show the absence of such traditions in the writings of historians who were contemporary or nearly contemporary with Tiberius. Cf., G. A. Harrer, "Tacitus and Tiberius," *American Journal of Philology*, XLI (1920), 57–68. The inscriptional evidence seems to indicate the absence of a tradition of evil. See, for example, *C.I.L.*, V¹, 3675; VI, 93, 902, 3674; XI, 3872; XIII, 941, 1769, 4635. In these inscriptions Tiberius is called the "best and most just prince," the "best of princes," or the "best of princes and most clement preserver of the country." There was hatred in the city of Rome at the time of his death. Suetonius, *Tib.*, LXXV; *Caligula*, XIII–XIV. A coin struck at Lyons in 37 as a memorial to Tiberius did not bear the legend, "Divus Tiberius," that apparently had been planned. H. Mattingly, "Some Historical Coins of the First Century A.D.," *Journal of Roman Studies*, X (1920), 37.

[164] Klinger, "Tacitus," in *loc. cit.*, 155.

to the melancholy conclusion that virtue and public order really were irreconcilable.[165] Freedom, for him, was little more than a desirable mean between rebellion and servility.[166] Monarchy, if elective, he considered compatible with such freedom, provided it was the rule of the best men, supplemented by the nominal concurrence of the aristocracy, and enlightened by free expression of opinion.[167] Although he expressed a nostalgic longing for a republic founded on virtue, he had no hope for a republican restoration.[168] He therefore attempted to teach the nobles of the imperial era to avoid the mistakes of the past, for even under the principate the aristocracy could still find a proper place, with opportunities to serve the state and acquire distinction.[169]

The reign of Tiberius eludes understanding unless the traditional concept of the gradual revelation of a depraved character is repudiated. The thesis of moral degeneration after the withdrawal to Capri is irreconcilable with the evidence of the continuance of excellent administration to the very end of the reign. A modern historian cannot follow Tacitus on his psychological explorations into the labyrinth of the mind as he purports to expose hidden thoughts and motives. The oft-repeated encomium that the historian was a masterly character analyst is only tenable if one unquestioningly assumes the validity of his allegations of motivation. The balance of good and bad traits, which ultimately yields to the preponderance of evil, need not beguile us, for this rhetorical convention is discernible in the ancient accounts of the reigns of other emperors. One is confronted with the alternative of frank

---

[165] *Ibid.*, 168–69.
[166] E. Fraenkel, "Tacitus," *Neue Jahrbücher für Wissenschaft und Jugendbildung*, VIII (1932), 225.
[167] Reitzenstein, "Tacitus und sein Werk," in *loc. cit.*, 9.
[168] *Ibid.*, 10.   [169] *Ibid.*, 20.

THE RETIREMENT TO CAPRI 163

acceptance of Tiberius as a dual personality or skepticism toward the character portrayals of the ancient authorities, unless, indeed, it can be assumed that an individual who dared not appear at Germanicus' funeral, lest his joy at the prince's death be detected, was such a consummate master of hypocrisy that he could hide his true character for years.

Grave errors of judgment doubtless were made by the emperor. His appointment of Piso to the Syrian governorship was a blunder of prime magnitude, for even the most sanguine could hardly have expected a man of his background and temperament successfully to perform the delicate mission entrusted to him. A mistake of tragic proportions was the reposal of excessive confidence in Sejanus. It was little short of folly to invest the favorite with power and honor while permitting him to retain command of the only formidable military force in Italy. If Sejanus did not cherish ambitions for the throne, conditions were created which were best calculated to arouse such aspirations. There is also reason to believe that after Sejanus' fall the *princeps* relied on Macro almost to the same degree as he had upon his former favorite.

While Agrippina and her partisans were guilty of indiscretion and probably of conspiracy, there is reason to believe that Tiberius was gulled by Sejanus into exaggerating the gravity of the threats to his security. In any event, a wiser and more courageous course would have been for the emperor to return to Rome to deal at first hand with the Agrippinians.

Indeed, the withdrawal to Capri was a fundamental mistake, although the charges of immorality can be ignored, and there is no evidence that governmental business was neglected. The necessity for the employment of intermediaries to keep the emperor in touch with the

Senate certainly did much to frustrate the attainment of his hopes for harmonious collaboration with the Fathers. More, of course, was involved in the retirement than a mistake of judgment. The emperor's decision doubtless was the expression of an excessively introverted nature, but it would be difficult to invest this failing, if failing it was, with moral significance.

The emperor indubitably lacked a tactful regard for the impressions made by his deeds and words, and his reserve frequently bordered upon haughtiness. Perhaps nothing better illustrates the personal contrasts between Augustus and his successor than their handling of the Senate when they presumably relinquished ruling powers. Augustus twice relinquished powers, only to have the Fathers invest him with proconsular and tribunician authority without hesitation. On the other hand, Tiberius' efforts to strengthen his constitutional position at his accession engendered taunts and recriminations, with the senators conveying the impression that they succumbed to necessity rather than acted in accordance with their desires. Seldom did Tiberius succeed in evoking sincere co-operation on the part of the Fathers, for his cold, austere demeanor probably prevented them from accepting at face value his assurances of freedom of thought and discussion. It seems strange that so monstrous a hypocrite as Tiberius was, according to the ancient historians, proved unable to dissemble more convincingly; indeed, his directness, even bluntness, apparently were the very qualities that so effectively militated against his popularity.

His conduct at Germanicus' funeral was bound to be misinterpreted, however sincere may have been his desire to set an example of resignation and constancy in the face of bereavement. While he quite properly checked efforts to augment Livia's influence in public affairs, his failure to visit her during her last illness seems to have been as impolitic as it was unfilial. Magnanimity toward Julia likewise would have been a popular gesture, although Tiberius certainly had no reason to feel kindly disposed toward her.[170] Greater sensibility and a more lively appreciation of public reactions doubtless would have gone a long way to secure for the emperor the popular esteem which the general wisdom and effectiveness of his policies merited. "In spirit he was a man of an earlier generation, dignified in bearing, hating flattery, frugal in his personal habits and cordially detesting the frivolous luxury then common in high society." [171]

It is as necessary to avoid the extreme of considering Tiberius as a paragon of competence and virtue as it is to temper the derogation of the ancient writers. Serious personal defects he doubtless possessed, and his policies were by no means invariably wise in conception or fortunate in outcome. Nevertheless, his comprehension of the German problem was fully demonstrated by the sequel to Germanicus' recall, and his eastern policy, based as it was on the Augustan tradition, maintained Roman interests in Armenia and evaded a major clash with Parthia. Mistakes and lack of tact in dealing with the smoldering aristocratic opposition in the capital, which bulk so large in the Tacitean account, actually were of little consequence when the history of the empire is considered on a sufficiently broad scope. It is only when we turn to a study of the administration of the larger interests of the empire that we are able to gauge adequately the emperor's abilities and arrive at a valid estimate of the significance of his reign.

[170] E. Groag, "Der Sturz der Julia," *Wiener Studien*, XLI (1919), 74-88.
[171] Marsh, *Reign of Tiberius*, 47.

Chapter VIII

LÈSE MAJESTÉ PROSECUTIONS UNDER TIBERIUS

In no respect does Tacitus more clearly betray his prejudices against Tiberius than in his treatment of the prosecution of cases of *lèse majesté*. His purpose is to show that "between the time of the Republic and the imperial period yawns a deep, complete cleavage; a fundamental contrast exists between these two periods of Roman history which no intermediary element compensates for or reconciles." ¹ The historian claims that "thanks to the art of Tiberius the accursed thing crept in, and, after a temporary check, at last broke out an all-devouring conflagration." ² Tiberius also is charged with instituting the practice of prosecuting persons for seditious or defamatory speeches or writings.³

It is further alleged that the emperor was the first to avail himself of the services of professional accusers, whose zeal he rewarded by permitting them to share in the distribution of the properties confiscated from those whose

---

¹ Schott, *Die Kriminaljustiz unter dem Kaiser Tiberius*, 2. For a summary of the lurid source and secondary accounts of the "terror," see, *id.*, *Studien zur Geschichte des Kaisers Tiberius* (Bamberg, 1904), 1–30. For a recent repetition of the "terror" version, see, E. G. Sihler, "The First Twelve Roman Emperors," *Bibliotheca Sacra*, XC (1933), 170–74.

² Tacitus, *Ann.*, I, 73; IV, 33. Dio, *R.H.*, LVII, xix, makes substantially the same charge.

³ Tacitus, *Ann.*, I, 72. See, Paulus, *Libri Quinque Sententiarum*, V, xxi, 1; Ciaceri, "L'imperatore Tiberio e i processi di lesa maesta," in *loc. cit.*, 259.

condemnations their denunciations had secured.[4] It must be remembered, however, that under the Roman Law there was no official corresponding to the modern attorney-general to prosecute cases for the state. This naturally encouraged the rise of a class of professional informers, who zealously performed their assumed duties because of the rewards and the prospect of rhetorical fame, and the employment of such informers was an established procedure before Tiberius' reign was inaugurated.[5] Tacitus further points out that delators who lodged false accusations were punished [6] or deprived of the customary rewards for their activities.[7] Tiberius also ruled that senatorial sentences could not be executed until the expiration of ten days, and this proviso made possible the

[4] Tacitus, *Ann.*, IV, 19, 35, 52. The *quaestiones* for criminal cases continued, with dwindling powers, during the first century. C. Jullian, *Les transformations politiques de l'Italie sous les empereurs romains*, (Paris, 1883), 48-51. The jurisdiction of the emperor and the city prefect seriously curtailed the operation of the *quaestiones* in Tiberius' reign. E. Ciaceri, "La responsibilità di Tiberio nell'applicazione della Lex Maiestatis," *Studi Storici per l' Antichità Classica*, II (1909), 402-405.
[5] A. Dürr, *Die Majestätsprocesse unter dem Kaiser Tiberius* (Heilbronn, 1880), 13, points out that since *accusatio* was the standard procedure in criminal cases, the use of delators was not only justified but necessary. The delators in the better sense of the term were the custodians of the law. Gentile, *L'imperatore Tiberio secondo la moderna critica storica*, 53. See also, Flint, "The Delatores in the Reign of Tiberius," in *loc. cit.*, 37. Cicero, *Catiline*, IV, 5, considered delation justified, and Tacitus himself, in his *Dialogus de Oratoribus*, XL, 34, thought that delation brought glory and excellence to rhetoricians. R. Laqueur, "Kaiser Augustus und der Delator," *Hermes*, LXVII (1932), 237-40, presents the interesting suggestion that Sextius Sceva, mentioned in the second Cyrene Edict, was a delator who had failed to prove his case. He further holds that the edict shows that Augustus did not wish to discourage the practice of delation.
[6] Tacitus, *Ann.*, III, 12, 37; IV, 31, 36; VI, 9, 30. See, Rogers, "Lucius Arruntius," in *loc. cit.*, 38. Jerome, *Some Aspects of Roman History*, 340, counts 43 delators in the reign of Tiberius. Of these, 10 were punished for failing to substantiate their charges, and 16 were punished for *maiestas* or other offenses.
[7] Tacitus, *Ann.*, VI, 47. There were more cases of punishment than reward. Schott, *Die Kriminaljustiz unter dem Kaiser Tiberius*, 45.

annulment of such sentences or the extension of imperial clemency.[8]

The law of *maiestas* actually was the product of a long process of legal evolution. In the early Republic all offenses against the well-being and safety of the state constituted *perduellio*. Maiestas ultimately came to have the more specialized meaning of betrayal of the state to an enemy or physical attack upon a magistrate.[9] Sulla, with the issue of his *Lex Cornelia de Maiestate*, was a forerunner of the emperors in the use of *maiestas* proceedings against political opponents. He utilized the procedure of *aquae et ignis interdictio*, virtually equivalent to the death sentence, since those so outlawed could be slain with impunity.[10] During the Sullan proscriptions many persons sought safety in exile, which was tantamount to forced renunciation of Roman citizenship [11] as distinct from voluntary renunciation resulting from assumption of civic status in a state the independence of which was recognized by Rome.[12]

The *Lex Julia* enacted during the dictatorship of Caesar was largely responsible for a broader interpretation of the law of *lèse majesté*. As interpreted in the *Digest*, it held that "the law of majesty provides that he who injures the dignity of the state shall be liable, just as one who has submitted to the enemy in war, or occupied a castle, or

---

[8] R. S. Rogers, "Two Criminal Cases Tried before Drusus Caesar," *Classical Philology*, XXVII (1932), 79.
[9] Schott, *Die Kriminaljustiz unter dem Kaiser Tiberius*, 3–6.
[10] Strachan-Davidson, *Problems of Roman Criminal Law*, II, 51.
[11] Mommsen, *Römisches Strafrecht*, 68.
[12] Strachan-Davidson, *Problems of Roman Criminal Law*, II, 53. For a fuller discussion of the early development of the law, see, I. Brunner, *Das Maiestättverbrechen und die Majestäts-gesetze bis auf die Zeit des Tiberius* (Aarau, 1877); P. M. Schisas, *Offenses against the State in Roman Law* (London, 1926).

surrendered a camp."[13] It was invoked particularly to protect the inviolability of tribunes.[14]

In the imperial period the protection extended by law to the persons of tribunes was applied to the *princeps*, who, of course, held tribunician powers.[15] An attempt to overthrow Augustus was considered, by a legal fiction, equivalent to an effort to betray the state.[16] The *Lex Julia*, as first interpreted, held that the crime of *maiestas* was committed against the safety of the Roman people. The security of the people was held to be endangered when anyone maliciously retaliated for the death of a hostage without the emperor's consent. An assemblage for seditious purposes, a plot to assassinate the ruler, or to communicate with or aid the enemy with malicious intent "by means of which the enemies of the Roman people [might] be assisted in their designs against the government" likewise constituted *maiestas*.[17] The law also provided for the regulation of provincial officials and their relations to the government, and forbade the solicitation of soldiers for seditious purposes. Governors were required to relinquish their posts when their successors arrived and were forbidden to falsify their accounts on pain of prosecution under the Julian law of *maiestas*.[18] Under the principate,

---

[13] *Digest*, XLVIII, xiv, 3. Ciaceri, "L'imperatore Tiberio e i processi di lesa maesta," in *loc. cit.*, 251, thinks that the *Lex Julia* was issued by Augustus. Cf., Mommsen, *Römisches Strafrecht*, 554. Dürr, *Die Majestätsprocesse unter dem Kaiser Tiberius*, 8, suggests that both Caesar and Augustus issued such laws.

[14] Schott, *Die Kriminaljustiz unter dem Kaiser Tiberius*, 10-11.

[15] Ciaceri, "L'imperatore Tiberio e i processi di lesa maesta," in *loc. cit.*, 252. Tribunes henceforth were protected by the *minuta maiestas* which represented the older specialized conception of the law. *Ibid.*, 253; Mommsen, *Römisches Strafrecht*, 538.

[16] Ciaceri, "L'imperatore Tiberio e i processi di lesa maesta," in *loc. cit.*, 253.

[17] *Digest*, XLVIII, iv, 1-2; XLVIII, iii. [18] *Ibid.*

however, the law was not so strictly delimited, for the powers of the citizenry had been concentrated in the person of the emperor, an indispensable concomitant with his status.[19] The Julian law also provided that "he who injures the dignity of the state shall be liable, just as one who has submitted to the enemy in war, or occupied a castle, or surrendered a camp." [20] When the dignity of the state was identified with the person of the emperor, offenses against him were punishable as offenses against the state. Moreover, since Julius Caesar and Augustus had been deified, open disrespect toward their memories might be punished as blasphemy or sacrilege.

The first cases in the reign of Tiberius were those of the Roman knights, Falanius and Rubrius, who were prosecuted on *maiestas* charges in 15. The former was charged with the admission of a mime among the votaries of Augustus and with the sale of a statue of the late emperor. Rubrius allegedly had sworn falsely by the memory of Augustus. Both cases were quashed by Tiberius' orders.[21]

Granius Marcellus, praetor of Bithynia, was accused of treason by his quaestor. He was charged with circulation of calumnies against the emperor's character and disrespect toward statues of Augustus and Tiberius. According to the Tacitean account, the emperor was incensed against the defendant and announced his intention of vot-

---

[19] Gentile, *L'imperatore Tiberio secondo la moderna critica storica*, 51; E. Pollack, *Der Maiestätsgedanke im Römischen Recht* (Leipzig, 1908), 125–41, 206–207.

[20] *Digest*, XLVIII, xiv, 3. "The empire outwardly changed nothing in regard to the law of lèse majesté. The text remained the same, but the effects became wholly different. The emperor was substituted for the people; he profited by applying to his own security and grandeur the law which had protected the greatness and security of the Republic." Boissier, *L'opposition sous les Césars*, 174.

[21] Tacitus, *Ann.*, I, 73.

ing with the Senate. When the point was subtly made by Gnaeus Piso that this in reality would be an attempt to coerce the Fathers, the emperor voted for acquittal.[22]

A famous case prosecuted in 16 was that of Libo Drusus, scion of the Scribonian family. The youth, who certainly lacked discretion, was noted for his luxuries, debaucheries, debts, and implicit belief in magic and soothsaying. Firmius Catus, an apparent friend, encouraged him in his licentiousness and aroused his ambitions by harping on the past glories of his family.[23] Catus then attempted to lodge accusations against the youth, but found that the *princeps* already was cognizant of Libo's indiscretions because of information furnished him by Vescularius Flaccus.[24] Libo, however, was admitted to the praetorship, and continued to enjoy the emperor's hospitality. Eventually, his consultation with soothsayers was discovered by Fulcinius Trio, a professional informer, who hastened to the consuls and demanded senatorial inquiry. Libo, realizing his peril when senatorial investigation was begun, was unable to secure the aid of relatives or friends. His efforts to curry sympathy by feigning illness and his entreaties to the emperor failed, and the prosecution continued.[25]

[22] *Ibid.*, 74. For sketch of his career, see, Pauly, Wissowa, and Kroll (eds.), *Real-Encyklopädie*, VII, 1822–23.
[23] Tacitus, *Ann.*, II, 27. "Some of the optimates, imbecilic in mind and dedicated to superstitions, had faith in all signs by which their hopes were confirmed." Levy, *Quo modo Tiberius Claudius Nero se gesserit*, 16. Tacitus apparently condemns Libo's belief in magic, yet in *Ann.*, IV, 58; VI, 20, the historian's skepticism is by no means clear. Pohlmann, *Die Weltanschauung des Tacitus*, 64, 65–66. Libo's "family connections in a sense justified his puerile and foolish aspirations." Strazzulla, "Il processo di Libone Druso," in *loc. cit.*, 71. In view of the fact that the Julio-Claudian dynasty was by no means secure it was impossible for the emperor to overlook Libo's activities. Dürr, *Die Majestätsprocesse unter dem Kaiser Tiberius*, 14. Catus was exiled in 24 for lodging a false accusation against his sister. Tacitus, *Ann.*, IV, 31.
[24] Tacitus, *Ann.*, II, 28; VI, 10.
[25] *Ibid.*, II, 29. Lang, *Beiträge zur Gesch. des Kaisers Tiberius*, 31–32, thinks there was a plot, and that Libo was a mere tool of the

A number of specific charges were submitted to the Senate. A list of names of members of the imperial family and of senators was found, to which were appended marks allegedly expressive of sinister intentions against them. Slaves of the defendant, subsequently purchased by the state, were put to torture to procure evidence against the defendant, and, under torment, they declared that the incriminating document was authentic.[26]

Libo refused to await the verdict and committed suicide. The emperor declared that he would have extended clemency to the youth despite his guilt had he not taken his own life.[27] Libo's property then was confiscated and parceled out among the accusers, showing that the defendant's suicide had not served to forestall loss of property. Days of thanksgiving were decreed to commemorate the rescue of the state from imminent peril, and astrologers and magicians were banished from Italy. The fact that the conspiracy was taken so seriously indicates that more was involved than was implied in the Tacitean account, which in all likelihood was based on the aristocratic tradition.[28]

In A.D. 17 Appuleia Varilla was prosecuted on charges

---

leaders. F. B. Marsh, "Tacitus and the Aristocratic Tradition," *Classical Philology*, XXI (1926), 294–300, believes that Tacitus' account of Libo's conspiracy is a good example of the historian's reliance upon the aristocratic tradition.

[26] Tacitus, *Ann.*, II, 30. Torture of slaves was necessary to validate their evidence. See, T. Mommsen (ed.), *Zum ältesten Strafrecht der Kulturvölker* (Leipzig, 1905), 43. R. S. Rogers, "Ignorance of the Law in Tacitus and Dio: Two Instances from the History of Tiberius," *Transactions and Proceedings of the American Philological Association*, LXIV (1933), 24–27, has shown that the slaves were purchased by the *fiscus* after they were questioned.

[27] Tacitus, *Ann.*, II, 31. In *ibid.*, VI, 29, the historian claims that defendants committed suicide to avoid loss of testamentary rights and sepulture. Rogers, "Ignorance of the Law in Tacitus and Dio," in *loc. cit.*, 18–27, has shown that this did not apply to *maiestas* cases.

[28] Tacitus, *Ann.*, II, 32.

of *maiestas* and adultery. The ground for the former accusation was found in allegedly scandalous remarks made against Tiberius and Livia as well as sacrilege committed against the deified Augustus. The emperor ordered that the *maiestas* charge should be dropped unless it could be shown that the defendant was guilty of sacrilege against Augustus. Derogatory remarks against him and his mother were not to be considered grounds for punishment. The charge of sacrilege apparently could not be sustained, and the defendant was tried and punished for adultery.[29]

Another celebrated case was that of Lepida Aemilia in A.D. 20. She was accused of adultery, poisoning, and forgery. *Maiestas* apparently was involved in the charge that she had made contacts with astrologers in order to work evil on the imperial house.[30] Tiberius interceded and requested that the treason charge be dropped, and he would not permit the defendant's slaves to be tortured to elicit evidence of plots against his family.[31] The emperor, however, was represented at the trial by his son, Drusus, as consul-designate. This was interpreted by some as an indication that the emperor desired the defendant's conviction on the other charges without incurring personal obloquy. Despite evidences of elaborately incited popular sympathy, the defendant was convicted on some of the charges and exiled, although she was spared from confiscation of her property.[32]

In A.D. 21 Clutorius Priscus, who had earned a measure of fame as the author of a poem mourning the death of Germanicus, was charged with the composition of verses

---

[29] *Ibid.*, 50. For the case of Flavius Clemens, see, *ibid.*, 39-40. "Where several counts figure in an indictment Tacitus is sure to stress that of *maiestas* as if it were the chief factor in the case. It is the black paint in which he is always ready to dip his brush." Jerome, *Some Aspects of Roman History*, 331.
[30] Tacitus, *Ann.*, II, 27; XII, 22, 52; XVI, 14, 30.
[31] *Ibid.*, III, 22.   [32] *Ibid.*, 23.

during a serious illness of Drusus in which he prematurely bemoaned the prince's death, a contingency he allegedly desired.[33] The defendant accordingly was accused of plotting against Drusus' life, and, despite the arguments of Manius Lepidus,[34] he was convicted and executed.[35] There was evidence in this case that the Senate was willing to exceed the emperor in zeal in the enforcement of the *maiestas* law, and the severity exercised was certainly unwarranted.[36]

The following year Lucius Ennius, a knight, was arraigned on charges that he had melted a silver statuette of the emperor and converted the metal into household silver. The emperor forbade the trial of the case in the face of a strong protest from Ateius Capito who insisted that the Senate should be free to proceed against those who had injured the state.[37] This case, like that of Priscus, indicated that the senators, on occasion, were willing to go further than the emperor desired, possibly in the hope of currying favor.

In 24 the case of Gaius Silius (Gaius Silius A. Caecina Largus) incited considerable interest. It was charged that he had boasted that Tiberius owed his throne to the defendant's valor in the Sacrovir war.[38] Sejanus apparently pushed prosecution of the case, for Silius and his wife Sosia were known to be partisans of Agrippina.[39] The defendant was guilty of extortionate practices during the

---

[33] *Ibid.*, 49. Knabe, *De Fontibus Historiae Imperatorum Julianorum*, 10, presents the interesting view that the banned works nevertheless were widely read and served as sources for later historians, including Tacitus.
[34] Tacitus, *Ann.*, III, 50. [35] *Ibid.*, 51.
[36] *Ibid.* [37] *Ibid.*, 70.
[38] *Ibid.*, IV, 18. He is the Caecina who helped Germanicus suppress the mutiny and served in the German campaigns. Pauly, Wissowa, and Kroll (eds.), *Real-Encyklopädie*, IIIa, 74–77.
[39] Tacitus, *Ann.*, IV, 19.

LÈSE MAJESTÉ PROSECUTIONS   175

tenure of his Gallic command, and with the realization that his conviction, at least on extortion charges, was assured, he committed suicide.[40] His death, however, did not forestall confiscation of his estate. Sosia was banished and probably lost one fourth of her estate, which was assigned to her accusers in the normal fashion.[41] Titius Sabinus also was prosecuted about this time, according to the Tacitean account, as a member of the Agrippinian faction.[42]

Calpurnius Piso,[43] who had inveighed against the *maiestas* trials and who had deprecated the influence of Livia in the government, was accused of conversations derogatory to the emperor, a poison plot, and the wearing of a sword into the Senate House. The last count of the indictment was dropped as "too atrocious to be true," and the defendant forestalled condemnation on the other charges by committing suicide.[44] Cassius Severus, who had been relegated to Crete, was deported to Seriphos and stripped of his property.[45]

Prosecution of the celebrated case of Vibius Serenus also took place in the year 24. The defendant's son accused him after his return from exile to stand trial. It was charged that, with the aid of Caecilius Cornutus, the defendant had attempted to incite rebellion in Gaul. Cornutus committed suicide, but Serenus confronted his son and denied his guilt.[46] Two additional defendants, both prominent nobles and friends of the emperor, then were accused in connection with the same case.[47] Serenus' slaves were put to the torture, but his son, terrified by evidences of popu-

---

[40] *Ibid.*, 20.
[41] *Ibid.* See, *infra*, Chap. IX, n.8.
[42] Tacitus, *Ann.*, IV, 20.
[43] *Ibid.*, II, 33-34.
[44] *Ibid.*, IV, 21. Cassius Severus was a famous orator of the Augustan age. See, *ibid.*, I, 72; IV, 21; Suetonius, *Caligula*, XVI.
[45] Tacitus, *Ann.*, IV, 21.
[46] *Ibid.*, 28.
[47] *Ibid.*, 29.

lar hostility, fled from Rome. The Senate, apparently convinced of Serenus' guilt, was in favor of the death penalty, but Tiberius vetoed the extreme sentence. When banishment was substituted, the emperor insisted that the accused be banished to a habitable place, and he accordingly was sent to Amorgus.[48] Since Cornutus had committed suicide, it was proposed that the accusers should be deprived of their customary rewards, but Tiberius vetoed the suggestion on the ground that it would endanger the state.[49]

About the same time Gaius Cominius Proculus, a knight, was convicted of the authorship of a lampoon against the emperor, but he was spared by the intercession of the object of his spleen.[50] This case moved Tacitus to observe that "the fact heightened the general wonder that, cognizant as he was of better things and of the fame that attended mercy, he still should prefer the darker road."[51] The effect of this clemency at the time was somewhat offset by the emperor's insistence on the banishment of Publius Suillius, but Tacitus admits that subsequent events vindicated his judgment.[52]

In A.D. 25 Votienus Montanus was prosecuted on the charge of circulating scurrilities against the *princeps*. Tiberius presumably was considerably excited by the recital of the calumnies that were current against him. The defendant was convicted and "suffered the penalties of treason," apparently death.[53]

---

[48] *Ibid.*, 30.
[49] *Ibid.*
[50] *Ibid.*, 31; Dio, *R.H.*, LVII, xxii, 5.
[51] Tacitus, *Ann.*, IV, 31.
[52] *Ibid.* Suillius was a famous delator. *Ibid.*, 31; XIII, 42. He had served as a quaestor of Germanicus. *Ibid.*, IV, 31.
[53] Tacitus, *Ann.*, IV, 42. For other cases, see, *ibid.*, 66; *infra*, 203–207. Votienus Montanus was a famous orator and declaimer, known as the "Ovid of the rhetorical schools." An amusing case of ridiculing the emperor was that of Lucius Caecianus who was charged with having poked fun at his baldness. Dio, *R.H.*, LVIII, xix, 1–2.

Six years later Vitellius and Pomponius Secundus were arraigned on *maiestas* charges. The former, it was claimed, had offered to hand over the keys of the treasury and the army fund to those plotting revolution in behalf of Agrippina and her sons. Secundus was charged with the offer of shelter to Aelius Gallus. Vitellius committed suicide, but Secundus, who probably was banished, outlived the emperor.[54]

Cotta Messalinus, who had distinguished himself as an accuser in *maiestas* cases, was indicted for impugning the sex of Gaius and circulating scurrilities against Livia and the emperor. The *princeps*, recalling the defendant's past devotion, declared that "mischievously perverted phrases and the frankness of table-talk should not be turned into evidence of guilt."[55] In the famous letter in which the emperor made this decision, he declared that "may gods and goddesses destroy me more wretchedly than I feel myself to be perishing every day." Doubtless he was considerably disgusted at the accusations and counteraccusations that beset him.[56]

In 32 Sextus Vistilius, a former praetor, was accused of attacks on the morals of Gaius, or of other calumnies of an undisclosed nature. He was excluded from the em-

---

[54] Tacitus, *Ann.*, V, 8. Pomponius Secundus was a writer of tragedy. See, *ibid.*, XII, 28; Quintilian, *Institutio Oratoria*, X, i, 98.

[55] Tacitus, *Ann.*, VI, 5. The emperor apparently prided himself on his clemency toward those accused of political offenses and his moderation in the enforcement of the criminal law. A number of his coins bear the inscription *Clementia* and *Moderatio*. Mattingly, *Coins of the Roman Empire*, I, cxxxvi.

[56] Tacitus, *Ann.*, VI, 6. Cotta Messalinus frequently had served as a delator. He was instrumental in securing the damnation of Libo's memory and had attempted to secure senatorial concurrence in his proposal to make provincial officials accountable for the actions of their wives. He also was one of the first to advocate punitive action in response to Tiberius' letter complaining about the actions of Agrippina and Nero. Rogers, "Der Prozess des Cotta Messalinus," in *loc. cit.*, 122. See, Tacitus, *Ann.*, II, 32; IV, 20; V, 3; VI, 5.

peror's society, and, alarmed at this evidence of Tiberius' anger, he committed suicide.[57] Vitia, mother of Fufius Geminus, allegedly was put to death because of her sign of grief at the death of her son, which was interpreted to indicate her involvement in his treasonable activities.[58] Vescularius Flaccus and Julius Marinus were executed, apparently because of complicity in the schemes of Sejanus.[59] Toward the end of the year, Geminius, Celsus, and Pompeius, all knights, were put to death or impelled to commit suicide because of their connections with the fallen minister.[60] The cases of Considius Proculus and his sister Sancia also were probably attributable to this fatal connection,[61] and later in the year a number of adherents of Sejanus who had been held in prison since his condemnation were executed.[62]

Mamercus Scaurus, who had escaped condemnation as Sejanus' adherent,[63] committed suicide in 34 to forestall execution on charges of libel, adultery, and addiction to the practice of magic. His wife shared his fate, and Macro, whose influence with Tiberius now was very strong, served as accuser.[64]

The following year saw the end of several notorious delators, among them Fulcinius Trio. Tacitus declares that, notwithstanding the three years that had elapsed since

[57] Tacitus, *Ann.*, VI, 9.
[58] *Ibid.*, 10. C. Fufius Geminus was consul in 29. He was a close friend of Livia. *Ibid.*, V, 2. His wife, Mutilia Prisca, also had great influence with the emperor's mother. *Ibid.*, IV, 12. In 31 he and his wife were accused of *maiestas*, and both committed suicide. Dio, *R.H.*, LVIII, iv, 5–7.
[59] Tacitus, *Ann.*, VI, 10. Marinus had been a companion of Tiberius both at Rhodes and Capri. See Pauly, Wissowa, and Kroll (eds.), *Real-Encyklopädie*, X, 669, for good sketch of his career.
[60] Tacitus, *Ann.*, VI, 14.   [61] *Ibid.*, 18.
[62] *Ibid.*, 19. Under the circumstances, some injustice might have been expected. Ihne, *Zur Ehrenrettung des Kaisers Tiberius*, 71–72. Suetonius, *Tib.*, LXI, gives the number executed as 20.
[63] Tacitus, *Ann.*, VI, 9.   [64] *Ibid.*, 29.

Sejanus' execution, "not time nor prayers nor satiety, influences that soften other breasts, could mollify Tiberius or arrest his policy of avenging half-proved or forgotten delinquencies." Other charges may well have been brought against these delators; in considerable measure, however, their ruin was the result of their activities as informers, during the course of which they probably launched a number of ill-founded or wholly false charges. Sextius Paconianus, however, was executed upon conviction of the authorship of libelous verses.[65]

As we have seen, a number of cases of *lèse majesté* prosecutions were based on charges of sacrilege, libel, or magical practices with seditious intent. Several cases developed from the open disaffection of the Agrippinians, and Sejanus, as the foe of this element, naturally played a part in bringing about the condemnations of a few of the defendants. A considerable number of cases were the result of the ruin of Sejanus. At no time, however, was the number of such prosecutions of proportions sufficient to justify the claim that a "reign of terror" existed. There was also a considerable volume of cases where charges of extortion or maladministration in the provinces were involved. These really were in line with the emperor's policy of reform in provincial administration, and will be discussed under that heading. In any event, the applicability of the *maiestas* law to such cases was clearly established by the Julian law, and the prosecutions in Tiberius' reign seem to have been abundantly justified. Tacitus enhanced the darkness of the picture which he drew of these prosecutions by including cases where adultery, murder, and other crimes were involved.[66] Tiberius did not institute

---

[65] *Ibid.*, 38–39. Boissier, *L'opposition sous les Césars*, 208, says Tiberius only permitted prosecution of the delators after they had outlived their usefulness to him.

[66] Freytag, *Tiberius und Tacitus*, 296–99.

the practice of utilizing the services of informers, nor was he the innovator of the custom of rewarding them. Even Tacitus, a hostile source, admitted his efforts to curb unwarranted prosecutions and pointed out that frequently he attempted to check the zeal of the Senate in the punishment of the defendants.

In all there were, during the reign, fifty-two prosecutions for treason as defined and interpreted by the *maiestas* law. Twelve of the defendants were executed, while four committed suicide, and one died before trial. Five convicted defendants were banished, four were imprisoned or kept under surveillance, and two lost their citizenship. Proceedings were dropped against seven persons, while fourteen were acquitted. Of those convicted, only four seem clearly to have been innocent—Lutorius and the children of Sejanus—and these were condemned by the Senate without the personal participation of the emperor in the proceedings. The eight persons whom the emperor himself ordered executed seem to have been guilty. These were the pseudo Agrippa, Titius Sabinus, Sejanus, the alleged murderers of Drusus, and the two adherents of Sejanus who were executed at Capri.[67] Despite the varia-

[67] *Ibid.*, 307. Sievers, *Studien zur Gesch. der Röm. Kaiser: Tacitus and Tiberius*, 95, counts 48 criminal cases of all kinds after Sejanus' fall. Gentile, *L'imperatore Tiberio secondo la moderna critica storica*, 54-55, lists 87 cases in which *maiestas* was at least partially involved. Of these cases, 36 resulted in the sentencing of the defendants, 19 in acquittal, 19 in quashing of the charges, and 13 in the suicide of the defendant. Freytag's computation is the most acceptable, for he included only the cases of *maiestas*. Strazzulla, "Il processo di Libone Druso," in *loc. cit.*, 63, declares that even when the defendants were guilty "a noble soul would not have treated so cruelly Libo, Sabinus, Cordus, Agrippina, as well as others who were such fine examples of the old Roman character." It is difficult to share his admiration for these individuals as representatives of the "old Roman character." Dürr, *Die Majestätsprocesse unter dem Kaiser Tiberius*, 15 ff., distinguishes between *maiestas* cases and those involving attempts on the life of the ruler, making war on the state or against another power, aiding enemies of the state, or betrayal of the army. He lists 39 cases of the

tions in the compilations of the cases, we are inclined to agree with Professor Marsh's statement that "the number of prosecutions is much smaller than might have been expected after what had passed, and the proceedings seem to show that a real attempt was made to secure justice; in short the whole picture of the Tiberian terror is a product of imagination and rhetoric quite unsupported by the evidence." [68]

former type and 27 of the latter. Of the *maiestas* cases he lists 13 resulting in condemnation of the accused, 14 in suicide, and 12 in acquittals or quashing of the indictments. It must be remembered that reports of cases are not complete, and since a number of counts frequently were involved in the indictments, the cases are difficult to classify. *Ibid.*, 14-15. Jerome, *Some Aspects of Roman History*, 336-38, cites 58 cases of which 22 resulted in condemnations (13 capital), 26 in acquittals, and 10 in the suicides of the defendants.

[68] Marsh, *Reign of Tiberius*, 200. The emperor used his judicial powers "reluctantly and indulgently." Marchesi, *Tacito*, 234-35.

CHAPTER IX

WAR AND PEACE IN THE PROVINCES

In A.D. 17 the Roman province of Africa was seriously menaced by the major revolt incited and led by Tacfarinas, a native Numidian and deserter from Roman auxiliary forces. He recruited a hardy army, made up in large measure of tribesmen inured to the rigors of desert warfare and accustomed to brigandage. A formidable military force soon was evolved, for Tacfarinas possessed sufficient ability and forcefulness as a leader to impose discipline and organization on his motley horde.

The formidable Musulami, south of the Saltus Aurasius, revolted under the leadership of Mazippa, and they soon were joined by tribesmen of eastern Mauretania. Tacfarinas retained command of the picked troops whom he drilled and equipped in Roman fashion, while Mazippa's light-armed forces concentrated on plundering and terrorizing forays. Mazippa's tactics ultimately forced the Cenithians to join him.[1]

Furius Camillus, proconsul of Africa, led the III (Augusta) legion and a force of auxiliaries against the rebellious tribesmen. The modest size of the proconsul's army tempted Tacfarinas to offer battle, the very thing Camillus hoped he would do. The legion was posted in the center of the Roman line and was flanked by the auxiliary infantry and cavalry. The charging natives were repulsed

[1] Tacitus, *Ann.*, II, 52. There had been an uprising in Augustus' reign which was suppressed by L. Sempronius Atratinus and L. Cornelius Balbus. R. Cagnat, *L'armée Romaine d'Afrique et l'occupation militaire de l'Afrique sous les empereurs*, 2 vols. (Paris, 1912), I, 4–8.

and scattered, and Camillus subsequently was granted the triumphal insignia in recognition of his apparently decisive victory.[2]

In the year A.D. 20, however, Tacfarinas, despite the check he had sustained, resumed his aggressions. His dashing raids ultimately were followed by more serious inroads into the provinces, where villages were destroyed and much booty was taken. Finally he led his army against a Roman cohort stationed near the Pagyda (Pazida) river. Decrius, the cohort commander, hoped to avoid the ignominy of undergoing a siege by barbarian troops, and accordingly drew up his line before the camp to offer battle in the open. His confidence in his troops was unwarranted, however, for they broke at the first onset, and, despite the heroic efforts of their commander to rally them, fled in wild confusion. Decrius stood his ground until he fell mortally wounded.[3] When the news of the disaster reached Lucius Apronius,[4] who had been made proconsul in A.D. 18 to succeed Camillus, he decided on drastic punishment for the cowardly cohort. Decimation, a penalty resorted to only in extreme cases, was prescribed, and every tenth man of the cohort accordingly was chosen by lot and flogged to death. This severity, barbarous as it was, doubtless had a salutary effect, for when Tacfarinas assaulted the stronghold of Thala (Haidra), in Tunis, he was turned back by an inferior force of Roman veterans. A private soldier who had distinguished himself by conspicuous bravery in this engagement was decorated by the proconsul, and Tiberius added the civic crown to his honors. The Roman military strength under Apronius

[2] Tacitus, *Ann.*, II, 52. The third legion was stationed in Africa by Augustus in 27 B.C. See, C. Halgen, *Essai sur l'administration des provinces senatorials sous l'empire romain* (Paris, 1898), 267.
[3] Tacitus, *Ann.*, III, 20; Cagnat, *L'armée Romaine d'Afrique*, I, 12-13.
[4] Tacitus, *Ann.*, I, 56, 72; III, 64; IV, 13, 22, 73; VI, 30; XI, 10.

had been considerably augmented by sending the IX legion from Pannonia to reinforce the III (Augusta).⁵

Tacfarinas was driven to resort to mere guerrilla warfare. So long as he persisted in these harrying tactics, there was little the Roman commander could do to restore order. When the chieftain became bold enough to venture close to the coast, however, he was forced to approach a Roman camp. Apronius Caesianus, son of the proconsul, accordingly was able to defeat him with a light force and compel his retirement to the desert.⁶

By A.D. 21 the African situation was sufficiently disturbing to impel Tiberius to send an official communication to the Senate from Campania. The Fathers were directed to select a proconsul to assume charge of the African province, and, in view of the anticipated necessity for major military operations, they were admonished to choose someone with considerable experience as well as a physique able to withstand the rigors of a campaign. Marcus Lepidus' name was mentioned for the post, but he was bitterly assailed by Sextus Pompeius who labeled him a "spiritless and poverty-stricken degenerate." Pompeius argued that not only should Lepidus be denied the African appointment, but that the Asiatic command likewise should be withheld. The Senate, however, disapproved these strictures and decided that Lepidus should be sent to Asia. On the more important point of the African command, the Fathers decided to leave the choice up to the emperor.⁷

The incident is an enlightening one, for it shows that

⁵ *Ibid.*, III, 21; Cagnat, *L'armée Romaine d'Afrique*, I, 13.
⁶ Tacitus, *Ann.*, III, 21.
⁷ *Ibid.*, 32. D. McFayden, "The Princeps and the Senatorial Provinces," *Classical Philology*, XVI (1921), 40, holds that this incident shows that Tiberius possessed no *imperium* in Africa nor did he have a *maius imperium*. He merely used his right of *relatio* to report the African situation to the Senate. See, however, Tacitus, *Ann.*, III, 21, 47.

Tiberius apparently was willing to entrust major responsibilities to the Senate, which, however, it was not prepared to assume. In the course of the discussion of the African appointment, Caecina Severus moved that no magistrate assigned to a province should be permitted to take his wife with him to his post. He pointed out that women were prone to jealousy, petty intrigues, and interference with civil and military affairs. Experience had demonstrated that the wives of provincial governors frequently had been responsible for grave abuses. The Senate, however, refused to take action on the suggestion.[8]

At the next meeting of the Senate another letter from the emperor was read, in which he chided the body for its evident disposition to leave all matters of importance to him. He then went on to nominate Manius Lepidus and Junius Blaesus for the African post. Already Lepidus had apparently been rejected for the African command, probably at his own request, and it had been decided at the preceding session to invest him with the Asiatic command. He now addressed the Senate, and, with all earnestness, pleaded that his ill-health, as well as the ages of his children and the fact that he had a marriageable daughter, should be sufficient to excuse him from assuming the African post. Blaesus, the uncle of Sejanus, accordingly accepted the tendered position with at least feigned reluctance.[9] Tacitus implies that Lepidus in reality declined the African appointment so as not to be a rival of so formidable a competitor as the uncle of the reigning favor-

[8] Tacitus, *Ann.*, III, 34. In *ibid.*, IV, 20, Tacitus points out that a *Senatus Consultum* was passed in A.D. 24 making provincial officials legally responsible for the misdeeds of their wives in the provinces. I agree with O. Hirschfeld, "Über ein Senatus Consultum von Jahre 20 nach Chr.," *Kleine Schriften*, 405–406, who maintains that the law was passed in A.D. 20 as an aftermath of the trial of Plancina, wife of Piso. See, *Digest*, I, xvi, 4; *infra*, 114.

[9] Tacitus, *Ann.*, III, 35.

ite.¹⁰ Nevertheless, the historian specifically says that Lepidus offered his excuses with "particular earnestness," and, of course, the Senate apparently had decided not to appoint him to Africa before the emperor submitted the name of Blaesus.¹¹ Blaesus apparently spent the first year of his command in making preparations, for there is no report of military actions, and his term was thereupon extended.¹²

Tacfarinas, in the meantime, recruited additional troops and, with unparalleled boldness, sent an embassy to Tiberius demanding territorial grants for himself and his army, with war as the alternative to acceptance of the terms of his ultimatum. The emperor was enraged by the assumption of the status of a belligerent power by what he considered a mere bandit horde. He therefore ordered Blaesus to make every effort to suppress the uprising and to capture Tacfarinas by whatever means seemed expedient. Blaesus was authorized to grant amnesty to the other leaders of the rebellion as well as to any of the rebel troops that would desert. Many apparently accepted the terms, but Tacfarinas was able to continue his operations, weakened, but not irreparably crippled, by the defections.¹³

¹⁰ *Ibid.*   ¹¹ *Ibid.*, 32.
¹² *Ibid.*, 58. The African and Asiatic proconsulships were filled by lot from the eldest consulars, usually from 4 to 14 years after expiration of their consular terms. The proconsul was empowered to raise troops, inflict punishments, including decimation, bestow rewards, coin money, and administer justice. Cagnat, *L'armée Romaine d'Afrique*, I, 122–23. The African proconsuls were assisted by *beneficarii* (lieutenants), *immunes* (scribes), and *singulares* (bodyguards). *Ibid.* See also, Halgen, *Essai sur l'administration des provinces senatoriales sous l'empire romain*, 215–18.
¹³ The main objective of the rebels was to secure fertile land. Their revolt might be interpreted basically as a manifestation of land hunger. Cantarelli, "Tacfarinata," in *loc. cit.*, col. 8. This article was reprinted in *Studi Romani e Bizantini* (Rome, 1915). Cagnat, *L'Armée Romaine d'Afrique*, I, 18, agrees with Cantarelli's interpretation. The Romans signally failed to understand that the African herdsmen frequently had to migrate in search of new pasturage, and their attempts to restrain

WAR AND PEACE IN THE PROVINCES 187

In order to cope with the guerrilla tactics of the rebels, Blaesus wisely decided to divide his troops into three columns. One column, under Cornelius Scipio, held control of the road between Labda and Fezzan, hitherto much used by Tacfarinas in his forays. A second contingent under Blaesus the Younger, son of the proconsul, protected towns and villages in the vicinity of Cirta (Constantine) from the danger of ravaging. The proconsul himself held a central position with the best troops. Each of the three contingents, in turn, was subdivided into smaller detachments under carefully selected centurions. A considerable number of bases and camps thereupon was established, with the result that the area of Roman operations was greatly extended.[14] The approach of winter was not permitted to interrupt operations, as usually was the case. At least small detachments of Roman troops continued to harass the native forces all through the winter. Tacfarinas' brother finally was captured, and since the rebel forces had apparently dispersed, Blaesus felt justified in terminating the campaign. Tiberius approved the conduct of the proconsul, for he permitted him to be saluted as *imperator* by his soldiery.[15] As further indication of his belief that the campaign had been brought to a definitive conclusion, the emperor withdrew the ninth legion and ordered its return to Pannonia.[16]

Such optimism proved unfounded, however, for Tacfarinas rallied his forces and resumed the raids that so greatly plagued the province. Mauretania, which under

---

such migrations did much to cause hostilities. T. R. S. Broughton, *The Romanization of Africa Proconsularis*, in *Johns Hopkins University Studies in History and Political Science*, Extra Volumes, New Series, V (Baltimore, 1929), 90.

[14] Tacitus, *Ann.*, III, 74. The camps naturally were located near springs. Many of these camps later developed into towns. Broughton, *The Romanization of Africa Proconsularis*, 94-95.

[15] Tacitus, *Ann.*, III, 74.   [16] *Ibid.*, 9; IV, 23.

King Juba II had aided the Romans, now was under the weak rule of Ptolemy. Many of his subjects rebelled against him and joined forces with Tacfarinas. The Garamantian ruler in Fezzan also was to some degree an ally of Tacfarinas, since he served as custodian of the booty taken by the rebels and sent light-armed troops to their assistance. Matters reached a critical stage when Tacfarinas laid siege to the town of Thubuscum (Tiklat).[17]

Publius Dolabella, who had succeeded Blaesus as proconsul, mustered every available man and marched to the relief of the beleaguered city. As on many previous occasions, the rebel troops proved unable to withstand the advance of the Roman infantry and withdrew. Dolabella continued prudently, establishing bases at strategic points, and discouraging further affiliation with Tacfarinas by executing Musulamian chieftains who were contemplating rebellion. Ptolemy of Mauretania, whose throne was in jeopardy because of desertion of many of his warriors to Tacfarinas, was prevailed upon to furnish all available contingents to the Romans for service as auxiliaries. The joint forces were organized in four columns under the command of legates or tribunes, while scouting and raiding parties, accompanied by Ptolemy's subjects, still further widened the field of Roman activities.[18]

Eventually the main force of Tacfarinas was located in a camp near the ruins of a fort adjoining Auzea (Aumale) which it had destroyed some time before. The site was surrounded by forests, which apparently Tacfarinas thought could not be penetrated by large Roman forces. When Dolabella received news of the enemy position, however, he ordered his light infantry and cavalry to ad-

---

[17] *Ibid.*, IV, 23-24. Cantarelli, "Tacfarinata," in *loc. cit.*, col. 10-11, identifies the site with Tiklat. Cagnat, *L'armée Romaine d'Afrique*, I, 23, argues for Khamessa.
[18] Tacitus, *Ann.*, IV, 24.

WAR AND PEACE IN THE PROVINCES 189

vance as rapidly as possible, with the result that they arrived in time to surprise the rebels at daybreak. Their cavalry were unable to form, since most of the horses still were tethered in distant pasturages; the infantry likewise were disordered as the Roman attack developed. With the rebels virtually helpless, the Roman soldiery soon turned the engagement into a massacre. Orders were given that Tacfarinas was to be taken or slain at all costs, for peace was illusory until the leader who had so sorely tried the Roman government of Africa should be eliminated. Early in the fray his son was captured, and he, surrounded by hopelessly outnumbered guards who defended him to the last, impaled himself on the spears of the onrushing Romans.[19]

Dolabella's request for triumphal insignia was refused by the emperor. It is indeed difficult to acquit the *princeps* of the charge of injustice or gross partiality. Certainly the exploit of Dolabella had ended the African war. His achievement at Auzea seems to have been as deserving of recognition as the tentative success enjoyed by Blaesus. Furthermore, the death of Tacfarinas led to the submission of the Garamantians, who sent emissaries to seek pardon for their connection with the rebellion.[20] Another constructive result was the solidification of friendly relations with Ptolemy, who received an embroidered robe, an ivory scepter, and the salutation of king, ally, and friend from a senatorial deputation sent to confer these distinctions upon him.[21] A considerable strip of territory joined to the province of Africa had the ultimate

[19] *Ibid.*, 25.
[20] *Ibid.* Cagnat, *L'armée Romaine d'Afrique*, I, 21, considers Blaesus' triumph unwarranted. If so, denial of Dolabella's request for recognition of his exploits was all the more unjust.
[21] Tacitus, *Ann.*, IV, 26. Victory coins issued by Ptolemy show the curule chair, a diadem, and a scepter. L. Müller, *Numismatique de l'ancienne Afrique*, 3 vols. in 1 (Copenhagen, 1860), 129, nos. 185-95.

effect of stabilizing Roman control and curtailing the migrations of the desert tribes into the fertile areas.[22]

Roman occupation of Africa was stabilized with the successful termination of the war against Tacfarinas. Major military operations had been requisite to attain objectives of fundamental importance to the empire, and Tiberius had not shrunk from the employment of sufficient forces to ensure victory. He continued, however, to profit by the lessons taught by his predecessor, and accordingly utilized diplomatic means in preference to military force whenever such a course was feasible. The complex situation in Thrace gave him abundant opportunity for patient diplomacy.

When Rhoemetalces, king of Thrace, died, Augustus had intervened to partition the kingdom between Cotys, son of the late ruler, and Rhescuporis, a brother. Cotys received the more valuable share of the kingdom, for most of the fertile areas, as well as virtually all the towns, came under his control, while his uncle was assigned the relatively poor western portion largely inhabited by barbarians.[23] As could be anticipated, Rhescuporis was dissatisfied with Augustus' territorial allocation and gradually

[22] Cagnat, *L'armée Romaine d'Afrique*, I, 25. Caligula added an African military legate to the staff of the province. Tacitus, *Histories*, IV, 48. A great temple built in Tiberius' reign at Bulla Regia was testimony of the prosperity of the African province in the later years of the period. M. Besnier, "Fouilles recentes en Tunisie," *Journal des Savants*, New Series, XII (1914), 217-18. Mommsen, "Das Verhältnis des Tacitus zu den Acten des Senats," in *loc. cit.*, 258-59, points out that the discussion of the war with Tacfarinas by Tacitus is a good example of how he arranged the material in accordance with the connection of the Senate with the affair. The historian, however, frequently departed from the purely annalistic approach. See, O. Hirschfeld, "Zur Annalistischen Anlage des Taciteischen Geschichtswerkes," *Kleine Schriften*, 855-64.

[23] Tacitus, *Ann.*, II, 64. Tacitus, to some degree, exaggerated the poverty of the western half of the kingdom which was within the radius of the Roman legion camps in Moesia. V. Parvan, "I primordi della civiltá Romana alle foci del Danubio," *Ausonia*, X (1921), 192.

encroached on his nephew's domain, although he avoided overt aggression, which he feared would occasion Roman intervention. Upon receipt of the news of Augustus' death, however, Rhescuporis was emboldened, and the operations of his predatory bands, as well as his demolition of frontier fortresses, were acts of an unmistakably belligerent nature.[24]

Tiberius responded to the challenge by warning both Thracian kings to refrain from hostilities, but only Cotys sincerely desired to preserve peace. Rhescuporis feigned willingness to negotiate, and, after preliminary haggling, he invited Cotys to a banquet to signalize the conclusion of a treaty. While the festivities were in progress, Rhescuporis ordered the seizure and imprisonment of his rival and hastened to assure Tiberius that such action had been necessary to forestall a similar plot against himself. He also strengthened his military forces on the plea that new contingents were needed for imminent service against the Bastarnae and Scythians. Tiberius, still apparently hopeful for a peaceful and equitable solution of the Thracian problem, replied that he would not prejudge the matters at issue, and urged the release of Cotys as a necessary preliminary to a hearing of the case at Rome. Only by such a step could Rhescuporis vindicate his contention that he was the aggrieved party.[25]

Tiberius' first letters insisting upon the preservation of peace had been delivered by a mere centurion. The growing gravity of the situation now was reflected by the dispatch of a letter demanding Cotys' release. This communication was taken to Rhescuporis by Latinius Pandusa, propraetor or *Legatus Legionis* of Moesia, who was accompanied by soldiers ostensibly to take custody of Cotys.[26] Tiberius had established Moesia as an adminis-

[24] Tacitus, *Ann.*, II, 64.   [25] *Ibid.*, 65.   [26] *Ibid.*, 66.

trative, fiscal, and military entity in 15, and his policy in Thrace was closely connected with the evolution of the Moesian province.[27] Rhescuporis anticipated the arrival of the Roman official by ordering Cotys' execution and announcing that he had committed suicide. Tiberius, despite this provocation, did not alter his policy; indeed, Pandusa's death made it necessary to defer action until his successor arrived.[28]

The emperor proved more than able to deal with Rhescuporis by his own methods. Pomponius Flaccus, a friend of the Thracian ruler, was appointed legionary legate for Moesia. This action disarmed Rhescuporis' apprehensions and seemed to be a tacit recognition of his plea that Pandusa had been prejudiced against him.[29]

With guile worthy of the best efforts of oriental despots, Flaccus persuaded Rhescuporis to appear in his camp. Here he was attended by a bodyguard, nominally in deference to his royal status. While negotiations between the king and Flaccus continued, enough of his followers apparently were induced to desert so that the king ultimately found himself under surveillance that became constantly closer, until he finally realized that he actually was a prisoner. He then was sent to Rome with an escort of Roman centurions and tribunes and placed on

---

[27] A. von Premerstein, "Die Anfänge der Provinz Moesien," *Jahreshefte des Österreichischen Archäologischen Instituts in Wien*, I (1898), Beiblatt, 173. See also, Tacitus, *Ann.*, I, 80; *C.I.L.*, XI, 1825; XIV, 3608. According to Von Premerstein, Caecina was governor from 9 to 14 only of the military district of Moesia, which he carefully distinguishes from the province. He maintains that the province was not organized until 15 when Poppaeus Sabinus was appointed consular legate. S. E. Stout, *The Governors of Moesia* (Princeton, 1911), 2, rightly regards the evidence in support of this thesis as inconclusive.

[28] Tacitus, *Ann.*, II, 66.

[29] *Ibid.* Stout, *The Governors of Moesia*, 4, suggests that Flaccus was *Legatus Legionis* under Sabinus, and his authority was increased when Sabinus was assigned Macedonia and Achaea in addition to Moesia.

trial before the Senate. Cotys' widow appeared as an accuser against him, and her husband's death was avenged by the sentence of his murderer to banishment. He subsequently was taken to Alexandria, where he was executed or committed suicide.[30]

The Thracian kingdom was divided between Rhoemetalces, son of Rhescuporis who had opposed his father's policies, and the minor children of Cotys. The latter were placed under the guardianship of Trebellenus Rufus and educated at Rome, while their guardian, an ex-praetor, represented their interests in Thrace.[31]

Trebellenus' task was not an easy one, and his administration aroused considerable criticism by the Thracians, who were unfamiliar with Roman administrative practices. Rhoemetalces, however, was equally unpopular for his failure to deal effectively with the incursions of the barbarous Coelaletae, Odrysae, and Dii. Fortunately, the attacks of these marauders were not co-ordinated; nevertheless, Rhoemetalces was besieged in Philippolis and needed Roman help to extricate himself from danger.[32]

Publius Vellaeus, who succeeded Pomponius Flaccus in command of Moesia, in 21 sent his cavalry and auxiliaries to deal with plundering bands, while he led the legionaries to Philippolis. There, dissension among the besiegers and an effective sally by the beleaguered Thracians conjoined with the arrival of the Roman legions to bring overwhelming victory.[33]

In 26 Roman interests in Thrace were jeopardized by a major insurrection. The levying of auxiliaries, presumably for service with the two legions in Moesia, was a fundamental cause of the rebellion, and the disaffection had been aggravated by rumors of tribal deportations

[30] Tacitus, *Ann.*, II, 67.
[31] *Ibid.*
[32] *Ibid.*, III, 38.
[33] *Ibid.*, 39.

and resettlements.[34] C. Poppaeus Sabinus, governor of Macedonia, Achaea, and Moesia, temporized until one of the Moesian legions, under the command of Pomponius Labeo, praetorian legate of Moesia, arrived.[35] Rhoemetalces furnished auxiliaries recruited from his subjects who had remained loyal. Sabinus, after consolidating his forces, established a base and employed his auxiliaries in skirmishing until a second camp, closer to the main body of the rebels, could safely be built.[36] The rebels refused to be lured into open battle, and a prolonged siege of their stronghold thereupon was begun with a Roman circumvallation that was gradually drawn closer as the investment continued.[37] The beleaguered garrison, demoralized by privation, especially the dearth of water, was urged to surrender by several of its leaders, but more courageous younger chieftains successfully advocated a last desperate attack on the Roman lines. A ferocious night assault resulted in several minor penetrations of Roman positions, but the main body of the attackers was beaten back. An ensuing Roman counterattack on the Thracian stronghold resulted in its prompt surrender.[38] Sabinus was decreed a triumph by the Senate for his part in the campaign.[39]

The suppression of the Thracian rebellion was connected with the larger project of assuring Roman control of the right bank of the Danube to its mouth. A permanent camp had been established at Ratiaria, on the road

---

[34] *Ibid.*, IV, 46. The Moesian legions were the III (Scythica), based at Ratiaria, and the V (Macedonia), stationed at Viminacium. Von Premerstein, "Die Anfänge der Provinz Moesien," in *loc. cit.*, 177.

[35] Tacitus, *Ann.*, IV, 47. For the Moesian administrative structure, see, Von Premerstein, "Die Anfänge der Provinz Moesien," in *loc. cit.*, 173-74. Sabinus was the grandfather of Poppaea, mistress of Nero. See, Tacitus, *Ann.*, I, 80; V, 10; VI, 39.

[36] Tacitus, *Ann.*, IV, 47-48.   [37] *Ibid.*, 49.
[38] *Ibid.*, 50-51.   [39] *Ibid.*, 46.

to Dardania through Nis, and a second camp was founded before 33-34 near Viminacium.[40] Pacification of Thrace opened the way from Moesia to the Aegean and safeguarded the Roman occupation of the Lower Danube basin.[41] No important Roman colonization of the lower basin ensued until the reign of Hadrian, despite this early penetration of the area.[42]

Germanicus' diplomacy, for the time being at least, had restored Roman prestige in Armenia and Parthia. A pro-Roman king was installed on the Armenian throne, and the Parthians had evinced no disposition to resort to arms to dispute the Roman policy. Upon the death of Artaxias, however, Arsaces, son of Artabanus III of Parthia, was crowned king of Armenia. Artabanus then gradually developed an anti-Roman policy and threatened to expand his empire by the annexation of a number of territories under native chieftains. In 35 an embassy of Parthian nobles came to Rome to complain in secret about their king's actions. Tiberius gave a favorable answer to their request for his aid in installing Phraates, a son of the former king Phraates IV, on the Parthian throne. The prince, who with his brothers had been living in Rome, was sent to the East with funds and equipment designed to ensure the success of his mission.[43]

Artabanus learned of the plan and executed several of the nobles who had instigated it. Phraates died soon after

[40] Von Premerstein, "Die Anfänge der Provinz Moesien," in *loc. cit.*, 175-77.
[41] W. Weber, "Studien zur Chronik des Malalas," *Festgabe für Adolf Deissmann* (Tübingen, 1927), 44.
[42] Von Premerstein, "Die Anfänge der Provinz Moesien," in *loc. cit.*, 177-82. Domitian installed a governor of Lower Moesia. Monuments of Trajan's reign have been found in considerable number, and the civil infiltration in Hadrian's reign was a natural concomitant with the defeat of the Dacians by Trajan. Parvan, "I primordi della civiltá Romana alle foci del Danubio," in *loc. cit.*, 192-203.
[43] Tacitus, *Ann.*, VI, 31-32.

his arrival in Syria, but not before his weakness had demonstrated that his candidacy for the Parthian throne was destined to failure. Tiberius then sent Phraates' brother, Tiridates, to succeed him as the Roman candidate. Mithridates of Iberia was advanced as the imperial nominee for the Armenian throne, since Armenia was the crux of the whole situation from Tiberius' standpoint.[44] Lucius Vitellius was put in charge of the Syrian legions and assigned the task of ensuring the success of the traditional Roman policy.[45]

Mithridates and his brother Pharasmanes, together with their allies, then invaded Armenia, the defense of which Artabanus had confided to his son, Orodes.[46] The Parthians soon were surrounded, and Orodes was forced to give battle to allay the disaffection of his subordinates. In a pitched engagement the Parthians were forced to retreat, after a rumor circulated through their ranks that Orodes, who had been wounded in a personal encounter with Pharasmanes, had been killed.[47]

Artabanus then prepared to send a punitive expedition into Armenia, but he was deterred by the threat that Vitellius would lead his legions against Parthia. This sign of weakness, in turn, encouraged the disgruntled Parthian nobles to revolt, and the king was forced to flee to Scythia, where he made vain efforts to secure reinforcements. Vitellius then proceeded with the legions to the Euphrates, where he secured the approval of a number of Parthian nobles for the recognition of Tiridates as their king.[48] With the Roman efforts apparently crowned with success, Vitellius withdrew his forces to Syria.

Tiridates secured the allegiance of a number of important Parthian towns and cities. Seleuceia was prompt

[44] *Ibid.*, 33.   [45] *Ibid.*   [46] *Ibid.*
[47] *Ibid.*, 34-35.   [48] *Ibid.*, 36.

WAR AND PEACE IN THE PROVINCES 197

to recognize him as the legitimate Parthian ruler, and greeted him enthusiastically when he arrived in the city. In gratitude, he confirmed the democratic regime that had been established.[49] The Parthian capital was transferred to Ctesiphon, and arrangements were made to proceed with Tiridates' coronation.[50] Phraates and Hiero, two of the most important satraps, asked that the coronation be deferred until their arrival, but when they delayed their appearance unreasonably long, the ceremonies were carried out.[51]

The disgruntled satraps then professed allegiance to the exiled Artabanus, whom they found in dire want. With the satraps' aid, however, Artabanus raised an army and advanced against Tiridates, whom he denounced as a usurper. Tiridates, deferring to the advice of his court favorite, retired to Mesopotamia, where it was hoped aid from Rome would be forthcoming. Disappointed in these hopes, Tiridates then fled to Syria and placed himself under Roman protection,[52] and this was the situation at the end of Tiberius' reign.

The insurrection of the year 21 in Gaul was an upheaval comparable in potential danger to that of the first year of Vespasian's reign. *Gallia Lugdunensis* and *Belgica* were involved in the rebellion, the causes of which were largely economic.[53] Julius Florus fomented the uprising among the Treveri in *Belgica*, while Julius Sacrovir served as the leader of the Aedui in *Gallia Lugdunensis*. Both men were Roman citizens, of families that had attained civic status in recognition of distinguished service to Rome. Both leaders exploited long standing grievances of the provincials, and emphasized the burdens of taxation and usurious rates of interest exacted from debtors. They

[49] *Ibid.*, 41.
[50] *Ibid.*, 42.
[51] *Ibid.*
[52] *Ibid.*, 44.
[53] *Infra*, 243, 249.

believed, or professed to believe, that the Rhine legions were still undisciplined as an aftermath of the great mutiny of A.D. 14, and held forth the prospect of the impotence of Rome to quell a provincial rebellion.[54]

The Andecavi (Anjou) and Turoni (Touraine) began the rebellion. Acilius Aviola defeated the former with only a cohort of the garrison at Lyons, while the Turoni were reduced to submission with the aid of a contingent of legionaries sent from Lower Germany.[55] Sacrovir as yet masked his intention to rebel; he and many of his followers, awaiting a more favorable opportunity to strike, actually served with the Roman auxiliaries in the campaigns against the Andecavi and Turoni.[56]

In the meantime, Florus led a premature uprising near Treves. His nondescript army was intercepted while proceeding toward the Ardennes Forest by legions sent by Visellius Varro from Lower Germany and by Gaius Silius from Upper Germany. The Roman forces, aided by Julius Indus, a Gallic enemy of Florus, attacked and dispersed the rebels before their troop dispositions could be effectively arranged. Florus forestalled capture by committing suicide.[57]

The uprising of the Aedui, led by Sacrovir, was a more serious matter. Augustodunum (Autun) was seized by the rebels, and Gallic youths, scions of prominent provincial families, who were receiving Roman education in the capital city, probably were held as hostages to force the support of their families for the rebellion. Some 40,-000 men presumably were at the disposal of Sacrovir, and

---

[54] Tacitus, *Ann.*, III, 40. Gaul furnished very few senators or officials in the early empire. It is hardly likely, therefore, that the families of the rebel leaders had performed anything but local services for the government. H. Dessau, "Die Herkunft der Offiziere und Beamten des Römischen Kaiserreichs," *Hermes*, XLV (1910), 11-12.

[55] Tacitus, *Ann.*, III, 41.   [56] *Ibid.*   [57] *Ibid.*, 42.

of these about 8,000 were equipped with arms comparable with those of the Roman legions, while the rest possessed at least hunting weapons. The rebel army was considerably augmented by a contingent of gladiatorial slaves and a steady influx of recruits from the surrounding countryside.[58]

Roman action was delayed by jealousy between Varro and Silius, but the former finally gave way and permitted Silius to assume command of the operations. Silius ordered his auxiliaries to ravage the villages of the Sequani to prevent them from lending effective aid to the Aedui and marched with the greatest speed against Augustodunum. Some twelve miles from the city, the rebels were encountered, drawn up in battle line, with the gladiators in the vanguard.[59]

Silius ordered an immediate assault. The high morale of the Romans was fostered by their commander, who affected disdain for the rebels whose temerity in appearing in the field against the legionaries he denounced as insulting to Roman prestige. The Roman cavalry turned the flanks of the enemy, and the center, defended by the heavily armed gladiators, ultimately gave way. Sacrovir could not rally a sufficient force to attempt to defend Augustodunum, and thereupon fled to a near-by villa where he and other leaders of the revolt committed suicide.[60]

Tacitus censures Tiberius who, he charges, did not officially inform the Senate of the rebellion until he could accompany announcement of the outbreak with the report that it already had been suppressed. The failure of the *princeps* to send an official communication to the Senate before the termination of the rebellion probably was largely responsible for the wild rumors that excited

[58] *Ibid.*, 43.   [59] *Ibid.*, 45.   [60] *Ibid.*, 46.

the capital to the effect that all Gaul was in rebellion, aided by the Germans, and that there was danger that Spain likewise would join in the insurrection.[61]

In 31 Asia and Achaea were considerably disturbed by the circulation of a rumor that Drusus, son of Germanicus, had appeared in the Cyclades and in Asia. It was alleged that he was mustering an army preparatory to an invasion of Syria or Egypt. As a matter of fact, a pretender had recruited a considerable following of freedmen, slaves, and adventurers, especially among the Greeks with their "avidity for the new and strange." The situation became sufficiently serious to induce Sabinus, governor of Macedonia, Achaea, and Moesia, to make an extensive trip throughout Greece to secure reliable information about the activities of the pretender. Upon his arrival at Nicopolis he learned that the impostor finally had admitted the fraudulent nature of his claims and had fled after his followers deserted him.[62]

The most important provincial acquisition of the reign was that of Cappadocia. In 36 B.C. the kingdom, strategically located because it commanded the route to Armenia and Mesopotamia by way of Sophene, was assigned by Marcus Antonius to Archelaus.[63] Augustus permitted Archelaus to retain his position, despite his adherence to Antonius before Actium, and subsequently assigned Armenia Minor and a part of Cilicia Trachea to him.[64] The

---

[61] *Ibid.*, 47.

[62] *Ibid.*, V, 10. E. S. Bouchier, *Spain under the Roman Empire* (Oxford, 1914), 34, believes that the attack on Lucius Piso, governor of Hither Spain, had political significance. It is far more likely that the attack was the work of brigands. See, Tacitus, *Ann.*, IV, 45; VI, 27.

[63] Dio, *R.H.*, LI, ii, 2. See, W. E. Gwatkin, *Cappadocia as a Roman Province*, in *University of Missouri Studies*, V (Columbia, Mo., 1930), 1-8.

[64] Tacitus, *Ann.*, II, 42; Dio, *R.H.*, LVII, xvii, 3.

Cappadocian ruler, however, incurred the ill will of Tiberius during his voluntary exile at Rhodes by ignoring him while Gaius, Augustus' grandson, was in the East.[65]

In 17 Livia, possibly in response to complaints lodged against the Cappadocian king by his subjects, summoned Archelaus to Rome with the promise of clemency if the charges against him were sustained.[66] No explanation is given by Tacitus to account for Livia's assumption of responsibility to deal with the king. Tacitus leaves the impression that the monarch's trial was the result of the hostility occasioned years before, but this does not seem to be an adequate motive for his deposition,[67] although the statement that Archelaus had ruled his kingdom for fifty years seems to imply that he was deprived of his ruling authority as early as 14, the year of Tiberius' accession.[68] According to the Tacitean account, Archelaus came to Rome and was arraigned on unspecified charges before the Senate, but he committed suicide before termination of the trial. His kingdom was declared a Roman province [69] and was so organized by Germanicus, who installed Quintus Veranius as temporary governor.[70]

It is probably safe to assume that the sentiment for Roman rule was as strong in Cappadocia as it was in Commagene and Cilicia, where the warlike propensities of the native rulers caused many of their subjects to yearn for peace under Roman control.[71] Then, too, Archelaus was the grandfather of Tigranes V, whom Zeno had expelled as king of Armenia. The activities of Archelaus in behalf of his grandson's aspirations for the Armenian

---

[65] Tacitus, *Ann.*, I, 4; II, 42; Dio, *R.H.*, LVII, xvii, 3.
[66] Tacitus, *Ann.*, II, 42.
[67] Gwatkin, *Cappadocia as a Roman Province*, 9.
[68] Tacitus, *Ann.*, II, 42; Gwatkin, *Cappadocia as a Roman Province*, 8.
[69] Tacitus, *Ann.*, II, 42.   [70] *Ibid.*, 56.   [71] *Ibid.*, 54.

throne may well have been an important cause of his removal, since Roman policy, as implemented by Germanicus, was opposed to the recognition of Tigranes.⁷²

The financial administration of Cappadocia under an imperial procurator was much more efficient than it had been under the king. Archelaus' crown estates passed to Tiberius, and the augmentation of imperial revenues was so great as to make possible reduction of the unpopular tax in Italy from 1 to ½ per cent.⁷³

The Cietae, a barbarian people subject to Cappadocia, had stanchly resisted efforts of Archelaus to conduct a census as a preliminary to the imposition of tribute. Inauguration of Roman administration in the province naturally was accompanied by efforts to systematize tax collection, but the Cietae in their strongholds in the Taurus mountains were no more amenable to Roman exactions than they had been to those of Archelaus. Finally in 36 Vitellius, legate of Syria, sent Marcus Trebellius with 4,000 legionaries and a force of auxiliaries to reduce them to obedience. The Roman forces surrounded the barbarians, who had fortified themselves on two hilltops, and forced them to surrender primarily because of their lack of an adequate water supply.⁷⁴

A significant change in provincial arrangements was the termination of senatorial jurisdiction in Achaea and Macedonia, which thereupon were grouped with Moesia and placed under imperial control. The change doubtless was dictated primarily by the desire for more economical and efficient government, since only one staff of officials now was requisite for the government of the

⁷² Gwatkin, *Cappadocia as a Roman Province*, 14; Asdourian, *Die pol. Beziehungen zw. Armenien und Rom*, 80.
⁷³ Tacitus, *Ann.*, II, 42; *infra*, 248.
⁷⁴ Tacitus, *Ann.*, VI, 41.

consolidated province.⁷⁵ It is interesting to note that Tiberius, despite the fact that he constantly adhered to precedents set by Augustus, did not hesitate to change the status of provinces from senatorial to imperial. This alone would go far to show that Tiberius did not consider the government of the empire a "dyarchy," nor did he believe that his predecessor had established such a regime.

Corruption on the part of provincial officials was severely punished. Several cases involving this offense originated in the rich province of Asia. In 23 Lucilius Capito, an imperial procurator, was tried before the Senate and convicted on the charge that he had usurped the authority of a governor, even to the extent of attempting to exercise command over the troops. The emperor properly pointed out during the course of the trial that the authority of an imperial procurator in a senatorial province "extended merely to the slaves and revenues of the imperial domains." ⁷⁶

A more serious case arose from the extortions of Gaius Silanus, proconsul of the Asiatic province. The charges of cruelty and malversation were supported by Gellius Publicola and Marcus Paconius, quaestor and legate of the proconsul, and advocates were sent by the aggrieved provincials to support the charges which were coupled with an indictment for *maiestas*. Junius Otho, one of the praetors, and Bruttedius Niger, an aedile, joined in the prosecution. Tacitus inveighs against Otho as a former school teacher who had attained senatorial rank by the

⁷⁵ *Ibid.*, I, 76, 80. See, Halgen, *Essai sur l'administration des provinces senatoriales sous l'empire romain*, 21.

⁷⁶ Tacitus, *Ann.*, IV, 15. Small units of the imperial army were stationed in several of the senatorial provinces. "At no time can a garrison of that kind ever have been absent from the great proconsular province of Asia." Ritterling, "Military Forces in the Senatorial Provinces," in *loc. cit.*, 29.

aid of Sejanus, and denounces Bruttedius as a man of real talent who had allowed his excessive ambition to induce him to play the ignoble role of accuser in this case. Despite the historian's obvious effort to enlist sympathy for the "solitary man devoid of forensic knowledge and beset by that personal fear which enfeebles even professional eloquence," there seems to have been no doubt of the defendant's guilt, although no effort was made to substantiate the *maiestas* charge. Tiberius took a major part in the interrogation of accusers and witnesses, and the defendant's slaves, presumably purchased by the *fiscus*, were questioned under torture.[77] Silanus requested a delay for a few days to enable him to prepare his defense, but before the expiration of this customary recess, he announced his decision to waive contest of the case.

Tiberius then read as precedents reports of similar cases in Augustus' reign. When the senators were asked to give their *sententiae*, Lucius Piso began by advising the outlawry of the defendant and his relegation to the island of Gyarus in the Aegean.[78] The Fathers agreed with this recommendation, but Gnaeus Lentulus proposed that since the defendant's property had been inherited from his mother, it should not be confiscated but assigned to his son, and Tiberius approved this mitigation of the sentence.[79]

Cornelius Dolabella suggested that men of scandalous life and evil reputation should be debarred from provincial positions. The emperor demurred, however, pointing out that judgments could not be passed on mere rumors. "Many a man by his conduct in his province had reversed the hopes or fears concerning him: some natures were roused to better things by great position, others became sluggish. . . . Princes had enough of burdens—enough,

[77] Tacitus, *Ann.*, III, 67. [78] *Ibid.*, 68. [79] *Ibid.*, 69.

even of power; and where it was possible to proceed by law, it was a mistake to employ the fiat of the sovereign."[80] He concluded his remarks by proposing that Silanus be banished to the island of Cythanus, a less forbidding place of exile, and this extension of clemency was approved.[81]

The provincials showed their gratitude for the prosecution of Capito and Silanus by building a temple in the emperor's honor.[82] He refused, however, to permit a similar edifice to be constructed in Hither Spain to honor him and his mother.[83] Tacitus reports the speech in which he attempted to justify this decision, ostensibly inconsistent with his reception of such honors from the Asiatic provincials. The emperor reminded the Senate that Augustus had permitted a temple to be dedicated to himself at Pergamum, and, therefore, he "followed the precedent already sealed by his approval, with all the more readiness that with worship of [himself] was associated veneration of the Senate." Although he thought it permissible to accept honor on one occasion "yet to be consecrated in the image of deity through all the provinces would be vanity and arrogance."[84]

He then went on to express the following noble sentiments:

As for myself, Conscript Fathers, that I am mortal, that my functions are the functions of men, and that I hold it enough if I fill the foremost place among them—this I call upon you to witness, and I desire those who shall follow us to bear it in mind. For they will do justice, and more, to my memory,

[80] *Ibid.* [81] *Ibid.* [82] *Ibid.*, IV, 15. [83] *Ibid.*, 37.
[84] *Ibid.* There probably was no temple to Augustus in Spain at this time or Tiberius would have mentioned it. M. Krascheninnikoff, "Ueber die Einführung des provinzialen Kaisercultus," *Philologus*, LIII (1894), 179. I agree with his thesis that introduction of the imperial cult came first in the new provinces that were most in need of Romanization. *Ibid.*, 169, 172, 184–85.

if they pronounce me worthy of my ancestry, provident of your interests, firm in dangers, not fearful of offenses in the cause of the national welfare. These are my temples in your breasts, these my fairest and abiding effigies: for those that are reared of stone, should the judgment of the future turn to hatred, are scorned as sepulchres! And so my prayer to allies and citizens and to Heaven itself is this: to Heaven, that to the end of my life it may endow me with a quiet mind, gifted with understanding of law human and divine; and to my fellow-men, that, whenever I shall depart, their praise and kindly thoughts may still attend my deeds and the memories attached to my name.[85]

In 21 Ancharius Priscus accused Caesius Cordus of corrupt practices in Crete, but apparently failed to prove his case.[86] Some years later, however, Priscus secured conviction of the same defendant for extortion in Cyrene.[87] Pomponius Labeo, legate of Moesia, committed suicide in 34 after being accused of maladministration of the province.[88] Charges of extortion in Gaul played at least a minor role in the prosecution of Gaius Silius on the charge of *maiestas* that culminated in his suicide in 29.[89] Granius Marcellus, propraetor of Bithynia, was accused of treason by his quaestor, and misgovernment of the province entrusted to him may have been involved in the indictment.[90]

Tacitus, who generally betrays a disposition to con-

---

[85] Tacitus, *Ann.*, IV, 38. The emperor during the course of his reign accepted in various parts of the empire virtually all the divine honors he had refused. "It is clear that Tiberius, though he may have objected oftener and with more effect than other emperors, was not alone in his depreciation of divine honors and was not effective in his opposition." L. R. Taylor, "Tiberius' Refusal of Divine Honors," *Transactions of the American Philological Association*, LX (1929), 101. A temple and priesthood were established in his honor at Cyprus. *I.G.R.R.*, III, 933. He was deified in Crete and Baetica. *C.I.L.*, II, 1516; III, 12036. For additional inscriptional evidence of the establishment of priesthoods, see, *I.G.R.R.*, III, 474, 1344, 1473; IV, 256, 257.

[86] Tacitus, *Ann.*, III, 38.   [87] *Ibid.*, 70.   [88] *Ibid.*, VI, 29.
[89] *Ibid.*, IV, 20.   [90] *Ibid.*, I, 74.

demn the emperor's conduct or to impugn the motives behind actions he approves, does not qualify his favorable verdict on the administration of the provinces. He declares that the emperor "saw to it that the provinces were not disturbed by fresh impositions and that the incidence of the old was not aggravated by magisterial avarice or cruelty: corporal punishment and the forfeiture of estates were not in vogue." [91]

Most of the cases of provincial misrule originated in the senatorial provinces. The reasons for this are not hard to discover. Senatorial governors held office usually for but one year; moreover, the allocation of even the most important provinces to eligible ex-magistrates continued to be by lot. Short tenure of office and the persistence of the late republican tradition that a provincial governor should accumulate enough wealth in his province to live in subsequent luxurious retirement at Rome encouraged abuses.[92]

In the imperial provinces, on the other hand, terms of five years or more were common during Tiberius' reign. Tacitus narrates:

It was one of the peculiarities of Tiberius to prolong commands, and, as often as not, to retain the same man at the head of the same army or administrative district till his dying day. Various reasons are given. Some hold it was the weary dislike of recurring trouble which caused him to treat a decision once framed as eternally valid; others that he grudged to see too many men enjoying preferment; while there are those who believe that as his intellect was shrewd, so his judgment was hesitant; for, on the one hand, he did not seek out

[91] *Ibid.*, IV, 6.
[92] Lang, *Beiträge zur Gesch. des Kaisers Tiberius*, 60. The Senate did not ordinarily deal with cases involving the imperial provinces so it is possible that the preponderance of cases from the senatorial provinces is attributable to Tacitus' use of the Senate acts. Mommsen, "Das Verhältnis des Tacitus zu den Acten des Senats," in *loc. cit.*, 261. See, W. T. Arnold, *The Roman System of Provincial Administration*, 3rd ed. (Oxford, 1914), Chap. III.

pre-eminent virtue, and, on the other, he detested vice: the best he feared as a private danger, the worst as a public scandal. In the end, this vacillation carried him so far that he gave provinces to men whom he was never to allow to leave Rome.[93]

Suetonius attributes the failure to change provincial officials to the general neglect of governmental affairs which, he alleges, was the result of the emperor's retirement to Capri.[94] Yet no policy could have been more calculated to raise the standard of provincial government than that of keeping able, conscientious officials at their posts. Such men were thoroughly familiar with their duties and responsibilities, cognizant of local conditions, and free from the temptation to make a fortune in a short time.[95] Then, too, it was not always easy to secure men who had executive and military ability coupled with unimpeachable integrity.[96]

Many examples of the policy of prolonged provincial commands could be given. Lucius Apronius served from 28–37 as legate of Lower Germany,[97] while Cornelius Lentulus Gaetulicus served a ten-year term (29–39) in Upper Germany.[98] C. Calvius Sabinus was legate of Pannonia for almost the entire reign of Tiberius.[99] P. Cornelius Dolabella served from 14–18/19 in Dalmatia,[100] and C. Poppaeus Sabinus was in charge of Macedonia, Achaea, and Moesia from 15 until his death in 35.[101]

The emperor's regard for the well-being of the provin-

[93] Tacitus, *Ann.*, I, 80.
[94] Suetonius, *Tib.*, XLI. See, Dio, *R.H.*, LVIII, xxiii, 5.
[95] Josephus, *Antiquities*, XVIII, lxv. Lang, *Beiträge zur Gesch. des Kaisers Tiberius*, 64.
[96] Tacitus, *Ann.*, VI, 27. [97] *Ibid.*, IV, 73; VI, 30; XI, 19.
[98] *Ibid.*, VI, 30.
[99] E. Ritterling, "Die Statthalter der Pannonischen Provinzen," *Archaeologisch-Epigraphische Mitteilungen aus Oesterreich-Ungarn*, XX (1897), 7–8.
[100] Velleius, *R.H.*, II, 125; *C.I.L.*, III, 1741, 2908, 3198, 3199.
[101] Dio, *R.H.*, LVIII, xxv, 4.

cials was expressed further by his prompt action in 17 to relieve distress in twelve cities of Asia occasioned by a violent nocturnal earthquake and resultant fires. Loss of life was heavy, as many of the inhabitants of the affected cities were engulfed in yawning chasms while attempting to flee to open ground. Sardis, which was most severely damaged, received a subvention of 10,000,000 *sesterces* and a five-year remission of taxes. Magnesia also received substantial cash relief, while the other cities were aided by five-year moratoria on tax collections. A senatorial commissioner was sent to determine what additional relief was requisite, and probably to ensure expenditure of the cash advances solely for the purposes intended by the grant. Marcus Ateius, an ex-praetor, was appointed commissioner, and his praetorian rank avoided the embarrassment that might have been caused if his rank were the same as that of the proconsul of the province.[102]

In 23 similar liberality was extended to the cities of Cibyra and Aegium, each of which received a three-year remission of taxes to enable them to recover from the disastrous effects of earthquakes.[103] Such relief to damaged cities, of course, was not entirely altruistic. "When the emperors gave quittance of all contributions to damaged cities and added to this from their own resources for the reconstruction of ruins and the support of the inhabitants, they gave, with little actual expense to themselves, a witness of their generosity which permitted them in ordinary times to demand enormous revenues from the province and cause it to submit without a murmur." [104]

---

[102] Tacitus, *Ann.*, II, 47; *C.I.L.*, III$^{1-2}$, 7096; X, 4842. See, Abbott and Johnson, *Municipal Administration in the Roman Empire*, 149.

[103] Tacitus, *Ann.*, IV, 13; *I.G.R.R.*, IV, 914, 915, 1351.

[104] Chapot, *La province Romaine proconsulaire d'Asie*, 67. For the frequency and destructiveness of earthquakes in Asia Minor, see, O. Weismantel, *Die Erdbeben des Vorderen Kleinasiens in Geschichtlichen Zeit* (Marburg, 1891).

A constructive measure was the limitation of the rights of asylum. These rights of sanctuary developed originally to safeguard altars from sacrilege. From altars such rights were extended so as to embrace entire temples, and, ultimately, considerable territories. Debtors, slaves, and criminals often availed themselves of the protection afforded by privileged sites, and the priesthoods or municipal authorities frequently found opportunities for financial exploitation.[105] Disputes over jurisdiction, perennial suits to collect fines from alleged transgressors, and the tenuous claims to the enjoyment of asylum rights further complicated the situation that imperatively needed reform.

Tiberius submitted the problem to the Senate for settlement. Cities and shrines that claimed rights of asylum were directed to send emissaries to submit the evidence upon which their claims were based. A number of cities tacitly abandoned their alleged rights by failing to send representatives. Ephesus, Magnesia, and a considerable number of other cities, however, submitted their evidence. The Senate, wearied by the reading of charters and the copious references to mythology, authorized the consuls to make the final decision. Cities that received confirmation of their claims were directed to record such recognition on brass plates to be set up in the favored temples.[106] In 23 the grants were enlarged by recognition of asylum rights for the temples of Hera in Samos and Asclepius in Cos.[107] Cyzicus, however, was deprived of its liberties, civic and religious, because of its neglect of the Augustan cult and violence committed on Roman citizens.[108]

The emperor's conscientious effort to promote the wel-

[105] Chapot, *La province Romaine proconsulaire d'Asie*, 406–407.
[106] Tacitus, *Ann.*, III, 60–63; *Corpus Inscriptionum Graecarum*, I, 2943.
[107] Tacitus, *Ann.*, IV, 14.   [108] *Ibid.*, 36; Suetonius, *Tib.*, XXXVII.

WAR AND PEACE IN THE PROVINCES

fare of the provinces also was manifested by the building enterprises fostered by him. In recent years there has been great interest in the study of milestones set up along the great roads of the empire. These stones call attention to repairs made to existent roads and give the date and information as to the nature of the repairs; some give considerable information about new construction. Tiberius was active in the promotion of road building and repairing, particularly in Spain. "The importance of Roman roads as the arteries along which were poured the forces of Roman civilization was in no place better exhibited than in Spain. Soldier, trader, priest and scholar used them in quick succession. At their intersections and terminals sprang up flourishing cities. They made for unity and uniformity as did perhaps no other single work of the Romans." [109] In 25–26 the emperor built the road from Merida to Salamanica. Some repairs to this road were undertaken in the reigns of Claudius and Nero, but no extensive renovation apparently was necessary until the early years of Trajan. In 32–33 a road was built from Braga to Chaves, which was continued beyond Chaves by Trajan. A road from Bribiesca over the western Pyrenees also was built during Tiberius' reign, but as yet little is known about this route. Extensive repairs were made during the reign to the road built by Augustus from Braga to the northwest through Tuy and Pontevedra.[110]

In Dalmatia a road was built from Salonae to Ditionum, [111] as well as to Anderitum [112] and Daesitrate.[113]

[109] J. J. Van Nostrand, *The Reorganization of Spain by Augustus*, in *University of California Publications in History*, IV (Berkeley, 1916), 106–107.
[110] C. E. Van Sickle, "The Repair of Roads in Spain under Tiberius," *Classical Philology*, XXIV (1929), 77–87; J. J. Van Nostrand, "Roman Spain," in T. Frank (ed.), *An Economic Survey of Ancient Rome*, 5 vols. and index (Baltimore, 1933 ff.), III, 195.
[111] *C.I.L.*, III, 3198.   [112] *Ibid.*, 3200.   [113] *Ibid.*, 3201.

Tacitus mentions road construction in Pannonia in the vicinity of Nauportus.[114] Along the right bank of the Danube, in Moesia, a great road was built, part of it cut into solid rock cliffs, to establish effective communications between the fourth and the fifth legions permanently stationed in the Moesian province.[115] Many inscriptions recording road repairs in *Gallia Narbonensis* have been found,[116] and there is evidence of similar activity in Africa.[117] There was probably some road construction and repair in Syria during the reign,[118] and the road from Coptos to the Red Sea may have been repaired by Tiberius' officials.[119]

The construction of bridges is recorded at Vaga in Africa over the Wed Bedja,[120] at Cirminium, [121] Garovilla,[122] Brixia,[123] and Nicopolis in Syria.[124] In Syrian Antioch the emperor built a great wall to protect the city from dangerous landslides, and also probably constructed a temple and a theater in that city.[125] Recent excavations on the site of Pisidian Antioch have uncovered the remains of the square of Tiberius.[126] In Sicily the emperor

---

[114] Tacitus, *Ann.*, I, 20. [115] *C.I.L.*, III, 1698.

[116] *Ibid.*, XII, 5441, 5445, 5449, 5478, 5492, 5554, 5557, 5588, 5592, 5596, 5598, 5600, 5605, 5606, 5619, 5628, 5638, 5649, 5652, 5654, 5657, 5659, 5665. See, A. Grenier, "La Gaule Romaine," in Frank (ed.), *An Economic Survey of Ancient Rome*, III, 513, n.11.

[117] *C.I.L.*, VIII, 10023; M. P. Charlesworth, *Trade-Routes and Commerce of the Roman Empire* (Cambridge, 1924), 136.

[118] F. M. Heichelheim, "Roman Syria," in Frank (ed.), *An Economic Survey of Ancient Rome*, IV, 209.

[119] A. C. Johnson, "Roman Egypt," in Frank (ed.), *An Economic Survey of Ancient Rome*, II, 636.

[120] *C.I.L.*, VIII, 10568. [121] *Ibid.*, XI, 367.

[122] *Ibid.*, II, 4651. [123] *Ibid.*, V, 4307.

[124] *Ibid.*, III, 6703.

[125] Weber, "Studien zur Chronik Malalas," in *loc. cit.*, 48–56; A. Schenk, *Die Römische Kaisergeschichte bei Malalas* (Stuttgart, 1931), 17.

[126] D. M. Robinson, "A Preliminary Report on the Excavations at Pisidian Antioch and at Sizma," *American Journal of Archaeology*, XXVIII (1924), 438–40.

repaired a temple on Mount Eryx,[127] and there is a record of his dedication of a "Pronaos to Aphrodite" in the great temple at Denderah in Egypt.[128] The evidence of ancient historians and the votive offerings of the provincials [129] bear witness to their gratitude that the emperor "treated the provinces of Rome outside Italy in a human unity with the whole of the state instead, as happened before him, of treating them as possessions to be shorn or to be ground according to circumstances." [130]

[127] V. M. Scramuzza, "Roman Sicily," in Frank (ed.), *An Economic Survey of Ancient Rome*, III, 372, 376.
[128] Johnson, "Roman Egypt," in *loc. cit.*, 641, n.4.
[129] *C.I.L.*, II, 1516; III, 12032; IX, 652; X, 688, 7257; XI, 3308; XIII, 1769; *I.G.R.R.*, III, 157, 474, 1344, 1473; IV, 254, 256, 257; *C.I.G.*, I, 2943.
[130] Stahr, *Tiberius*, 167.

Chapter X

RELATIONS WITH THE SENATE AND THE ADMINISTRATION OF ITALY

The question of Tiberius' relations with the Senate is one of prime importance in any study of his reign. Immediately after the Senate had concluded ceremonies incident to Augustus' deification, Tiberius had accepted ruling authority, ostensibly in response to the importunities of the Fathers. Yet his conduct after his predecessor's demise indicated that he had no hesitancy in exercising tribunician and proconsular powers without awaiting senatorial sanction. The Senate had ratified these powers at the behest of Augustus, and, in the absence of any direct renunciation of such specific powers by Tiberius, his emulation of Augustus' abdications was not particularly fortunate. When he appeared before the Senate on this memorable occasion, he already was as much a constitutional ruler as Augustus ever had been. His problem was to give the appearance that the Senate retained freedom of action without reopening the whole succession issue, and such an objective naturally was difficult, if not impossible, to attain.

The Fathers did nothing to ease the embarrassment of his position. By groveling before him they tacitly impugned his "despotism," the very appearance of which he was so anxious to avoid. They had no disposition to counter his expressed reluctance to assume the burden of sovereignty by investment with constitutional or quasi-constitutional powers. Gallus' professed willingness to proceed with serious consideration of Tiberius' suggestion for a division of authority, even to the extent of partitioning the empire, was intended to embarrass him, and Haterius' reference to the tribunician power was added evidence that the senators, while not daring openly to challenge his claim to the throne, would not take the initiative in strengthening the constitutionality of his assumption of it. A number of measures could have been taken by the Senate to give the nominally official approval Tiberius so patently desired. A motion could have been passed providing for the extension of his tribunician and proconsular powers for life, or for a period beyond the date of their theoretical expiration. The *maius imperium* extending throughout the entire empire, including Italy, could have been voted, either for life or for a designated term of years, or the newly elevated emperor could have been named *princeps senatus*. Any of these actions by the Senate, while not altering the *de facto* position of Tiberius in the least, would have been an expression of confidence and constitutional sanction which he desired far more than mere empty titles. The senators, many of whom had lived through the reign of Augustus and were familiar with his methods, certainly realized what Tiberius desired, and their failure to adopt a more co-operative attitude toward him was indicative of the smoldering opposition that was to express itself in a number of ways during the course of his reign.[1]

The emperor, nevertheless, made substantial efforts to gain senatorial support and co-operation in the administration of the empire. According to Suetonius, "There was no matter of public or private business so small or so great that he did not lay it before the senators, consulting them about revenues and monopolies, constructing

[1] Levy, *Quo modo Tiberius se gesserit*, 34-35.

and restoring public buildings, and even about levying and disbanding the soldiers, and the disposal of the legionaries and auxiliaries; finally about the extension of military commands and appointments to the conduct of wars, and the form and content of his replies to the letters of kings."[2] He further declares that the emperor insisted upon freedom of speech, and in his own addresses he exceeded the requirements of courtesy in his deference to the Fathers.[3] Tacitus corroborates this praise of the emperor's relations with the Senate by declaring that the "public affairs—together with private affairs of exceptional moment—were treated in the senate, and discussion was free to the leading members, their lapses into subserviency being checked by the sovereign himself."[4]

Such testimony from Tacitus is particularly significant since his use of the *Acta* of the Senate as an important source for the *Annals* gave him an understanding of senatorial business unequaled by the other ancient writers who dealt with this period.[5] The *Acta*, or protocols, of the Senate were kept in the archives. They included a brief summary of the matters that came before the Fathers and the *Sententiae*, or decisions. Annual compilations were made by the quaestors, who were entrusted with the preservation of the records. Both Caesar and Augustus provided for the publication of these summaries, but after Augustus' reign only such excerpts as were of popular interest and could be made public without embarrassment

---

[2] Suetonius, *Tib.*, XXX.   [3] *Ibid.*, XXVII–XXIX.
[4] Tacitus, *Ann.*, IV, 6. See, Pfitzner, *Das Verhalten des Tiberius im Senate bei der Uebernahme der Herrschaft*, 17–18.
[5] Stein, "Tacitus als Geschichtsquelle," in *loc. cit.*, 371; *id.*, "Die Protokolle des römischen Senates und ihre Bedeutung als Geschichtsquelle für Tacitus," *Jahresbücher der I. deutschen Staats-Realschule in Prag*, XLIII (1904), 7–29; Mommsen, "Das Verhältnis des Tacitus zu der Acten des Senats," in *loc. cit.*, 253 ff.; Reitzenstein, "Tacitus und sein Werk," in *loc. cit.*, 22.

to the emperor or the Fathers were made available, either by the issue of certified copies by the government or by private publication on the part of individual senators.⁶ There are many indications of Tacitus' use of these documents, to which he, as a senator, had free access.⁷ Indeed, the annalistic form of his work may be attributable to his use of the *Acta*. It must always be remembered, however, that many matters affecting the imperial provinces or the legions never came before the Senate, and, therefore, probably did not come under the scrutiny of the historian.⁸

A number of examples can be cited to show to what degree the Senate participated in the government. Senatorial decision in regard to the arrangements for Augustus' funeral was taken as binding, and the Fathers likewise enjoyed a free hand in the deification of the late emperor.⁹ A number of important state trials, including those of Libo, Piso, and Archelaus of Cappadocia, took place before the Fathers.¹⁰ Trials of provincial officials before them included cases in which imperial officials were involved, as well as those which concerned only the administration of senatorial provinces.¹¹ Proconsuls who did not report to the Senate were censured by the emperor for

---

⁶ Stein, "Die Protokolle des römischen Senates," in *loc. cit.*, 7–22.
⁷ Tacitus, *Ann.*, I, 14, 72, 76; II, 35–36; III, 38, 58, 71; IV, 13; VI, 4, 11.
⁸ Mommsen, "Das Verhältnis des Tacitus zu der Acten des Senats," in *loc. cit.*, 258–61.
⁹ Tacitus, *Ann.*, I, 8; Dio, *R.H.*, LVI, xxxv–xlii.
¹⁰ Tacitus, *Ann.*, II, 29; III, 10–12; II, 42. See, Levy, *Quo modo Tiberius se gesserit*, 66. The importance of the Senate as a criminal court began in Tiberius' reign. McFayden, *The Rise of the Princeps' Jurisdiction Within the City of Rome*, in *loc. cit.*, 181–264; Dessau, *Gesch. der röm. Kaiserzeit*, Vol. I, Pt. I, 140. Augustus, however, as shown by the famous Cyrene edicts, set up senatorial machinery for the trial of provincial officials on charges that did not involve the loss of *caput*. A Senate committee was to decide such cases within thirty days after the hearing. Anderson, "Augustan Edicts from Cyrene," in *loc. cit.*, 45–48.
¹¹ *Infra*, 203.

failing to do so.¹² Prosecution of *maiestas* cases took place before the Senate on the ground that the state was in danger. Only in the case of Agrippina was there any evidence of concerted senatorial opposition to the exercise of judicial functions;¹³ indeed, the emperor on several occasions found it necessary to restrain the ardor of the Fathers in taking cognizance of accusations and condemning the defendants.¹⁴

The adjudication of the whole issue of the confirmation or termination of asylum rights in eastern cities was submitted by the emperor to the Senate, but the Fathers eventually authorized the consuls to act for them.¹⁵ After defendants in criminal and civil cases evaded the authority of the praetors by grasping images or portraits of members of the imperial family and claiming rights of asylum, the Senate legislated against this practice and ordered the imprisonment of a certain Annia Rufilla, who had defied the praetors by resort to such assumed immunity.¹⁶ Sumptuary legislation was passed by the Senate in 16, apparently without the initiative of the emperor; at least he expressed his conviction of the futility of such legislation when similar measures were under discussion six years later.¹⁷ Embassies protesting against diversion of the courses of streams to avoid floods of the Tiber were heard by the Senate,¹⁸ and the laws ordering the banishment of astrologers and magicians from Italy,¹⁹ as well as the repressive measures directed against Jews and devotees of the cult of Isis, were passed by that body,²⁰ although such measures may have been taken in response to the emperor's

---

¹² Suetonius, *Tib.*, XXXII. Dio, *R.H.*, LVII, xvii, 9, declares that all embassies were referred to the Senate.
¹³ Tacitus, *Ann.*, V, 4–5.
¹⁴ *Ibid.*, II, 28, 50; III, 41; IV, 30; VI, 5.   ¹⁵ *Ibid.*, III, 60–63.
¹⁶ *Ibid.*, 36.   ¹⁷ *Ibid.*, 54.   ¹⁸ *Ibid.*, I, 79.
¹⁹ *Ibid.*, II, 32; Suetonius, *Tib.*, XXXVI.   ²⁰ Tacitus, *Ann.*, II, 85.

RELATIONS WITH THE SENATE 219

suggestion. Proconsular powers were voted to Germanicus by the Fathers at Tiberius' request,[21] and in 17 they bestowed on the prince the *maius imperium* necessary for the performance of his eastern mission.[22] After the death of Germanicus the emperor commended Drusus and Nero to the care of the Senate.[23]

Suetonius reports several instances where the Senate adopted proposals against the expressed desires of the emperor. In one case, the city of Trebia was permitted to utilize funds for the construction of a theater, despite Tiberius' recommendation that the money be employed to finance the building of a road. In another instance a praetor was permitted to go abroad during his term of office, although the emperor expressed the eminently proper view that civic magistrates should remain in the capital until expiration of their terms.[24]

On the other hand, there are instances where the emperor's wishes prevailed. The transfer of Macedonia and Achaea from senatorial to imperial control could hardly have been approved by the senators, whose opportunities to secure lucrative offices thereby were curtailed.[25] The emperor refused to permit the use of certain titles voted to him by the Fathers, and he likewise curbed the honors voted to Livia.[26] Despite the protest of Ateius Capito, he refused to allow trial of Lucius Ennius on *maiestas* charges.[27] In the case of Granius Marcellus the emperor exercised his right of casting a vote in the Senate, despite the protest of Gnaeus Piso that this action might be inter-

---

[21] *Ibid.*, I, 14, 39.
[22] *Ibid.*, II, 43. See, Schulz, "Das Wesen des römischen Kaisertums," in *loc. cit.*, 60–66.
[23] Tacitus, *Ann.*, III, 29; Dio, *R.H.*, LVII, xxii, 4.
[24] Suetonius, *Tib.*, XXXII. See, S. Reinach, "Une séance du Senate Romain sous Tiberè," *Revue Historique*, CLXII (1930), 95-99.
[25] *Infra*, 202.   [26] Tacitus, *Ann.*, I, 14.
[27] *Ibid.*, III, 70.

preted as an effort to coerce the Fathers.[28] *Maiestas* indictments brought before the Senate in the cases of Appuleia Varilla,[29] Lepida Aemilia,[30] and Cotta Messalinus [31] were quashed by order of the emperor, and he exercised his clemency to spare Proculus from the death penalty voted by the Senate.[32]

During the ascendancy of Sejanus, senators were largely denied access to the emperor and were presumably forced to lay their business before the favorite. After Tiberius' retirement to Capri, it was impossible for the Fathers to secure an audience with him.[33] Dolabella's request for the triumphal insignia upon the termination of his African campaign was refused by the emperor, apparently without reference of the question to the Senate.[34] The proposal to bar men of evil reputation from provincial commands was voted down by the Senate, probably in response to the disapproval of the motion expressed by the emperor,[35] and the attempt to extend the scope of censorial legislation in 22 likewise was frustrated by his intercession.[36]

Freedom of debate certainly was permitted in the allocation of the African command. Although the emperor strongly suggested the need for a capable military commander in view of the projected campaign against Tacfarinas, he insisted that the Senate name the proconsul, despite its desire for him to make the choice.[37] The proposal to ban wives of provincial commanders from the provinces does not seem to have been originated by any

---

[28] *Ibid.*, I, 74; Schott, *Die Kriminaljustiz unter dem Kaiser Tiberius*, 22–24.
[29] Tacitus, *Ann.*, II, 50.   [30] *Ibid.*, 27.
[31] *Ibid.*, VI, 5. See, Rogers, "Der Prozess des Cotta Messalinus," in *loc. cit.*, 123.
[32] Tacitus, *Ann.*, IV, 31.   [33] *Ibid.*, 74.
[34] *Ibid.*, 26.   [35] *Ibid.*, III, 69.
[36] *Infra*, 228–29.   [37] Tacitus, *Ann.*, III, 32–35.

word of the emperor, and although the legislation was not passed, the introduction of the measure indicated the continued exercise of at least a modicum of senatorial initiative.[38] During the course of a debate in 16, Asinius Gallus is reported to have declared that matters affecting Italy and the provinces should not be discussed unless the emperor were present. This view was vigorously contested by Gnaeus Piso, who held that the senators should demonstrate their ability to perform their duties in his absence.[39]

The emperor exhibited concern for the continuance of prominent senatorial families. Since "high birth required the help of money," he refused to accept two intestate bequests, which he turned over to Aemilius Lepidus and Marcus Servilius.[40] He refused, however, to comply with the brazen request of Marcus Hortalus for a subvention. Hortalus was a grandson of Hortensius, the famous orator. Augustus had granted him 100,000 *sesterces* to subsidize his marriage and rearing of a family. Hortalus now appeared with his four sons and virtually said in so many words that, since he had begotten children in accordance with the wish of Augustus, he was entitled to financial relief, since "he had inherited or acquired nothing." The emperor properly labeled this request "an unseasonable and unexpected demand." Favorable reception of such pleas would mean eventual exhaustion of the treasury, an orgy of selfish intrigue, and the promotion of indolence. If such a precedent were set, the emperor continued, "We shall have the whole populace waiting, without a care in the world, for outside relief, incompetent to help itself and an incubus to us."[41] He did, however, express his willingness to agree if the Senate should desire to give each

[38] *Ibid*. Dio, *R.H.*, LVII, vii–xiii, makes much of the freedom of discussion enjoyed by the Senate.
[39] Tacitus, *Ann.*, II, 35.   [40] *Ibid*. Cf., Suetonius, *Tib.*, XLIX.
[41] Tacitus, *Ann.*, II, 37–38.

of the sons 200,000 *sesterces*, but the grant apparently was not made, for the Hortensian house "kept sinking deeper into ignominious poverty."[42]

In view of the efforts made by the emperor to encourage senatorial participation in governmental affairs, it is probably just to say that "The policy of Tiberius could be expressed in two principles: all power to the emperor and effective cooperation of the Senate. Never in the course of the history of the empire was the cooperation of the two powers practiced with any sincerity and liberalism on the emperor's part except in the first part of the reign of Tiberius."[43] The Senate, however, did not justify his hopes. In 21 he reproved the Fathers for their disposition to entrust everything to his decision.[44] On occasion, Senate sessions were sparsely attended, indicating a lack of interest in public business on the part of the members.[45] The ascendancy of Sejanus and the retirement of the emperor to Capri, of course, were largely responsible for curtailment of opportunity for the Senate effectively to co-operate in the government.[46] Then, too, independence of the Senate could hardly have been expected when the Praetorian Guard, exclusively under the command of the emperor, was concentrated in the capital.[47] Nevertheless, the Fathers were only too prone to hide their opposition

---

[42] *Ibid.*, 38; Suetonius, *Tib.*, XLVII.

[43] Homo, *L'empire Romain*, 32. O. Hirschfeld, "Zur Geschichte der römischen Kaiserzeit," *Kleine Schriften*, 909, makes the unjustified charge that Tiberius was responsible for the failure of Augustus' plan to admit the Senate to a real share in the government of the empire.

[44] Tacitus, *Ann.*, III, 35.

[45] *Ibid.*, VI, 12. Dio, *R.H.*, LVIII, xxi, 3, says that the emperor insisted on regularity and punctuality of attendance. Such insistence probably was necessary.

[46] Hirschfeld, *Die Kaiserlichen Verwaltungsbeamten*, 471; Abraham, *Tiberius und Sejan*, 15-16.

[47] Herzog, *Gesch. und System der Röm. Staatsverfassung*, Vol. II, Pt. I, 248. Maroni, "Uno sguardo ai fasti dei prefetti al pretorio," in *loc. cit.*, 342.

to the emperor under the cloak of flattery and adulation,[48] and he, in turn, could not entirely free himself of suspicion toward them.[49] "Tiberius had not the patience of his predecessor; the tension between the pride of the Senate, and the irritation of Tiberius was only accentuated when the latter retired to Capreae. His communications must have sounded to the Senate more and more like commands rather than proposals; its inefficiency must have seemed to him more and more like opposition concealed under superficial obsequiousness." [50]

One of the governmental changes inaugurated by Tiberius was the abolition of the electoral rights of the *Comitia Tributa*. Since the practice of submitting lists of candidates had been begun by Augustus, the electoral rights of the assembly were merely nominal. There was, therefore, little evidence of popular resentment against the policy. The senators, "relieved from the necessity of buying or begging votes," approved the change.[51] Since the emperor continued the practice of suggesting approved candidates the measure "took no real power from the people and gave none to the Senate." [52] The emperor named twelve candidates for the praetorship, and despite senatorial request that the number be increased, he swore never to submit more than twelve.[53] At times he directly suggested candidates for the consulship to the Senate. On other occasions he outlined the qualifications desired, such as ancestry, career, distinctions, and honors, in a fashion that left no doubt as to the identity of his favored candi-

[48] Jerome, *Some Aspects of Roman History*, Chap. XIV. See, S. Dill, *Roman Society from Nero to Marcus Aurelius* (New York, 1905), 185–86.
[49] Niese, *Grundriss der römischen Geschichte*, 305.
[50] Hammond, *The Augustan Principate*, 126; Marsh, *Reign of Tiberius*, 117.
[51] Tacitus, *Ann.*, I, 15.   [52] Marsh, *Reign of Tiberius*, 62.
[53] Tacitus, *Ann.*, I, 14. See, Dio, *R.H.*, LVIII, xx, 1–5.

dates. In years when he resorted to neither of these procedures, candidates applied directly to him, and he, in turn, called the attention of the incumbent consuls to their candidacies.[54] There is no question that Tiberius, like his predecessor, took measures to ensure against tenure of the consulships by persons inimical to him, but the verdict of Tacitus that his policy was "nugatory or perfidious and destined to issue in a servitude all the more detestable the more it was distinguished under a semblance of liberty" [55] seems unwarranted. Indeed, the historian points out that "in conferring offices, he took into view the nobility of the candidate's ancestry, the distinction of his military service, or the brilliance of his civil attainments, and left it sufficiently clear that no better choice had been available. The consulate had its old prestige; so had the praetorship: the powers even of the minor magistracies were exercised; and the laws, apart from the process in cases of treason, were in proper force." [56]

A spirited contest for a vacant praetorship ensued after the death of an incumbent in the year 17. Germanicus and Drusus actively supported the candidacy of Haterius Agrippa, but some senators took the legally correct position that the number of the candidate's children was, in this case, to be the determining factor. Haterius nonetheless received a majority of the votes, but the emperor, according to Tacitus, rejoiced that so many senators had chosen "to support the laws rather than his sons." [57]

Asinius Gallus, who often acted as an opposition leader, proposed that the incumbents for magistracies should be named for five years in advance. In the ensuing annual elections, candidates then would be named to assume

---

[54] Tacitus, *Ann.*, I, 81. See, Groag, "Zum Konsulat in der Kaiserzeit," in *loc. cit.*, 145.
[55] Tacitus, *Ann.*, I, 81.   [56] *Ibid.*, IV, 6.   [57] *Ibid.*, II, 51.

duties five years after the elections. This ingenious move really was aimed at the curtailment of the emperor's patronage, so as to strengthen the opposition. Filling the magistracies for five years would have created a considerable number of senators whose advancement would have been assured, and who, therefore, would have been free to adopt a more independent attitude toward the emperor. Tiberius realized that this was the objective of Gallus' proposal. He accordingly pointed out that men often became arrogant as soon as assured of the honors and perquisites of office. How would men of that type conduct themselves if they could take pride in their status as magistrates-designate for five years? It was difficult for him to avoid giving offense to disappointed candidates when the offices were merely to be filled for one year. Naturally, disappointment would be much more bitter if an aspirant for honor saw his ambitions frustrated, not for a single year, but for five years. After this pronouncement the proposal was dropped.[58]

An interesting demonstration of magisterial independence arose as a result of the activities of Lucius Piso, who, after inveighing against political intrigues and judicial corruption, had announced his intention to retire from public life, only to be dissuaded by the emperor. Some time later, Urgulania, a friend of Livia, was the defendant in a civil suit. Relying on the friendship of the emperor's mother, she ignored a summons to appear before the praetorian court and went instead to the imperial residence. In response to Livia's appeal, Tiberius promised to appear in the defendant's behalf, but he deliberately delayed his attendance at the trial until Piso, who conducted the

---

[58] *Ibid.*, 36. Bunting, "The Stoic Opposition to the Principate," 104, asks, "Was Asinius really trying to be disagreeable, and destructive, and anti-imperial?" I think the answer is decidedly affirmative.

prosecution, had won his case.⁵⁹ Urgulania subsequently recovered a modicum of her pride when she refused to appear as a witness before the Senate and was granted the right to have her deposition taken in her own home by a praetor.⁶⁰

The emperor was as prompt in relieving distress occasioned by disasters in Italy as he was in the provinces. In the year 15 incessant rains caused an abnormal rise of the Tiber, with the result that sections of the capital were flooded. With the recession of the flood a number of buildings collapsed and caused some casualties. When the problems incident to this disaster were discussed in the Senate, Asinius Gallus proposed consultation of the Sibylline Books. The emperor took no cognizance of this foolish suggestion, but appointed Ateius Capito and Lucius Arruntius as commissioners to study the flood problem with a view to making recommendations for avoiding danger in the future.⁶¹ They ultimately proposed the diversion of the courses of certain rivers and the lowering of the levels of a number of lakes to prevent abnormal rises of the Tiber. As a prelude to plans for a major program of public works, embassies and legations appeared from a number of Italian cities to protest against projected stream diversions. The Florentines insisted that diversion of the Chiana into the Arno would jeopardize their safety, and the populace of Terni and Reate likewise pleaded for abandonment of portions of the plans that threatened their interests. The familiar appeal to the inscrutable will of the gods was not wanting. "Nature had made the best provision for the interest of humanity when she assigned to rivers their proper mouths—their proper courses—

---

⁵⁹ Tacitus, *Ann.*, II, 34.   ⁶⁰ *Ibid.*
⁶¹ *Ibid.*, I, 76. Bunting, "The Stoic Opposition to the Principate," 102–103, calls Gallus' suggestion a typical conservative proposal.

their limits as well as their origins." [62] The opposition incited by the proposals doubtless was a fundamental cause for the abandonment of the entire scheme.

A fire in 26, which destroyed many structures on the Caelian Hill, caused much suffering, which the emperor promptly and liberally relieved. "Thanks were returned to him; in the senate, by the noble; in the streets, by the voice of the people: for without respect of persons, and without the intercession of relatives, he had aided with his liberality even unknown sufferers whom he had himself encouraged to apply." [63] The same year a flimsy amphitheater, built at Fidenae by a freedman, collapsed while games were in progress and caused many casualties. The stands had been overcrowded by the influx of spectators from the capital, where gladiatorial combats had become rare; indeed, the structure had been built in order to cater to the Roman clientele. Private homes were turned into hospitals to take care of the injured, and the necessary surgical attention was supplied without charge. An aftermath of the disaster was a senatorial act prohibiting the holding of games by anyone whose fortune did not equal at least 400,000 *sesterces*. The object of the law obviously was to prevent "shoestring" operators from erecting cheap, unsubstantial facilities for the presentation of such attractions.[64]

Ten years later a destructive fire in the *Circus Maximus* and on the Aventine induced the emperor again to exhibit his generosity, for, according to Tacitus, he made 100,000 *sesterces* available for relief and rehabilitation. The four

---

[62] Tacitus, *Ann.*, I, 79.   [63] *Ibid.*, IV, 64; Suetonius, *Tib.*, XLVII.
[64] Tacitus, *Ann.*, IV, 63; Suetonius, *Tib.*, XL. Tacitus' figure of 50,000 casualties, as well as Suetonius' 20,000, are too extreme to warrant serious consideration. Dio, *R.H.*, LVIII, i, 1, blames the emperor for the disaster because he was responsible for the cessation of gladiatorial shows in the capital!

husbands of the emperor's granddaughters were joined by Publius Petronius, nominated by the consuls, to form a commission of five to assess the damage and to supervise the disbursement of relief funds.[65]

Need for sumptuary legislation was a major topic of senatorial discussion during the year 16. Quintus Haterius [66] was a successful proponent of remedial laws, particularly to limit extravagance in the use of gold plate and costly fabrics. Efforts to pass more drastic prohibitions were frustrated, however, largely as a result of the opposition of Asinius Gallus. Tiberius apparently permitted free and full discussion of the issue, and, probably in response to a request that he assume censorial authority, declared that there was no need for a *lustrum*. If in the future comprehensive reform proved necessary, a suitable leader would be available, as on many occasions in the past.[67]

The legislation of 16 seemed to have had little effect on the trend toward luxury and extravagance, for six years later the Senate again took cognizance of complaints that emphasized the need for further prohibitions, especially to curb the vices of gluttony and intemperance.[68] The emperor expressed the wish that the Senate might deal with such matters in his absence. Accusing glances cast by the Fathers at some of their colleagues who were notorious for their excesses could not fail to direct his attention toward them, and he had no wish to seem to be arraigning anyone. He had little hope for effective measures against luxury and vice.[69] If the laws proved effective, all the senators would claim a share in the credit; if, on the other hand, general compliance proved impossible of attainment, the obloquy would fall on him. Legislation was a poor substitute for self-restraint, and he was ready to lend

---

[65] Tacitus, *Ann.*, VI, 45. [66] *Ibid.*, I, 13; III, 57; IV, 61.
[67] *Ibid.*, II, 33.   [68] *Ibid.*, III, 52.   [69] *Ibid.*, 53.

RELATIONS WITH THE SENATE

his support to any magistrate who believed he could cope with the problem, but no one was ready to assume such responsibility.[70] In line with his policy of discouraging extravagance, however, the emperor, in addition to setting a good personal example of economy, reduced the cost of games and gladiatorial shows by reducing the pay of actors and curtailing the number of gladiators that could be utilized.[71]

There is evidence that public order in Italy was vigorously maintained. Garrisons of troops were stationed at strategic points to suppress brigandage throughout the peninsula. Disturbances at theatrical performances came to a head in 15, when a riot in Rome resulted in the killing of a centurion and several soldiers, as well as the wounding of a member of the Praetorian Guard.[72] A proposal in the Senate to grant the praetors the right to sentence actors to the punishment of the lash was voted down, but measures were passed permitting the exile of spectators guilty of disturbances. Senators were forbidden to enter the houses of mimes, and *equites* were prohibited from congregating around them in the streets.[73] Most severe measures were employed in the interests of public order after a riot at Pollentia, where the populace rioted to force the heirs of a deceased chief centurion to donate money for a gladiatorial show. The emperor sent cohorts from the capital to suppress the demonstration, and the decurions, as well as a number of citizens who were held responsible for the outbreak, were imprisoned.[74]

---

[70] *Ibid.*, 54.
[71] Suetonius, *Tib.*, XXXIV. See, Dio, *R.H.*, LVII, iv, 5.
[72] Suetonius, *Tib.*, XXXVII.   [73] Tacitus, *Ann.*, I, 54, 77.
[74] Suetonius, *Tib.*, XXXVII. The emperor alone took responsibility for the policing of Italy. O. Hirschfeld, "Die Sicherheitspolizei im römischen Kaiserreich," *Kleine Schriften*, 591. In Rome, however, the magistrates were expected to exercise their authority. Tacitus, *Ann.*, VI, 13.

An important religious development was the creation of the *Augustales* to maintain the cult of Augustus. Twenty-one members of the college were drawn by lot from leading families, and to these were added Tiberius, Drusus, Germanicus, and Claudius, the future emperor.[75] The emperor also granted subsidies to the Vestals,[76] and the law of Augustus designed to ensure the authenticity of the Sibylline Books was enforced.[77] The qualifications for tenure of the position of *Flamen* of Jupiter were liberalized by abolishing the requirement that candidates be children of parents married according to the old sacred rites of *confarreatio*. Since this form of marriage was largely obsolete, it was becoming increasingly difficult to fill the ranks of the flamens and, at the same time, adhere to customary prerequisites. Since considerable opposition had developed to the practice of exempting the wives of flamens from the control of their parents, it was provided that henceforth they were to be subject to their husbands only in religious matters and were to retain normal legal relationship to their parents in all other respects.[78]

In 19 severe repressive steps were taken against the Jews.[79] In the reign of Tiberius there probably were about 50,000 Jews in a total population of 1,000,000 in the capital city. They lived in the Travastere region and in the Subura, a fringe of the *Campus Martius*, near Porta Capena. They virtually were all freedmen, the descendants of war captives who had been brought to Rome in great numbers, particularly after Pompey's capture of Jerusalem, and most of them were laborers or petty tradesmen. At least four of the thirteen synagogues of the im-

---

[75] Tacitus, *Ann.*, I, 54.   [76] *Ibid.*, II, 86.
[77] *Ibid.*, IV, 16; VI, 12.   [78] *Ibid.*, II, 86.
[79] *Ibid.*, 85; Suetonius, *Tib.*, XXXVI; Josephus, *Antiquities*, XVIII, iii, 5.

perial period were in existence in Rome in the first century A.D.[80]

According to Tacitus' account, four thousand freedmen were sent to Sardinia to campaign against brigands, while the remainder were ordered to renounce their faith or leave Italy,[81] possibly on pain of enslavement in the event of noncompliance with the decree.[82] Tacitus' account implies that only freedmen were ordered to Sardinia. As a matter of fact, many of the Jews were merely *peregrini*, who could be ordered to leave without further ceremony. Those with civic status, however, could not be banished without trial and conviction on charges that entailed relegation as a punishment. These, however, if within military age (18–45), were liable to service in the army, and they accordingly were impressed into service and sent into Sardinia. The *peregrini*, on the other hand, simply were ordered to renounce their faith or leave.[83] Josephus[84] states further that the consuls punished a great number of Jews aside from those sent to Sardinia or banished from Rome. Those so punished probably were military conscripts who refused to serve on the ground of religious scruple, or who successfully demonstrated their immunity from the obligation of service.[85] Josephus' account also furnishes what seems to be a plausible immediate cause for the harsh treatment of the Jews. A wealthy Roman matron allegedly had been converted to Judaism

[80] G. La Piana, "Foreign Groups in Rome," *Harvard Theological Review*, XX (1927), 344–70.
[81] Tacitus, *Ann.*, II, 85.   [82] Suetonius, *Tib.*, XXXVI.
[83] E. T. Merrill, "The Expulsion of the Jews under Tiberius," *Classical Philology*, XIV (1919), 365–68; La Piana, "Foreign Groups in Rome," in *loc. cit.*, 375.
[84] *Antiquities*, XVIII, iii, 5.
[85] Merrill, "The Expulsion of the Jews under Tiberius," in *loc. cit.*, 365.

and subsequently defrauded of considerable sums, which presumably were to be employed for the reconstruction of the temple in Jerusalem, and the resultant scandal precipitated governmental action.[86]

Priests and devotees of the worship of the Egyptian goddess Isis also were banished in 19, possibly as a result of revelations of the sordid practices that had attended the conversion of a Roman woman of position to the cult.[87] Three years before, astrologers and magicians had been expelled from Italy by a senatorial decree, in all likelihood issued with the full approval of the emperor.[88] These measures, like the efforts to curb the licentiousness of the theater, are indicative of the emperor's solicitude for the preservation of reasonable standards of public morality, and serve further to strengthen the impression of able, conscientious administration in Italy comparable with the excellent government of the provinces.

[86] *Antiquities,* XVIII, iii, 5. Dio, *R.H.,* LVII, xviii, 5, also states that the banishment of the Jews was attributable to their activities in converting Gentiles.

[87] Tacitus, *Ann.,* II, 85; Josephus, *Antiquities,* XVIII, iii, 4-5. W. A. Heidel, "Why were the Jews Banished from Italy in 19 A.D.?" *American Journal of Philology,* XLI (1920), 43-47, suggests that this case was connected with the banishment of the Jews. He believes that the Roman authorities were induced to move against the Jews because they thought that both Jews and devotees of Isis were attempting to encourage temple prostitution among Roman women. See, Z. Zmigryder-Konopka, "Les Romains et la circoncision des Juifs," *Eos,* XXXIII (1930-1931), 339; R. S. Rogers, "Fulvia Paulina C. Sentii Saturnini," *American Journal of Philology,* LIII (1932).

[88] Tacitus, *Ann.,* II, 32-33. See also, *ibid.,* III, 22-24; VI, 29; Dio, *R.H.,* LVII, xxi, 3. R. G. Bone, *Roman Persecution of Non-Christian Religions Before 200 A.D.* (Urbana, Ill., 1937), presents, in the form of a dissertation abstract, a full listing of references to the mention of such persecutions by the ancient historians.

Chapter XI

ECONOMIC CONDITIONS DURING THE REIGN OF TIBERIUS

The age of Tiberius forms part of the "period of incubation during which the assimilation of Latin culture and the material development of the western provinces went on without ceasing."[1] If a single feature characterized the age, it was the tendency toward urbanization[2]—the "formation of a city *bourgeoisie*, of a class of landowners, traders, and industrialists, who resided in the city and developed an energetic business activity on capitalistic lines."[3] In agriculture, this meant the accretion of huge, scientifically managed estates.[4] Tiberius was aware of this tendency,[5] as was a contemporary who has left his observations to posterity. Columella complained that luxury, ambition, avarice, intemperance, and idleness had replaced the old industry. Landowners who formerly had lived on their estates now left their management to over-

---

[1] A. N. Sherwin-White, *The Roman Citizenship* (Oxford, 1939), 180.
[2] M. I. Rostovtzeff, *The Social and Economic History of the Roman Empire* (Oxford, 1926), 82-83.
[3] *Ibid.*, 81-82; T. Frank, *An Economic History of Rome*, 2nd ed. (Baltimore, 1927), 407.
[4] Rostovtzeff, *Social and Economic History*, 89; L. Friedlander, *Roman Life and Manners under the Early Empire*, 7th ed., 4 vols. (New York, 1909), I, 114. Large estates resulted in large measure from indiscriminate leasing of the *ager publicus*. W. L. Westermann, "The Economic Basis of the Decline of Ancient Culture," *American Historical Review*, XX (1915-1916), 739. G. Mickwitz, "Economic Rationalism in Graeco-Roman Agriculture," *English Historical Review*, LII (1927), 587-89, points out that close examination of accounting practices on estates indicates the employment of many unscientific procedures.
[5] Tacitus, *Ann.*, III, 53.

seers, while they lived in the towns and devoted themselves to the pursuit of pleasure. Their wives, instead of engaging in domestic pursuits as they did in earlier times, had become so delicate that they required all sorts of costly articles to sustain themselves.[6]

Industry prospered during the first half of the first century, especially in the provinces.[7] There was a tendency toward large scale production in the manufacture of pottery, glass, silver and bronze ware, furniture, and wine,[8] but, as a general rule, most industrial enterprises were hindered by the slowness of transport, the absence of patent laws, and the continued employment of slaves in domestic manufacture.[9] Freedmen [10] usually managed the industries, and slaves performed most of the labor.[11] Workers in the same industry frequently were grouped into guilds, but there were no regulations concerning methods or apprenticeship, nor was there any attempt to exercise monopolies.[12] No important inventions or new industrial processes were evolved during the period.[13]

Capitalistic agriculture and rejuvenated industry produced a growing volume of commerce.[14] Enduring peace, a uniform currency, and a united empire gave trade an ex-

[6] Columella, *De Re Rustica*, I, i, 3, 6; xii.
[7] Frank, *Economic History of Rome*, 356–57.
[8] *Ibid.*, 271–72.
[9] *Ibid.*, 224; H. J. Loane, *Industry and Commerce of the City of Rome*, in *Johns Hopkins Studies in Historical and Political Science*, LV (1928), 156.
[10] A. M. Duff, *Freedmen in the Early Roman Empire* (Oxford, 1928), 66, 220.
[11] Rostovtzeff, *Social and Economic History*, 100. Tiberius had misgivings about the large number of slaves. Tacitus, *Ann.*, III, 53.
[12] J. P. Waltzing, *Étude historique sur les corporations professionelles chez les romains* (Louvain, 1895), 194, 478.
[13] Frank, *Economic History of Rome*, 408.
[14] Rostovtzeff, *Social and Economic History*, 91. The stigma attached to trade considerably diminished during the early empire. Charlesworth, *Trade-Routes and Commerce*, 236.

ECONOMIC CONDITIONS

cellent opportunity to develop.[15] Goods were transported across the seas and along the many roads to be sold at fairs and markets.[16] Not only was there an extensive trade within the empire, but also a considerable commercial contact with lands bordering upon the Roman world, and there was at least a modicum of organization among the merchants based on national or religious ties.[17]

The various regions of the empire evinced a general uniformity of prosperity. Italy enjoyed at least a modest prosperity;[18] her fields produced grain, wine, and olive oil, and the workshops of Campania and northern Italy were still active, stimulated as they were by immigration of artisans from the Aegean area.[19] In central and south Italy there appears to have been a considerable cattle- and sheep-raising industry.[20] Production does not seem to have been curtailed, even with the rise of provincial competition, for local consumption was able to absorb the output.[21] In fact, Italy was forced to import many commodities not produced in the peninsula in sufficient quantities. Tacitus quotes Tiberius' concern at the fact that

---

[15] Friedlander, *Life and Manners*, I, 304; H. Mattingly, *Roman Coins* (London, 1928), 184. Roman tariffs were low since they were designed for revenue only. M. R. Cagnat, *Les impots indirects chez les romains* (Paris, 1882), 4.

[16] Columella, *De Re Rustica*, I, 8; Charlesworth, *Trade-Routes and Commerce*, 9-11.

[17] Tacitus, *Ann.*, II, 62. For commercial organization, see, V. Parvan, *Die Nationalität der Kaufleute in römische Kaiserreiche* (Breslau, 1909), 123-26. The large number of coins of Tiberian stamp found in India suggest a sizeable volume of trade with that region. It is possible, however, that later emperors struck Tiberian pieces for use in this trade. E. H. Warmington, *The Commerce Between the Roman Empire and India* (Cambridge, 1928), 39, 78-79, 285.

[18] Frank, *Economic History of Rome*, 410; Rostovtzeff, *Social and Economic History*, 99.

[19] Frank, *Economic History of Rome*, 220-37, 418, 421, 424. For the immigration of Greek craftsmen, see, H. Gummerus, "Die römische Industrie," *Klio*, XV (1917), 259.

[20] Frank, *Economic History of Rome*, 411, 421, 424.

[21] *Ibid.*, 423.

Italy was dependent upon the provinces for sustenance and points out that the emperor had to import more grain than was necessary in the reign of Augustus.[22] In industry there was a tendency toward the employment of free labor;[23] in agriculture, however, Italian landowners were inclined to let their land to tenants,[24] although large scale slave labor was still quite prevalent.[25]

Gaul probably was the most economically undeveloped of the Roman provinces, although under Tiberius the Gallic tribes were afforded broadened opportunities to assimilate Roman culture.[26] While there seems to have been a slight economic recession at the beginning of Tiberius' reign, the Gallic provinces were in the main prosperous.[27] The growth of cities that had characterized Augustus' reign slackened, but the movement did not come to a complete halt because many of the garrisons established along the Rhine quickly became the nuclei for towns.[28] The few industries of the region were confined to metal work and pottery making, of which the Graufenesque ware is the best known.[29] Agricultural endeavors, pursued on

---

[22] Tacitus, *Ann.*, III, 54; IV, 13. The growing need for grain importations probably was attributable to the increase of population. Friedlander, *Life and Manners*, IV, 21. It has been estimated that Italy required some 150,000,000 bushels of grain. If she imported 7 per cent of this from Africa, 3½ per cent from Egypt, 1¼ per cent from Sicily, and a smaller amount from Spain she must have produced about 87 per cent of her own needs. Frank, *Economic History of Rome*, 430. See also, Scramuzza, "Roman Sicily," in *loc. cit.*, 349-50; Van Nostrand, "Roman Spain," in *loc. cit.*, 175; R. M. Haywood, "Roman Africa," in Frank (ed.), *An Economic Survey of Ancient Rome*, 43-44.

[23] Frank, *Economic History of Rome*, 209.

[24] Columella, *De Re Rustica*, I, 7.

[25] *Ibid.*; Tacitus, *Ann.*, IV, 27. Debtors sometimes were seized and forced to work on their creditors' estates. See, R. H. Barrow, *Slavery in the Roman Empire* (New York, 1928), 74-75.

[26] Grenier, "La Gaule Romaine," in *loc. cit.*, 509, 518, 528; W. T. Arnold, *Studies in Roman Imperialism* (Manchester, 1906), 92.

[27] *Ibid.*; Charlesworth, *Trade-Routes and Commerce*, 183.

[28] Grenier, "La Gaule Romaine," in *loc. cit.*, 488, 506-507.

[29] *Ibid.*, 471, 527-28.

ECONOMIC CONDITIONS

increasingly larger estates,[30] produced, besides what was raised for sustenance, hides, wool, and exportable quantities of cheese.[31]

During the early empire Spain prospered, as wealth and population simultaneously increased.[32] Diversified industry and commerce, unhindered by the government, flourished.[33] From the soil came wheat (especially in the Baetis valley), barley, peas, artichokes, lettuce, flax, olives, grapes, fruits, and nuts.[34] The mines yielded quantities of lead, iron, tin, silver, and gold,[35] while "the collection and preparation of dyes, drugs and ointments, formed a minor but highly remunerative industry." [36] Nor were livestock, fish, and bees neglected.[37] Practically every item enumerated was exported,[38] either in natural or processed form, from ports like Gades or New Carthage.[39] Spain enjoyed a favorable balance of trade; her relatively few imports included pottery, slaves, and articles of luxury.[40]

Augustus bequeathed to Tiberius a much more prosperous Sicily than he himself had acquired,[41] although the province had lost much of the commercial and industrial

---

[30] *Ibid.*, 539.
[31] Frank, *Economic History of Rome*, 312; Charlesworth, *Trade-Routes and Commerce*, 189.
[32] Frank, *Economic History of Rome*, 366; Van Nostrand, "Roman Spain," in *loc. cit.*, 148.
[33] Van Nostrand, "Roman Spain," in *loc. cit.*, 185, 196–97.
[34] Pliny, *Natural History*, XXXVII, 203; III, 7; XVIII, 20, 75; XIX, 1, 35, 152; XV, 8; XIV, 41; Columella, *De Re Rustica*, II, 11; XI, 3; V, 8; Strabo, *Geography*, III, 2, 6.
[35] Van Nostrand, "Roman Spain," in *loc. cit.*, 178; Pliny, *N.H.*, III, 30; XXXIII, 34.
[36] Van Nostrand, "Roman Spain," in *loc. cit.*, 179.
[37] Strabo, *Geography*, III, i, 8; ii, 6–7; iii, 1, 5, 7; iv, 5, 6, 11; v, 4; Pliny, *N.H.*, VIII, 75, 166, 170, 191; IX, 49, 68; XXX, 45; XXXI, 94; XXXII, 60; Columella, *De Re Rustica*, VI, 27; VII, 1; VIII, 16.
[38] Van Nostrand, "Roman Spain," in *loc. cit.*, 184.
[39] *Ibid.*, 185–86.   [40] *Ibid.*, 185–87.
[41] Scramuzza, "Roman Sicily," in *loc. cit.*, 372.

importance it had possessed during the Republican era, and was reverting to an agricultural economy,[42] practiced on estates that were becoming progressively larger.[43] The chief products of the island were wheat,[44] wine, livestock, fish,[45] sulphur, bitumen and pitch, alum, slate, and stone.[46] The most important industry was the manufacture of woolens.[47] There was a brisk trade between Sicily and Italy and Africa.[48]

The province of Africa enjoyed an embryonic prosperity which betokened the halcyon days of the following century.[49] The Roman sphere was expanding [50]—one might say that parts of Africa, like Gaul, were experiencing a frontier age. The region was pre-eminently agricultural; here, too, estates tended to increase in size.[51] A combination of free and slave labor produced principally cereals,[52] oil, wine, figs, livestock, dyes, and stone.[53]

[42] *Ibid.*, 368.   [43] *Ibid.*, 363.

[44] *Ibid.*, 349–50. "We do not know how much wheat Sicily sent to Rome in the first century of the empire. Tenney Frank's conjecture that she supplied one per cent of the entire demand of the peninsula, that is, about 1,500,000 bushels, represents 1,663,000 bushels less than the total exportable amount at the time of Cicero and postulates a shrinkage of more than fifty per cent in the cultivation of the wheat area. We should probably think in terms of larger exports, perhaps one and one-half per cent of the entire demand of Italy." Rostovtzeff, *Social and Economic History*, 505, n.26. See, Scramuzza, "Roman Sicily," in *loc. cit.*, 349.

[45] Mullets from Sicily were highly prized. Suetonius, *Tib.*, XXXIV, makes the unbelievable statement that three sold for 30,000 *sesterces*.

[46] Scramuzza, "Roman Sicily," in *loc. cit.*, 350 ff.

[47] *Ibid.*, 355. Tiberius' law against the use of silk may have benefited the industry. Tacitus, *Ann.*, II, 33.

[48] Scramuzza, "Roman Sicily," in *loc. cit.*, 357. See, Tacitus, *Ann.*, IV, 13.

[49] Haywood, "Roman Africa," in *loc. cit.*, 73.

[50] *Ibid.*, 34. See, Tacitus, *Ann.*, II, 52; III, 73.

[51] Haywood, "Roman Africa," in *loc. cit.*, 39 ff. In the reign of Nero six men allegedly owned half of Africa. Pliny, *N.H.*, XVIII, 35.

[52] Haywood, "Roman Africa," in *loc. cit.*, 39, 43.

[53] *Ibid.*, 49.

There appears to have been a scarcity of industrial and commercial organizations, except for the cloth industry,[54] although many "of the products, such as olives, grapes, wool, and fish were processed before being exported."[55] The chief exports were grain, oil, and pottery;[56] the imports included manufactured articles of luxury, cheap wholesale products, and particularly lamps.[57] Cities like Carthage, Lepcis, and Thapsus were the chief commercial centers.[58]

"The period of the civil wars with its heavy drain on Greece and Macedonia was followed by an era of peace such as these countries had never experienced." Although the literary sources paint a rather gloomy picture of the times, the archaeological evidence contradicts them.[59] There were fewer cities, now that an appreciable part of the region had turned to agriculture and grazing.[60] Grain, wine, honey, flax and hemp, livestock, stone, and dyes were the principal products, and all of these, except grain, seem to have been exported to some extent.[61] The mineral wealth of the land was exploited by the imperial government.[62]

Aided by prolonged peace, the provinces which composed Asia Minor enjoyed a moderate prosperity during this era.[63] Local building programs, revival of festivals, appearance of philanthropists, and resumption of local coinage denoted an improvement of conditions.[64] Cap-

[54] *Ibid.*, 73.   [55] *Ibid.*, 55, 59.   [56] *Ibid.*, 61-62.
[57] *Ibid.*, 64. Strabo, *Geography*, III, 2, 6, mentions a brisk trade between Africa and Ostia. See, Tacitus, *Ann.*, IV, 13.
[58] Haywood, "Roman Africa," in *loc. cit.*, 69.
[59] J. A. O. Larsen, "Roman Greece," in Frank (ed.), *An Economic Survey of Ancient Rome*, IV, 465.
[60] *Ibid.*, 467, 471.   [61] *Ibid.*, 483 ff.   [62] *Ibid.*, 460-65.
[63] Frank, *Economic History of Rome*, 314.
[64] T. R. S. Broughton, "Roman Asia Minor," in Frank (ed.), *An Economic Survey of Ancient Rome*, IV, 712-13, 716-33.

padocia was prosperous enough to permit tax reductions by Tiberius.[65] Progressive urbanization continued,[66] and places like Ephesus, Nicaea, Smyrna, Cos, and Rhodes thrived.[67] There were few centers of great wealth, few slaves, and an absence of capitalistic development.[68] From Asia Minor came grain, salt fish, timber, dried fruit, precious stones, wine, metals, tapestries, draperies and rugs; [69] the region enjoyed a favorable trade balance.[70]

"The most important trade routes of the ancient world passed through the Roman Near East." [71] Syria was ideally located to partake of the profits therefrom, for her ports connected with all the empire.[72] To the lands east of the empire went—through Syrian marts like Seleuceia, Tyre, Antioch, Palmyra, and Damascus—metal goods, minerals, and articles of craftsmanship, besides slaves, corals, textiles, and wine.[73] To the west went textiles, embroideries, furs, hides, silk cloths, perfumes, drugs, and spices.[74] Syria itself imported pottery, dried fish, wine, and various foodstuffs,[75] and produced wheat and barley, flax, hemp, cotton, vegetables, lumber, olives, dates, figs, grapes, livestock, glassware, parchment, cloth, perfumes, and drugs.[76] To the numerous cities already existing were added four new ones upon the accession of Tiberius.[77]

[65] Tacitus, *Ann.*, II, 42, 52.
[66] Broughton, "Roman Asia Minor," in *loc. cit.*, 733.
[67] *Ibid.*, 709; Tacitus, *Ann.*, IV, 55-56.
[68] Frank, *Economic History of Rome*, 314.
[69] *Ibid.*, 311; Broughton, "Roman Asia Minor," in *loc. cit.*, Chap. I.
[70] Broughton, "Roman Asia Minor," in *loc. cit.*, 888.
[71] Heichelheim, "Roman Syria," in *loc. cit.*, 198.
[72] *Ibid.* [73] *Ibid.*, 200.
[74] *Ibid.*, 201. A party of merchants bearing news of Germanicus arrived in Rome from Syria in A.D. 19. Tacitus, *Ann.*, II, 82.
[75] Heichelheim, "Roman Syria," in *loc. cit.*, 201-202.
[76] *Ibid.*, 127-30, 131, 133, 134-35, 138, 152-56. See, Bouchier, *Syria as a Roman Province*, 162. The actual mineral resources of Syria itself were meager. Charlesworth, *Trade-Routes and Commerce*, 44.
[77] Josephus, *Jewish Wars*, II, 9.

ECONOMIC CONDITIONS

During the reign of Tiberius, Egypt, and in particular Alexandria, was prosperous.[78] It is true that the standard of living was probably lower there than elsewhere, at least for the average worker, but wages were increasing.[79] There were good Nile floods during the period,[80] and favorable results had come from the partial liberation of industry from the monopolistic system that had characterized the Ptolemaic regime.[81] Commerce, especially with the East, was flourishing,[82] and a reduction of tariffs by Augustus had made possible a virtually unhampered trade.[83] The heavy tribute exacted by the Roman government was balanced by the favorable balance of trade, the great fertility of the soil, and Roman expenditures in the country.[84] The chief product of the Nile valley was grain,[85] which was cultivated on large estates by slaves (who were relatively rare), hired labor, tenants, or sharecroppers.[86] Industrial establishments produced cloth, glass,

---

[78] Johnson, "Roman Egypt," in *loc. cit.*, 253. Roman government was beneficial to production, since centralized control facilitated irrigation. But the wealth derived from agriculture benefited Romans and Jews rather than Egyptians. Anti-Semitic riots under Caligula indicated local discontent. J. G. Milne, "The Ruin of Egypt by Roman Mismanagement," *Journal of Roman Studies*, XVII (1927), 6–7.

[79] Johnson, "Roman Egypt," in *loc. cit.*, 306.

[80] *Ibid.*, 17.

[81] *Ibid.*, 327–33. Oil and papyrus seem to have been privately produced. There were private and state-owned breweries; goldsmiths and bricklayers were controlled by licensing; the weaving industry probably was state-controlled and privately operated. *Ibid.*, 328–29, 332, 332–33. Charlesworth, *Trade-Routes and Commerce*, 26, concludes that little trade was left to private enterprise.

[82] Johnson, "Roman Egypt," in *loc. cit.*, 353.

[83] Frank, *Economic History of Rome*, 394, 406.

[84] Johnson, "Roman Egypt," in *loc. cit.*, 353. The grain sent to Rome came from tribute and from "royal farmers" on imperial property. Charlesworth, *Trade-Routes and Commerce*, 30.

[85] Columella, *De Re Rustica*, II, 2, estimated a yield of 20–25 fold. Some 20,000,000 bushels went annually to Rome. Charlesworth, *Trade-Routes and Commerce*, 30.

[86] Johnson, "Roman Egypt," in *loc. cit.*, 277; Rostovtzeff, *Social and Economic History*, 267.

papyrus, and drugs in exportable quantities.[87] On the other hand, it was necessary to import some lumber, metals, oil, wine, and dyes.[88]

Augustus apparently had succeeded in fulfilling his promises to restore peace and prosperity, and the provinces especially had reason for gratitude.[89] "Credit has been restored in the forum," wrote Velleius, "justice, equity, and industry, long buried in oblivion, have been restored to the state.... When was the price of grain more reasonable, or when were the blessings of peace greater?"[90] In A.D. 16 there was an extended debate in the Senate anent the "present pitch of splendor." It finally was resolved that table plate should not be manufactured in solid gold, and that the wearing of silk garments should be restricted to women. Tiberius wisely realized the futility of restrictive legislation when the prevailing economy could support extravagance, and refused to recommend censorial measures.[91] Again in A.D. 22 "There was uneasiness at the prospect of stern measures against the luxury which had broken all bounds and extended to every object on which money can be squandered."[92] The senators referred the problem to the emperor, who questioned the wisdom of enacting measures that would be practically impossible to enforce. He replied to the Senate in writing: "For on what am I to make my first effort at prohibition and retrenchment to the ancient standard? On the infinite expanse of our villas? The miracles of bronze and canvas: The promiscuous dress of male and female—and the specially female extravagance by which for the sake of jewels, our

---

[87] Johnson, "Roman Egypt," in *loc. cit.*, 339; Frank, *Economic History of Rome*, 406.
[88] Johnson, "Roman Egypt," in *loc. cit.*, 350–52.
[89] Rostovtzeff, *Social and Economic History*, 49, 52.
[90] Velleius, *R.H.*, II, 126.   [91] Tacitus, *Ann.*, II, 38; *infra*, 245–46.
[92] *Ibid.*, III, 51; *infra*, 228–29.

ECONOMIC CONDITIONS

wealth is transported to alien or hostile countries?" He concluded by saying that if he attempted to enforce sumptuary legislation, he would incur obloquy rather than praise even from the senators themselves.[93]

That conditions failed to vary from this prosperous standard would be impossible to maintain. There were sporadic periods of depression in scattered parts of the empire during the era. The imperial treasury was in financial straits at the start of Tiberius' reign.[94] In A.D. 15 there were complaints from Macedonia and Achaea, obviously because of financial mismanagement.[95] Judaea and Syria claimed to be exhausted by their burdens in 17 and asked for a diminution of their usual tribute.[96] Germanicus in 18 brought relief to several cities and provinces.[97] The next year there was a "sudden and terrible famine" in Egypt,[98] one result of which was to raise the price of grain in Rome, for mention is made that the Romans protested against the high price of this commodity.[99] A grain shortage in Megalopolis in the early part of Tiberius' reign possibly came at this time also.[100] The year 21 saw "an incipient rebellion among the heavily indebted communities of the Gallic provinces." [101] Two years later the populace of Rome suffered as a result of exorbitant food prices, and the emperor spared neither pains nor expense to secure adequate supplies.[102] In 32 the excessive price of grain almost ended in rioting,[103] and the next year there was a

---

[93] *Ibid.*, III, 53. See, Suetonius, *Caligula*, XXXVII.
[94] Suetonius, *Caligula*, XLIX; Tacitus, *Ann.*, I, 78.
[95] Tacitus, *Ann.*, I, 76; Arnold, *Roman Imperialism*, 206-207.
[96] Tacitus, *Ann.*, II, 42.   [97] *Ibid.*, 54.
[98] *Ibid.*, 59; Suetonius, *Tib.*, LII.   [99] Tacitus, *Ann.*, II, 87.
[100] Larsen, "Roman Greece," in *loc. cit.*, 483.
[101] Tacitus, *Ann.*, III, 11. Many communities had started building programs far more pretentious than their resources permitted and were in a serious financial predicament as a result. Grenier, "La Gaule Romaine," in *loc. cit.*, 514 ff.
[102] Tacitus, *Ann.*, IV, 6.   [103] *Ibid.*, VI, 13.

financial panic in Rome of sufficient gravity to induce the emperor to make available 100,000,000 *sesterces* to alleviate the situation.[104]

Tiberius inherited a system of governmental finance wherein the emperor's private fortune was confused with the income of the state.[105] "During his reign there was a continuation of the gradual development of bureaucracy, the elimination of the Senate from the work of administration, and the concentration of it in the hands of the emperors. The most important side of the work was the management by the emperor of all the resources of the state, the exclusive right to dispose of the income of the Roman Empire, and to organize its expenditure. The assessment of taxes, both direct and indirect, the collection of the indirect, the management of the domains of the Roman state, were all gradually concentrated in the hands of the imperial administration." [106] Capable freedmen were widely used in administrative posts, although under Tiberius they never dominated the system.[107]

Tiberius apparently was a good financial administrator. He was generous but careful; during the early part of his

[104] *Ibid.*, 16–17; Dio, *R.H.*, LVIII, xxi; Suetonius, *Tib.*, XLVIII.
[105] Rostovtzeff, *Social and Economic History*, 57.
[106] *Ibid.*, 77–78. The *libertus a rationibus* existed first as a title in the reign of Tiberius. With the growth of the *fiscus* this official became "in effect the Chancellor of the Exchequer." A. D. Winspear and L. K. Geweke, *Augustus and the Reconstruction of Roman Government and Society*, in *University of Wisconsin Studies in the Social Sciences and History*, XXIV (Madison, Wis., 1935), 118; Duff, *Freedmen in the Early Empire*, 153. An official of the emperor, probably called *acceptor a subscriptionibus*, during Tiberius' reign received petitions and requests from all parts of the empire. Winspear and Geweke, *Augustus and the Reconstruction of Roman Government and Society*, 119. Cf., Suetonius, *Tib.*, XXX. The emperor refused to allow Italian cities to collect their own port dues. Abbott and Johnson, *Municipal Administration in the Roman Empire*, 147. "Many states and individuals were deprived of old immunities and the right of working mines and collecting revenues." Suetonius, *Tib.*, XLIX.
[107] Duff, *Freedmen in the Early Empire*, 176.

ECONOMIC CONDITIONS 245

reign he personally supervised the disbursement of money in an effort to prevent official abuses.[108] He discontinued the practice of publishing the accounts of the empire,[109] but many of his expenditures are recorded elsewhere. One might expect them to approach the scale of Augustus if Tiberius' praises of his predecessor in his funeral oration are indicative of his own predilections, for he pointedly recalled how Augustus "had provided public works, largesses, games, festivals, amnesty, food in abundance."[110] And if the words of a contemporary may be believed, such was the case, for "the munificence of the emperor claims for its province the losses inflicted by fortune not merely on private citizens but on whole cities,"[111] and "how often did he honor the people with his largesses."[112] Tiberius paid the bequests of Augustus' will, which amounted to 260 *sesterces* per man,[113] even doubling the legacies left to the soldiers.[114] When Germanicus celebrated his triumph on his return from the German campaigns, Tiberius gave, in the name of his nephew, "a distribution to the populace of three hundred sesterces per man."[115] He refused, however, to pay the bequests of Livia's will.[116] After the fall of Sejanus, he distributed 1000 *denarii* to each of the praetorians for refraining from supporting the prefect at the critical time of his denunciation before the Senate, and gifts were sent to the legions of Syria for the same reason.[117] In 33 he came to the rescue during a financial crisis by providing interest-free loans from a fund of 100,000,000 *sesterces*.[118] To these extraordinary expenses must be added the occasional

---

[108] Dio, *R.H.*, LVII, x.   [109] Suetonius, *Caligula*, XVI.
[110] Dio, *R.H.*, LVI, xli.   [111] Velleius, *R.H.*, II, 116.
[112] *Ibid.*, 129.   [113] Dio, *R.H.*, LVII, xiv.
[114] Tacitus, *Ann.*, I, 8; Suetonius, *Tib.*, XLVIII.
[115] Tacitus, *Ann.*, I, 42.
[116] Dio, *R.H.*, LVIII, i; Suetonius, *Tib.*, XLVIII.
[117] Suetonius, *Tib.*, XLVIII.   [118] *Ibid.*; Tacitus, *Ann.*, VI, 17.

cash bonuses he granted to senators facing destitution.[119] On the other hand, the emperor was opposed to expensive games and shows, even if sponsored by others,[120] and he objected to the practice of New Year's donatives.[121]

In the matter of building expenses, Tiberius is accused of having been niggardly. "While emperor he constructed no magnificent public works," says Suetonius,[122] and Tacitus adds that "he was far from extravagant in building on his own behalf and even on the public account." [123] Both authorities agree, however, that he erected a temple to Augustus [124] and rebuilt Pompey's theater.[125] Dio relates that Tiberius finished many of Augustus' buildings and spent much "for the common good, either rebuilding or adorning practically all the public works," [126] although he refused to have an honorary arch to Livia erected at public expense.[127] In 16 the emperor aided the victims of a conflagration in rebuilding,[128] and after a fire in 27 had ravaged the Caelian Hill section of the capital city, he distributed money to the sufferers in proportion to the losses sustained.[129] In 36 when another fire had destroyed part of Rome, he advanced 100,000 *sesterces* to help defray the cost of repairing the damage.[130] In the provinces, too, there was some building activity. In Sicily the emperor repaired a temple on Mount Eryx,[131] and, on

---

[119] Tacitus, *Ann.*, II, 37-38; Dio, *R.H.*, LVII, x; Suetonius, *Tib.*, XLVIII.
[120] G. Jennison, *Animals for Show and Pleasure in Ancient Rome* (Manchester, 1937), 68.
[121] Dio, *R.H.*, LVII, xvii.   [122] Suetonius, *Tib.*, XLVIII.
[123] Tacitus, *Ann.*, VI, 45.
[124] It was not complete in A.D. 35. See, Mattingly, *Coins of the Roman Empire*, I, cxxxvii, n.4.
[125] Tacitus, *Ann.*, III, 72; VI, 45; Suetonius, *Tib.*, XLVII.
[126] Dio, *R.H.*, LVI, xlvi.   [127] *Ibid.*, LVIII, i.
[128] *Ibid.*, LVII, xvi.
[129] Tacitus, *Ann.*, IV, 64; Suetonius, *Tib.*, XLVIII.
[130] Tacitus, *Ann.*, VI, 45; Dio, *R.H.*, LVIII, xxvi.
[131] Scramuzza, "Roman Sicily," in *loc. cit.*, 372, 376.

ECONOMIC CONDITIONS 247

more than one occasion, he aided cities of Asia Minor in rebuilding programs after they had been devastated by earthquakes.[132] There is record of his having dedicated the "pronaos to Aphrodite" at Denderah in Egypt,[133] and he is credited with having built a wall around Antioch to protect the city from landslides, as well as a temple, theater, and other public structures.[134] In Judaea an aqueduct was built during his reign to carry water to Jerusalem.[135] There was considerable building and repairing of roads during the reign, particularly in Spain.[136] In view of the facts cited, it is difficult to acquiesce in any charge of parsimony leveled against the emperor.

None of the emperors dared to encroach on the right of the Romans to free food and entertainment. "They limited themselves to reducing and fixing the numbers of participants in the distribution of corn and to organizing an efficient system of administration." [137] Tiberius had charge of the grain supply for a time during the reign of Augustus,[138] and hence was familar with the distributive organization. Perhaps to him can be attributed some of the changes in the relief system which resulted in its transfer entirely into the hands of the *fiscus* by the time of Claudius.[139] That he interested himself in the problem is indicated by his expressed misgivings over Rome's dependence upon imported grain,[140] his statement that he was compelled to import more grain than Augustus,[141] and the fact that he took measures to ensure an adequate

---

[132] Tacitus, *Ann.*, II, 47; IV, 13; Dio, *R.H.*, LVII, xvii.
[133] Johnson, "Roman Egypt," in *loc. cit.*, 641, n.4.
[134] *Infra*, 212-13.   [135] Josephus, *Jewish Wars*, II, ix.
[136] *Infra*, 211-12.
[137] Rostovtzeff, *Social and Economic History*, 80. See, Suetonius, *Caligula*, XXXIX.
[138] Suetonius, *Tib.*, VIII.
[139] A. Momigliano, *Claudius the Emperor and His Achievement* (Oxford, 1934), 49.
[140] Tacitus, *Ann.*, III, 54.   [141] *Ibid.*, IV, 13.

food supply for Rome,[142] even going so far as to guarantee to the sellers of grain a subsidy of two *sesterces* per peck in order to keep down the price.[143]

Tiberius inherited from Augustus a taxation system in which the burdens were reasonably well distributed, although Italy paid no direct taxes.[144] References to taxation during the reign are usually too general to be very informative. Tacitus' statement that there were no new impositions obviously refers to "the corn tribute, the monies from indirect taxation and other public revenues which are mentioned in the same chapter." [145] He also mentions a 1 per cent sales tax which had been in existence since the Civil Wars,[146] and its incidence undoubtedly was universal. At the time that Cappadocia became a province of the Roman empire, this tax was reduced to ½ per cent, at least in Italy, for the remainder of the reign.[147] There are references to Syrian taxes under Tiberius, and Judaea paid a poll tax of one *denarius*.[148] We also know that in A.D. 36 Vitellius abolished a market duty on Jerusalem which had existed from the time of the Jewish kings to the first procurators.[149] There is no reason to suppose that the *tributum soli* (12 ½ per cent of the grain harvest) which was imposed in A.D. 7 had been rescinded.[150] For the other provinces, the references are

---

[142] *Ibid.*, 6.   [143] *Ibid.*, II, 87.
[144] Frank, *Economic History of Rome*, 491.
[145] Tacitus, *Ann.*, IV, 6.   [146] *Ibid.*, I, 68.
[147] *Ibid.*, II, 42. Dio, *R.H.*, LVIII, xvi, states that the tax again was raised to 1 per cent in A.D. 31, but the evidence from Suetonius, *Caligula*, XVI, to the effect that Caligula abolished the tax of ½ per cent, plus a coin commemorating this act, supports the view we have taken. See, Cagnat, *Les impots indirects chez les romains*, 229–30. Cf., Mattingly, *Coins of the Roman Empire*, I, cxlvii; *id.*, *The Imperial Civil Service of Rome*, 8.
[148] Mark, XII, 13–17; Matthew, XXII, 15–22; Luke, XX, 2–26.
[149] Josephus, *Antiquities*, XVIII, iv, 3.
[150] Heichelheim, "Roman Syria," in *loc. cit.*, 234.

most indefinite. The procurator of Asia was expected to collect "the customary revenues," [151] and Tiberius reduced the "royal tribute" of Cappadocia.[152] Achaea and Macedonia protested their high taxes,[153] while the emperor was accused of having deprived states and individuals of the right to collect revenues.[154] Judaea and Syria pressed "for a diminution of the tribute," [155] and Tiberius made provision for the tributes of the tetrarch of Philip, brother of Herod.[156] Tacitus speaks of taxes due the national and imperial treasuries from the cities of Asia Minor,[157] and Suetonius refers to governors who recommended "burdensome taxes." [158] The instigators of the short-lived Sacrovir rebellion in Gaul tried to secure support by pointing to the "continuous tributes" imposed upon the people,[159] but again, as in other references, no information is given as to the nature of the levies. In spite of the dearth of specific information, it can be suggested that at this time the provinces paid a tax on land and a capitation tax; it is impossible to determine either the rate or the total from the early empire.[160] The usual indirect taxes included a 2 to 2 ½ per cent transport duty levied on goods as they passed through various customs areas, 5 per cent tax on inheritances and slave manumissions, and the sales tax of 1 per cent (4 per cent on slaves).[161] The cost of maintaining roads fell upon the country through which the highway passed, and this was a very unpopular burden.[162]

---

[151] Dio, *R.H.*, LVII, x.
[152] Tacitus, *Ann.*, II, 56.
[153] *Ibid.*, I, 66.
[154] Suetonius, *Tib.*, XLIX.
[155] Tacitus, *Ann.*, II, 42.
[156] Josephus, *Antiquities*, XVIII, iv.
[157] Tacitus, *Ann.*, II, 47.
[158] Suetonius, *Tib.*, XXXII.
[159] Tacitus, *Ann.*, III, 40; *infra*, 197–99.
[160] Grenier, "La Gaule Romaine," in *loc. cit.*, 500.
[161] Cagnat, *Les impots indirects chez les romains*, 1-2, 46, 69, 70, 80, 153, 175, 227, 232–33.
[162] Charlesworth, *Trade-Routes and Commerce*, 230.

Besides revenue from taxation, there was a sizeable income from bequests [163] and from the possessions of the emperor.[164] While at first Tiberius had few estates in Italy,[165] his possessions there and elsewhere were increased by confiscations later in the reign.[166] He had inherited large holdings in Sicily,[167] and the estates of Livia and Germanicus in Asia Minor indicate that there were imperial possessions in that region.[168] Indeed, the emperor himself stated that his procurator in Asia had charge of his slaves and private funds in that province.[169] In Cappadocia the emperor probably owned the former possessions of the native royal house,[170] and these were no doubt considerable since tax reductions in Italy and the provinces followed their acquisition, and such reductions could only have been possible if considerable revenues accrued directly from imperial estates.[171] The Thracian Chersonese was private imperial property.[172] But most extensive of all were the imperial possessions in Egypt,[173] even though Augustus had sold much of his property to Roman citizens.[174] In Spain there were a few imperial olive groves.[175] Tiberius inherited the ownership of mining

[163] Cagnat, *Les impots indirects chez les romains*, 176–77.
[164] O. Hirschfeld, "Der Grundbesitz der römischen Kaiser," *Kleine Schriften*, 517–22, 528, 541, 545, 553–54, 586–87; T. Frank, "Dominium in 'solo provinciale' and 'Ager Publicus,'" *Journal of Roman Studies*, XVII (1927), 160–61.
[165] Tacitus, *Ann.*, IV, 6.
[166] Suetonius, *Tib.*, XLIX; Dio, *R.H.*, LVIII, xvi.
[167] Scramuzza, "Roman Sicily," in *loc. cit.*, 365; *C.I.L.*, X, 7489.
[168] Broughton, "Roman Asia Minor," in *loc. cit.*, 648–49.
[169] *Ibid*. Cf., Dio, *R.H.*, LVII, xxiii.
[170] Tacitus, *Ann.*, II, 64.
[171] Broughton, "Roman Asia Minor," in *loc. cit.*, 650–51.
[172] Tacitus, *Ann.*, II, 64.
[173] Johnson, "Roman Egypt," in *loc. cit.*, 481 ff. See also, H. Stuart Jones, *Fresh Light on Roman Bureaucracy* (Oxford, 1920), 15–16.
[174] Frank, "Dominium in 'solo provinciale' and 'Ager Publicus,'" in *loc. cit.*, 159.
[175] Van Nostrand, "Roman Spain," in *loc. cit.*, 198.

ECONOMIC CONDITIONS

properties scattered in Spain, Gaul, Asia Minor, Dalmatia, Noricum, and Pannonia,[176] and proceeded to augment them by confiscations. He thus began a process which ultimately resulted in the ownership of all mines by the emperors.[177] Mention also must be made of his seizure of the treasure of Vonones, king of Armenia, when he sought refuge in Antioch.[178]

In charge of the returns from these personal possessions were the emperor's own procurators working under the *procurator a rationibus*.[179] In the matter of the collection of the regular taxes, there was a tendency during Tiberius' reign toward the removal of the tax-farming companies from their part in the system.[180] This change cannot have been very drastic, for Tacitus states that the grain tribute, the indirect taxes, and other revenues "were handled by companies of Roman knights," at least as late as A.D. 23, and he notes no change in the procedure during the latter years of the reign.[181] Suetonius mentions the fact that some new taxes of Caligula were levied "at first through the publicans," as though that were the usual method.[182] It is known that in the early part of the first century the customs duties of 2 per cent "were farmed to a group of private citizens." [183] Rostovtzeff states that in those instances in which the taxes still were farmed out, imperial procurators supervised their collection.[184] Yet there is some evidence which tends to support the view that tax

---

[176] Arnold, *Roman Imperialism*, 146; Van Nostrand, "Roman Spain," in *loc. cit.*, 163.
[177] Van Nostrand, "Roman Spain," in *loc. cit.*, 166; Tacitus, *Ann.*, VI, 19.
[178] Suetonius, *Tib.*, XLIX.
[179] Winspear and Geweke, *Augustus and the Reconstruction of Roman Government and Society*, 122.
[180] Rostovtzeff, *Social and Economic History*, 330.
[181] Tacitus, *Ann.*, IV, 6.   [182] Suetonius, *Caligula*, XL.
[183] Van Nostrand, "Roman Spain," in *loc. cit.*, 146.
[184] Rostovtzeff, *Social and Economic History*, 467.

collecting was done directly by imperial officials. Cassius Dio states that "in those days officials administering the imperial funds were not allowed to do anything more than collect the customary revenues." [185] In A.D. 44, a few years after Tiberius' death, the governor of Baetica was "summoned and expelled from the Senate because he had sent too little grain to the soldiers then serving in Mauretania." [186] In the first part of the century the 5 per cent inheritance tax was collected by the imperial procurators.[187] The poll and land taxes of the Roman Near East were collected by officials during the principate.[188] Tiberius' warning to an overzealous governor that it was better to shear a flock than to skin it [189] would indicate that the governor was directly concerned with tax collection. Finally, the cadastre made in Africa for the regions acquired as a result of the war with Tacfarinas suggests that the government was the collecting agency in that province.[190]

Augustus had set up a permanent bimetallic coinage based on the gold *aureus* and the silver *denarius*. He provided provincial currency with the *aes* of baser metals for Gaul, Asia, Syria, and Egypt, and encouraged the issue of small coins over the whole empire.[191] The Senate's share of minting was restricted to copper coinage for Italy.[192] Tiberius adhered closely to the Augustan system.[193] A severe restriction of local coinage in the West was virtually the only important change inaugurated by the Tiberean regime.[194] After the Sacrovir revolt in Gaul and that of Tacfarinas in Africa, local issues were restricted

[185] Dio, *R.H.*, LVII, xxiii.
[186] *Ibid.*, LX, xxiv.
[187] *C.I.L.*, II, 2029.
[188] Heichelheim, "Roman Syria," in *loc. cit.*, 234.
[189] Suetonius, *Tib.*, XXXII.
[190] *Infra*, 189–90.
[191] Mattingly, *Roman Coins*, 112.
[192] Momigliano, *Claudius*, 40.
[193] Mattingly, *Roman Coins*, 112.
[194] In Spain twenty-seven cities issued copper coins.

ECONOMIC CONDITIONS

on the ground that they were conducive to particularism.[195] The *aureus* and *denarius* continued to be issued without debasement throughout the reign from the mint at Lyons,[196] and adequate provision for the coinage needs of the West seems to have been made.[197] The small coins of Tiberius fall into three categories, according to the date of issue. In A.D. 15-16, *asses* only were issued; in 22-23, *sesterces*, *dupondii*, and *asses* in large volume were minted; while in 34-37, *sesterces* and *asses* were coined.[198] In the East, local and provincial issues continued,[199] and there were issues also from the imperial mints in Asia Minor.[200] In Egypt, Tiberius instituted, in A.D. 19-20, an impure silver *tetradrachm* for local use.[201]

The most significant factor about the monetary system of the period was the unusual contraction of the currency, in spite of the mintings of Tiberius. Several factors explain this phenomenon. After 9 B.C. and as late as A.D. 32, coinage amounted to but 5 per cent of the twenty years preceding.[202] This may have been partially attributable to the depletion of the bullion stocks of the treasury.[203] It is known that large amounts of metal were immobilized in plate,[204] and some metal was leaving the

---

[195] Mattingly, *Roman Coins*, 112.
[196] *Id., Coins of the Roman Empire*, I, cxxx.
[197] *Ibid.*, xxx.
[198] *Ibid.*, cxxxii.
[199] *Id., Roman Coins*, 194, 196-97. An *aureus* equaled 25 *denarii*, or 100 *sesterces*, or 200 *dupondii*, or 400 *asses*. For local coinage, see, K. Pink, "Römische Kaisermünzen als Geschichtsquelle," *Klio*, XXIX (1936), 229.
[200] Mattingly, *Coins of the Roman Empire*, I, cxli.
[201] Johnson, "Roman Egypt," in *loc. cit.*, 427; F. Heichelheim, "New Light on Currency and Inflation in Hellenistic-Roman Times," *Economic History*, III (1935), 4-6.
[202] T. Frank, "The Financial Crisis of 33 A.D.," *American Journal of Philology*, LVI (1935), 338.
[203] *Ibid.*, 341; Grenier, "La Gaule Romaine," in *loc. cit.*, 517.
[204] Tacitus, *Ann.*, III, 53.

empire as a result of the eastern trade.²⁰⁵ By far the larger part of the money seems to have been hoarded and thus withdrawn from circulation.²⁰⁶ An enormous part of the imperial revenue went to pay the legions, and this money was spent in the provinces for the most part.²⁰⁷ The flow from Italy was accelerated by the adverse trade balance,²⁰⁸ as well as by investments in the thriving provinces by Italians.²⁰⁹ Neither in Italy nor in the provinces ²¹⁰ did Tiberius indulge in spending programs comparable with the expenditures of his predecessor,²¹¹ but, on the contrary, he was accused of having kept a considerable amount of coin locked up in the imperial vaults.²¹²

Currency contraction in Italy culminated in a serious financial crisis in A.D. 33.²¹³ Scarcity of funds forced interest rates up beyond the legal maximum, and debtors began to complain. The government thereupon intervened and forced the usurers to legalize their accounts.²¹⁴ As a result loans were promptly called in, and debtors were forced to dump their property on the market for whatever price could be realized, with a falling land market as the inevitable consequence.²¹⁵ To remedy the situation the Senate "prescribed that every creditor was to

---

²⁰⁵ Warmington, *The Commerce Between the Roman Empire and India*, 285. Too much emphasis has been placed on the flow of gold and silver to the East; Rome had produce as well as metal to send to the Orient. Westermann, "The Economic Basis of the Decline of Ancient Culture," in *loc. cit.*, 727-29.
²⁰⁶ Grenier, "La Gaule Romaine," in *loc. cit.*, 517.
²⁰⁷ Frank, "Financial Crisis of 33 A.D.," in *loc. cit.*, 339.
²⁰⁸ *Ibid.*, 337.
²⁰⁹ *Ibid.*, 339.
²¹⁰ Grenier, "La Gaule Romaine," in *loc. cit.*, 512.
²¹¹ Frank, "Financial Crisis of 33 A.D.," in *loc. cit.*, 337, 338-39.
²¹² Tacitus, *Ann.*, VI, 16-17.
²¹³ *Ibid.*; Frank, "Financial Crisis of 31 A.D.," in *loc. cit.*, 337.
²¹⁴ Tacitus, *Ann.*, VI, 16-17.
²¹⁵ "The money lent had been largely invested in Italian land; the forced sale that followed led to a collapse in prices and a great scarcity of ready money." Mattingly, *Roman Coins*, 185, n.1.

invest two-thirds of his capital . . . in landed property in Italy." [216] On the face of it, this would indicate that the wealthy had been investing their capital largely outside Italy.[217] The investment law seems to have done little to alleviate conditions caused by lack of ready money and sagging land prices, and it, therefore, was necessary for Tiberius to make available 100,000,000 *sesterces* ($5,000,000), from which fund interest-free loans were made to those able to post collateral worth double the amount of the loan. The land market presumably was readjusted eventually, for the decree making mandatory the purchase of Italian land soon was ignored.

The reign of Tiberius was a period of general prosperity, marked by continued urbanization, the extension of capitalistic agriculture, modest industrial expansion, and generally favorable conditions for commerce, conducted in large measure without governmental interference. There were, to be sure, periods of temporary economic stringency, both in Italy and in the provinces, attributable to bad harvests, speculative practices, or excessive governmental exploitation, particularly in Gaul, Egypt, Asia Minor, and Syria. Tiberius' economic policies, so far as we can judge them, were basically sound. While he discouraged extravagance, he was by no means niggardly, as his building projects and the scope of his activities for the relief of distress both in Italy and the provinces show. No governmental policy seems to have been responsible for the financial crisis in A.D. 33, which can be attributed primarily to the drain of capital from Italy to the provinces and the resulting constricted credit facilities in the peninsula. Measures taken by the emperor to deal with the crisis seem to have sufficed to solve the joint

[216] Tacitus, *Ann.*, VI, 16.
[217] Scramuzza, "Roman Sicily," in *loc. cit.*, 366.

problem of a shortage of liquid capital and a falling land market in Italy.

There was no fundamental change in the taxation structure, although the tendency to place financial matters more and more under the control of imperial officials was strengthened. The emperor's personal revenues were augmented with the acquisition of Cappadocia, confiscation, and the extension of control over mineral resources. The coinage system was basically the same as in Augustus' reign, and the volume in circulation was adequate to meet the demands of trade, except in localized instances where other economic factors created temporary shortages. The emperor's economic policies were to some degree coupled with humanitarian objectives, particularly his efforts to prevent rises in the prices of foodstuffs and his prompt and generous efforts to aid victims of disasters.

BIBLIOGRAPHY OF SECONDARY WORKS

General Works

Abbott, F. F., and Johnson, A. C., *Municipal Administration in the Roman Empire* (Princeton, 1926).

Arnold, W. T., *The Roman System of Provincial Administration*, 3rd ed. (Oxford, 1914).

———, *Studies in Roman Imperialism* (Manchester, 1906).

Asbach, J., *Römisches Kaisertum und Verfassung bis auf Traian* (Cologne, 1896).

Baker, G. P., *Tiberius Caesar* (New York, 1928).

Cohen, H., *Descriptions historiques de monnaies*, 3 vols. (Paris, 1880).

Delbrück, H., *Geschichte der Kriegskunst im Rahmen der politischen Geschichte*, 2 vols. in 3 (Berlin, 1902).

Dessau, H., *Geschichte der römischen Kaiserzeit*, 2 vols. in 4 (Berlin, 1924 ff.).

Dill, S., *Roman Society from Nero to Marcus Aurelius* (New York, 1905).

Domaszewski, A. von, *Geschichte der römischen Kaiser*, 2 vols. (Leipzig, 1909).

Drumann, W., *Geschichte Roms in seinem Übergange von der republikanischen zur monarchischen Verfassung*, 2nd ed., 6 vols. (Leipzig, 1908).

Frank, T., *An Economic History of Rome*, 2nd ed. (Baltimore, 1927).

———, *Roman Imperialism* (New York, 1925).

Friedlander, L., *Roman Life and Manners under the Early Empire*, 7th ed., 4 vols. (New York, 1909).

Gutschmid, A. von, *Geschichte Irans und seine Nachbarländer* (Tübingen, 1888).

Hahn, L., *Das Kaisertum: Das Erbe der Alten*, 6 vols. (Leipzig, 1913).

Herzog, E., *Geschichte und System der Römischen Staatsverfassung*, 2 vols. in 3 (Leipzig, 1887).

Hirschfeld, O., *Die Kaiserlichen Verwaltungsbeamten bis auf Diocletian*, 2nd ed. (Berlin, 1905).
Holmes, T. R., *The Architect of the Roman Empire* (Oxford, 1928).
Homo, L., *L'empire Romain* (Paris, 1925).
Kolbe, W., "Von der Republik zur Monarchie," *Aus Roms Zeitwende: Das Erbe der Alten* (Leipzig, 1931).
Kornemann, E., "Die Römische Kaiserzeit," in Gercke, A., and Norden, E. (eds.), *Einleitung in die Altertumswissenschaft*, 3 vols. (Leipzig, 1923).
Marquardt, J., *Römische Staatsverwaltung*, 4 vols. (Leipzig, 1881–1885).
Merivale, C., *History of the Romans under the Empire*, 8 vols. (London, 1865).
Mommsen, T., *Römisches Staatsrecht*, 3 vols. (Leipzig, 1877).
———, *Römisches Strafrecht* (Leipzig, 1899).
Müllendoff, K., *Deutsche Altertumskunde*, 2nd ed., 5 vols. in 8 (Berlin, 1890–1908).
Niese, B., *Grundriss der römischen Geschichte*, 5th ed. (Munich, 1923).
Rostovtzeff, M. I., *The Social and Economic History of the Roman Empire* (Oxford, 1926).
Schmaus, J., *Charakterbilder römischer Kaiser aus der Zeit des Prinzipats (31 v. Chr.–284 n. Chr.)* (Bamberg, 1909).
Scott, W. P., *The Civil Law*, 10 vols. (Cincinnati, 1932).
Strachan-Davidson, J. L., *Problems of the Roman Criminal Law*, 2 vols. (London, 1912).

MONOGRAPHS, DISSERTATIONS, AND OTHER STUDIES

Abele, T. H., *Der Senat unter Augustus* (Paderborn, 1907).
Abraham, F., *Tiberius und Sejan* (Berlin, 1888).
———, *Velleius und die Parteien in Rom unter Tiberius* (Berlin, 1885).
Asdourian, P. P., *Die politischen Beziehungen zwischen Armenien und Rom von 190 v. Chr. bis 428 n. Chr.* (Venice, 1911).
Baehr, P., *Die Ortlichkeit der Schlacht auf Idistaviso* (Halle, 1888).

Barbagallo, C., *Tiberio* (Rome, 1922).
Barrow, R. H., *Slavery in the Roman Empire* (New York, 1928).
Bergmans, J., *Die Quellen der Vita Tiberii (Buch 57 der Historia Romana) des Cassius Dio* (Heidelberg, 1903).
Boissier, J., *L'opposition sous les Césars* (Paris, 1875).
———, *Tacite* (Paris, 1903).
Bone, R. G., *Roman Persecution of Non-Christian Religions Before 200 A.D.* (Ph.D. Dissertation Abstract, Urbana, Ill., 1937).
Bouchier, E. S., *Spain under the Roman Empire* (Oxford, 1914).
———, *Syria as a Roman Province* (Oxford, 1916).
Broughton, T. R. S., "Roman Asia Minor," in Frank, T. (ed.), *An Economic Survey of Ancient Rome*, 5 vols. and index (Baltimore, 1933 ff.), IV.
———, *The Romanization of Africa Proconsularis*, in *Johns Hopkins University Studies in History and Political Science*, Extra Volumes, New Series, V (Baltimore, 1929).
Brunner, I., *Das Maiestättverbrechen und die Majestätsgesetze bis auf die Zeit des Tiberius* (Aarau, 1877).
Bunting, E., "The Stoic Opposition to the Principate as Seen in Tacitus" (Ph.D. Dissertation, Yale, 1932).
Cagnat, M. R., *Les impots indirects chez les romains* (Paris, 1882).
Cagnat, R., *L'armée Romaine d'Afrique et l'occupation militaire de l'Afrique sous les empereurs*, 2 vols. (Paris, 1912).
Cantarelli, L., "La diarchia Romana," *Studi Romani e Bizantini* (Rome, 1915).
———, "Un prefetto di Egitto," *Studi Romani e Bizantini* (Rome, 1915).
Casagrandi, V., "Germanico Cesare secondo la mente di Tacito," *Storia e Archeologia Romana* (Genoa, 1886).
———, "Il partito dell'opposizione repubblicana sotto Tiberio," *Storia e Archeologia Romana* (Genoa, 1886).
Chapot, V., *La province Romaine proconsulaire d'Asie* (Paris, 1904).
Charlesworth, M. P., *Trade-Routes and Commerce of the Roman Empire* (Cambridge, 1924).

Cheesman, G. L., *The Auxilia of the Roman Imperial Army* (Oxford, 1914).
Ciaceri, E., "L'imperatore Tiberio e i processi di lesa maesta," *Processi politici e relazioni internazionali* (Rome, 1918).
Cichorius, C., "Die Ägyptischen Erlasse des Germanicus," *Römische Studien* (Berlin, 1922).
——, "Der Astrologe Thrasyllos und sein Haus," *Römische Studien* (Berlin, 1922).
Domaszewski, A. von, "Die Rangordnung des Römischen Heeres," *Bonner Jahrbücher*, CXVII (1908).
Duff, A. M., *Freedmen in the Early Roman Empire* (Oxford, 1928).
Dürr, A., *Die Majestätsprocesse unter dem Kaiser Tiberius* (Heilbronn, 1880).
Ferber, C., *Utrum metuerit Tiberius Germanicum necne quaeritur* (Hamburg, 1890).
Freytag, L., *Tiberius und Tacitus* (Berlin, 1870).
Gentile, I., *L'imperatore Tiberio secondo la moderna critica storica* (Milan, 1887).
Graindor, P., "Athènes de Tiberè à Trajan," *Université Égyptienne Recueil de travaux publiés par la faculté des lettres*, VIII (Cairo, 1931).
Grenier, A., "La Gaule Romaine," in Frank, T. (ed.), *An Economic Survey of Ancient Rome*, 5 vols. and index (Baltimore, 1933 ff.), III.
Groag, E., "Zur Aemterlaufbahn der Nobiles in der Kaiserzeit," *Strena Buliciana* (Zagreb, 1924).
Gwatkin, W. E., *Cappadocia as a Roman Province*, in *University of Missouri Studies*, V (Columbia, Mo., 1930).
Halgen, C., *Essai sur l'administration des provinces senatorials sous l'empire romain* (Paris, 1898).
Hammond, M., *The Augustan Principate* (Cambridge, Mass., 1933).
Haywood, R. M., "Roman Africa," in Frank, T. (ed.), *An Economic Survey of Ancient Rome*, 5 vols. and index (Baltimore, 1933 ff.), IV.
Heichelheim, F. M., "Roman Syria," in Frank, T. (ed.), *An Economic Survey of Ancient Rome*, 5 vols. and index (Baltimore, 1933 ff.), IV.

BIBLIOGRAPHY

Hirschfeld, O., *Kleine Schriften* (Berlin, 1913).
Hofer, P., *Der Feldzug des Germanicus in J. 16 n. Chr.* (Leipzig, 1885).
Holtzhausser, C. A., *An Epigraphic Commentary on Suetonius' Life of Tiberius* (Philadelphia, 1918).
Ihne, W., *Zur Ehrenrettung des Kaisers Tiberius* (Strassburg, 1892).
Jennison, G., *Animals for Show and Pleasure in Ancient Rome* (Manchester, 1937).
Jerome, T. S., *Some Aspects of Roman History* (New York, 1923).
Johnson, A. C., "Roman Egypt," in Frank, T. (ed.), *An Economic Survey of Ancient Rome*, 5 vols. and index (Baltimore, 1933 ff.), II.
Jones, H. Stuart, *Fresh Light on Roman Bureaucracy* (Oxford, 1920).
Jullian, C., *Les transformations politiques de l'Italie sous les empereurs romains* (Paris, 1883).
Kessler, G., *Die Tradition über Germanicus* (Berlin, 1905).
Knabe, C. A., *De Fontibus Historiae Imperatorum Julianorum* (Halle, 1864).
Knoke, F., *Gegenwärtiger Stand der Forschungen über die Römerkriege im nordwestlichen Deutschland* (Berlin, 1903).
———, *Die Kriegzüge des Germanicus in Deutschland* (Berlin, 1922).
E. Kornemann, *Doppelprinzipat und Reichsteilung im Imperium Romanum* (Leipzig, 1930).
Kromayer, J., *Die rechtliche Begründung des Principat* (Marburg, 1888).
Kuntz, O., *Tiberius and the Roman Constitution* (Seattle, 1924).
Kuthman, C., *Zur Schlacht im Teutoburger Wald und den Feldzügen des Germanicus* (Hanover, 1932).
Lange, A., *Beiträge zur Geschichte des Kaisers Tiberius* (Jena, 1911).
Larsen, J. A. O., "Roman Greece," in Frank, T. (ed.), *An Economic Survey of Ancient Rome*, 5 vols. and index (Baltimore, 1933 ff.), IV.

Lesquier, J., "L'armée romaine d'Égypte d'Auguste à Dioclétian," *Mémoires de l'institut français d'archéologie orientale du Caire*, XLI (1918).
Levy, L., *Quo modo Tiberius Claudius Nero erga senatum se gesserit* (Paris, 1901).
Loane, H. J., *Industry and Commerce of the City of Rome*, in *Johns Hopkins Studies in Historical and Political Science*, LV (1938).
Marchesi, C., *Tacito* (Messina, 1924).
Marsh, F. B., *The Reign of Tiberius* (Oxford, 1931).
Mattingly, H., *Coins of the Roman Empire in the British Museum*, 2 vols. (London, 1923).
———, *Roman Coins* (London, 1928).
———, *The Imperial Civil Service of Rome* (Cambridge, 1910).
McFayden, D., *The History of the Title Imperator under the Roman Empire* (Chicago, 1920).
———, *The Rise of the Princeps' Jurisdiction Within the City of Rome*, in *Washington University Studies*, Humanistic Series, Vol. X, Pt. II (1923).
Meyer, E., *Untersuchen über die Schlacht im Teutoburga Wald* (Berlin, 1893).
Momigliano, A., *Claudius the Emperor and his Achievement* (Oxford, 1934).
Mommsen, T., *Gesammelte Schriften*, 6 vols. (Berlin, 1906).
——— (ed.), *Zum ältesten Strafrecht der Kulturvölker* (Leipzig, 1905).
Neubourg, H., *Die Ortlichkeit der Varusschlacht* (Detmold, 1887).
Oldfather, W., and Canter, H., *The Defeat of Varus and the German Frontier Policy of Augustus* (Urbana, Ill., 1915).
Parker, H. M. D., *The Roman Legions* (Oxford, 1928).
Parvan, V., *Die Nationalität der Kaufleute in römische Kaiserreiche* (Breslau, 1909).
Pfitzner, W., *Das Verhalten des Tiberius im Senate bei der Uebernahme der Herrschaft* (Parchim, 1877).
Pohlmann, R. von, *Die Weltanschauung des Tacitus*, 2nd ed. (Munich, 1913).

Pollack, E., *Der Maiestätsgedanke im Römischen Recht* (Leipzig, 1908).
Reynolds, P. K. Baillie, *The Vigiles of Imperial Rome* (Oxford, 1926).
Ritter, J., *Die taciteische Charakterzeichnung des Tiberius* (Rudolstadt, 1895).
Sandels, F., *Die Stellung der Kaiserlichen Frauen aus dem Julisch-Claudischen Hause* (Darmstadt, 1912).
Schenk, A., *Die Römische Kaisergeschichte bei Malalas* (Stuttgart, 1931).
Schisas, P. M., *Offenses against the State in Roman Law* (London, 1926).
Schott, W., *Die Kriminaljustiz unter dem Kaiser Tiberius* (Erlangen, 1893).
———, *Studien zur Geschichte des Kaisers Tiberius* (Bamberg, 1904).
Schulz, O. T., "Das Wesen des römischen Kaisertums der ersten zwei Jahrhunderte," *Studien zur Geschichte und Kultur des Altertums*, Vol. VIII, Pt. II (1916).
———, *Vom Principat zum Dominat. Das Wesen des römischen Kaisertums des dritten Jahrhunderts* (Paderborn, 1919).
Scramuzza, V. M., "Roman Sicily," in Frank, T. (ed.), *An Economic Survey of Ancient Rome*, 5 vols. and index (Baltimore, 1933 ff.), III.
Seeck, O., *Kaiser Augustus* (Leipzig, 1902).
Sherwin-White, A. N., *The Roman Citizenship* (Oxford, 1939).
Sievers, G. R., *Studien zur Geschichte der Römischen Kaiser: Tacitus und Tiberius* (Berlin, 1871).
Spengel, A., "Zur Geschichte des Kaisers Tiberius," *Sitzungsberichte der philos.-philog. und historische Klasse der K. Bayerische Akademie der Wissenschaft* (Munich, 1904).
Stahr, A., *Tiberius* (Berlin, 1863).
Stein, A., *Albinovanus Pedo* (Vienna, 1901).
———, *Der Römische Ritterstand* (Munich, 1927).
———, *Untersuchen zur Geschichte und Verwaltung Aegyptens unter Roemischer Herrschaft* (Stuttgart, 1915).

Stout, S. E., *The Governors of Moesia* (Princeton, 1911).
Syme, R., *The Roman Revolution* (Oxford, 1939).
Tieffenbach, R., *Über die Ortlichkeit der Varusschlacht* (Berlin, 1891).
Tuxen, S. C., *Kejser Tiberius* (Copenhagen, 1896).
Van Nostrand, J. J., *The Reorganization of Spain by Augustus*, in *University of California Publications in History*, IV (Berkeley, 1916).
———, "Roman Spain," in Frank, T. (ed.), *An Economic Survey of Ancient Rome*, 5 vols. and index (Baltimore, 1933 ff.), III.
Viertel, A., *Tiberius und Germanicus* (Göttingen, 1901).
Vogt, J., *Römische Politik in Ägypten* (Leipzig, 1924).
———, *Tacitus als Politiker* (Stuttgart, 1924).
Waltzing, J. P., *Étude historique sur les corporations professionelles chez les romains* (Louvain, 1895).
Warmington, E. H., *The Commerce Between the Roman Empire and India* (Cambridge, 1928).
Weber, W., "Studien zur Chronik des Malalas," *Festgabe für Adolf Deissmann* (Tübingen, 1927).
Weismantel, O., *Die Erdheben des Vorderen Kleinasiens in Geschichtlichen Zeit* (Marburg, 1891).
Wiesner, E., *Tiberius und Tacitus* (Krotoschin-Ostrowo, 1877).
Wilamowitz-Moellendorff, U. von, and Zucker, F., "Zwei Edikte des Germanicus auf einem Papyrus des Berliner Museum," *Sitzungsberichte der Königlich Preussischen Akademie der Wissenschaften* (1911).
Willenbücher, H., *Tiberius und die Verschwörung des Sejans* (Gutersloh, 1896).
Willrich, W., *Livia* (Leipzig, 1911).
Winspear, A. D., and Geweke, L. K., *Augustus and the Reconstruction of Roman Government and Society*, in *University of Wisconsin Studies in the Social Sciences and History*, XXIV (Madison, Wis., 1935).

ARTICLES AND SHORTER STUDIES

Anderson, J. G. C., "Augustan Edicts from Cyrene," *Journal of Roman Studies*, XVII (1927).

Barini, C. C., "La tradizione superstite ed alcuni giudizi dei moderni su Livia," *Rendiconti della R. Accademia Nazionale dei Lincei*, Series V, Vol. XXXI (1922).
Besnier, M., "Fouilles recentes en Tunisie," *Journal des Savants*, New Series, XII (1914).
Bevan, R. H., "The Deification of Kings in the Greek Cities," *English Historical Review*, XVI (1901).
Bickermann, E., "Die Römische Kaiserapothéose," *Archiv für Religionswissenschaft*, XXVII (1929).
Blanchet, A., "Les armes Romaines," *Journal des Savants*, XXV (1927).
Boutterin, M., "La Villa de Tiberè à Capri," *Monumenta Antiques*, Supp. VI (1914).
Cantarelli, L., "La famiglia e il cursus honorum," *Bullettino della Commissione Archeologica Communale di Roma*, 2nd Series, XII (1884).
———, "Tacfarinata," *Atene e Roma*, IV (1901).
Cantineau, J., "Textes Palmyreniens du Temple de Bel," *Syria*, XII (1931).
Carcopino, J., "Le mariage d'Octave et de Livie," *Revue Historique*, CLXI (1929).
Charlesworth, M. P., "Livia and Tanaquil," *Classical Review*, XLI (1927).
———, "Tiberius and the Death of Augustus," *American Journal of Philology*, XLIV (1923).
Ciaceri, E., "La responsibilitá di Tiberio nell'applicazione della *Lex Maiestatis*," *Studi Storici per l'Antichità Classica*, II (1909).
Cichorius, C., "Zur Familiengeschichte Seians," *Hermes*, XXXIX (1904).
Columba, G. M., "Il processo di Cremuzeo Cordo," *Atene e Roma*, IV (1901).
Cortellini, N., "A proposito di alcune date incerte dell'ultimo decennio del regno di Tiberio," *Rivista di Storia Antica*, III (1898).
Dahm, O., "Die Feldzüge des Germanicus in Deutschland," *Westdeutsche Zeitschrift für Geschichte und Kunst*, XI (1902).
Dessau, H., "Die Herkunft der Offiziere und Beamten des Römischen Kaiserreichs," *Hermes*, XLV (1910).

Dexler, H., "Bericht über Tacitus für die Jahre 1913–1927," *Jahresbericht über die Fortschritte der klassischen Altertumswissenschaft*, CCXXIV (1927).
Dieckmann, H., "Die effective Mitregenschaft des Tiberius," *Klio*, XV (1918).
Domaszewski, A. von, "Der Truppensold der Kaiserzeit," *Neue Heidelberger Jahrbücher*, X (1900).
Fabia, P., "La carrière senatoriale de Tacite," *Journal des Savants*, XXIX (1926).
———, "L'avénement officiel de Tiberè," *Revue Philologie*, XXXIII (1909).
Ferguson, W. S., "Legalized Absolutism en Route from Greece to Rome," *American Historical Review*, XVIII (1913).
Ferrero, G., "The Women of the Caesars: Tiberius and Agrippina," *Century Illustrated Magazine*, LXXXII (1911).
———, "The Women of the Caesars: The Daughters of Agrippina," *Century Illustrated Magazine*, LXXXII (1911).
Flint, W. W., "The Delatores in the Reign of Tiberius," *Classical Journal*, VIII (1912).
Fraenkel, E., "Tacitus," *Neue Jahrbücher für Wissenschaft und Jugendbildung*, VIII (1932).
Frank, T., "Dominium in 'solo provinciale' and 'Ager Publicus,'" *Journal of Roman Studies*, XVII (1927).
———, "The Financial Crisis of 33 A.D.," *American Journal of Philology*, LVI (1935).
Gagé, J., "Divus Augustus," *Revue Archéologique*, XXXIV (1931).
———, "La Victoria Augusti et les auspices de Tiberè," *Revue Archéologique*, XXXII (1930).
Gelzer, M., "Die Nobilität der Kaiserzeit," *Hermes*, L (1915).
Glaser, K., "Bemerkungen zu den Annalen des Tacitus," *Mitteilungen des Vereines Klassischer Philologen in Wien*, VI (1929).
Groag, E., "Der Sturz der Julia," *Wiener Studien*, XLI (1919).
———, "Zum Konsulat in der Kaiserzeit," *Wiener Studien*, XLVII (1929).
Gummerus, H., "Die römische Industrie," *Klio*, XV (1917).

Harrer, G. A., "Tacitus and Tiberius," *American Journal of Philology*, XLI (1920).
Haverfield, F., "The Name Augustus," *Journal of Roman Studies*, V (1915).
Heichelheim, F., "New Light on Currency and Inflation in Hellenistic-Roman Times," *Economic History*, III (1935).
Heidel, W. A., "Why were the Jews Banished from Italy in 19 A.D.?" *American Journal of Philology*, XLI (1920).
Hohl, E., "Wann hat Tiberius das Principat übernommen?" *Hermes*, LXVIII (1933).
———, "Primum Facinus Novi Principatus," *Hermes*, LXX (1935).
Hohl-Rostock, E., "Ein Römischer Prinz in Ägypten," *Preuszische Jahrbücher*, CLXXXII (1920).
Kahrstedt, V., "Frauen auf antiken Münzen," *Klio*, X (1910).
Kingman, J. A., "Isle of Capri, an Imperial Residence and Probable Wireless Station of Ancient Rome," *National Geographic Magazine*, XXXVI (1919).
Kornemann, E., "Neues von Kaiser Tiberius," *Forschungen und Fortschritte*, V (1929).
Krascheninnikoff, M., "Ueber die Einführung des provinzialen Kaisercultus," *Philologus*, LIII (1894).
La Piana, G., "Foreign Groups in Rome," *Harvard Theological Review*, XX (1927).
Laqueur, R., "Kaiser Augustus und der Delator," *Hermes*, LXVII (1932).
Liebenam, W., "Zur Tradition über Germanicus," *Jahrbücher für classische Philologie*, CXLIII (1891).
Lord, L. E., "Notes on Tacitus' Summary of the Reign of Augustus," *Classical Review*, XLI (1927).
Lugand, R., "Le viol rituel les Romains," *Revue Archéologique*, XXXII (1930).
Maroni, C., "Uno sguardo ai fasti dei prefetti al pretorio," *Rivista di Storia Antica*, IV (1899).
Marsh, F. B., "A Modern Historical Myth. A Defense of Tacitus," *Classical Weekly*, XIX (1925–1926).
———, "Roman Parties in the Reign of Tiberius," *American Historical Review*, XXX (1926).
———, "Tacitus and the Aristocratic Tradition," *Classical Philology*, XXI (1926).

Mattingly, H., "Some Historical Coins of the First Century A.D.," *Journal of Roman Studies*, X (1920).
McFayden, D., "The Princeps and the Senatorial Provinces," *Classical Philology*, XVI (1921).
Merrill, E. T., "The Expulsion of the Jews under Tiberius," *Classical Philology*, XIV (1919).
Meyer, E., "Kaiser Augustus," *Historische Zeitschrift*, LV (1903).
Mickwitz, G., "Economic Rationalism in Graeco-Roman Agriculture," *English Historical Review*, LII (1927).
Mierow, C. C., "Two Roman Emperors," *Classical Journal*, XXXVI (1941).
Milne, J., "The Ruin of Egypt by Roman Mismanagement," *Journal of Roman Studies*, XVII (1927).
Mommsen, T., "Der Rechenschaftsbericht des Augustus," *Historische Zeitschrift*, LVII (1887).
Motzo, B. R., "I commentari di Agrippina madre di Nerone," *Studi di Storia e Filologia*, I (1927).
Müller, A., "Die Strafjustiz in römischen Heere," *Neue Jahrbücher für das klassische Altertum-Geschichte und Deutsche Literatur*, XVII (1906).
Otto, W., "Die Nobilität der Kaiserzeit," *Hermes*, LI (1916).
Parvan, V., "I primordi della civiltá Romana alle foci del Danubio," *Ausonia*, X (1921).
Pink, K., "Römische Kaisermünzen als Geschichtsquelle," *Klio*, XXIX (1936).
Poplawski, M. St., "L'apothéose de Sylla et d'Auguste," *Eos*, XXX (1927).
Premerstein, A. von, "Die Anfänge der Provinz Moesien," *Jahreshefte des Österreichischen Archäologischen Instituts in Wien*, I (1898).
Reid, J. S., "Tacitus as a Historian," *Journal of Roman Studies*, XI (1921).
Reinach, S., "Une séance du Senate Romain sous Tiberè," *Revue Historique*, CLXII (1930).
Reitzenstein, R., "Tacitus und sein Werk," *Neue Wege zur Antike*, IV (1926).
Ritterling, E., "Military Forces in the Senatorial Provinces," *Journal of Roman Studies*, XVII (1927).

———, "Die Statthalter der Pannonischen Provinzen," *Archaeologisch-Epigraphische Mitteilungen aus Oesterreich-Ungarn*, XX (1897).
Robinson, D. M., "A Preliminary Report on the Excavations at Pisidian Antioch and at Sizma," *American Journal of Archaeology*, XXVIII (1924).
Rogers, R. S., "The Conspiracy of Agrippina," *Transactions and Proceedings of the American Philological Association*, LXII (1931).
———, "Fulvia Paulina C. Sentii Saturnini," *American Journal of Philology*, LIII (1932).
———, "Ignorance of the Law in Tacitus and Dio: Two Instances from the History of Tiberius," *Transactions and Proceedings of the American Philological Association*, LXIV (1933).
———, "Lucius Arruntius," *Classical Philology*, XXVI (1931).
———, "Der Prozess des Cotta Messalinus," *Hermes*, LXVIII (1933).
———, "Tiberius' Reversal of an Augustan Policy," *Transactions and Proceedings of the American Philological Association*, LXXI (1940).
———, "Two Criminal Cases Tried before Drusus Caesar," *Classical Philology*, XXVII (1932).
Rostovtzeff, M. I., "L'empereur Tiberè et le culte impérial," *Revue Historique*, CLXIII (1930).
Savage, J. J., "Germanicus and Aeneas," *Classical Journal*, XXXIV (1939).
Schmidt, L., "Das Regnum Vannianum," *Hermes*, XLVIII (1913).
Scott, K., "The Dioscuri and the Imperial Cult," *Classical Philology*, XXV (1930).
———, "Drusus Nicknamed 'Castor,'" *Classical Philology*, XXV (1930).
———, "Tiberius' Refusal of the Title of Augustus," *Classical Philology*, XXVII (1932).
Sihler, E. G., "The First Twelve Roman Emperors," *Bibliotheca Sacra*, XC (1933).
Stein, A., "Die Protokolle des römischen Senates und ihre

Bedeutung als Geschichtsquelle für Tacitus," *Jahresbücher der I. deutschen Staats-Realschule in Prag*, XLIII (1904).

Stein, A., "Tacitus als Geschichtsquelle," *Neue Jahrbücher für das klassische Altertum Geschichte und Deutsche Literatur*, XXXVI (1915).

Stein, E., "Zur Kontroverse über die röm. Nobilität der Kaiserzeit," *Hermes*, LII (1917).

Strazzulla, V., "Il processo di Libone Druso," *Rivista di Storia Antica*, XII (1908).

Taylor, L. R., "Tiberius' Refusal of Divine Honors," *Transactions and Proceedings of the American Philological Association*, LX (1929).

Van Sickle, C. E., "The Repair of Roads in Spain under Tiberius," *Classical Philology*, XXIX (1929).

Westermann, W. L., "The Economic Basis of the Decline of Ancient Culture," *American Historical Review*, XX (1915–1916).

Wilcken, U., "Zum Germanicus-Papyrus," *Hermes*, LXIII (1928).

Willrich, H., "Augustus bei Tacitus," *Hermes*, LXII (1927).

Zmigryder-Konopka, Z., "Les Romains et la circoncision des Juifs," *Eos*, XXXIII (1930–1931).

INDEX

Achaea, 194, 200, 202-203, 208, 219, 239, 243
Actium, battle of, 1, 89
Adriatic sea, 86, 89
Aedui, 198
Aegean sea, 195, 204, 235
Aegium, 209
Aemilia, Lepida, 173, 220, 221
Aemilius, 71
Afer, Domitius, 131
Africa, province of, 118, 212; war with Tacfarinas in, 182-90; economic conditions, 238-39
Agricola, 161
agriculture, development of large estates, 233; Italy, 235-36; Gaul, 236; Spain, 237; Sicily, 237-38; Africa, 238-39; Greece and Macedonia, 239; Syria, 240; Egypt, 241-42
Agrippa, 5, 6, 7, 10, 18
Agrippa, Haterius, 224
Agrippa Posthumus, 8, 10, 17, 157, 180; banished by Senate, 12; alleged reconciliation with Augustus, 13; death, 14-16
Agrippina, wife of Germanicus, 10, 67, 104, 108, 112, 119-20, 122, 142, 143, 152, 153, 158, 163, 177, 218; conduct during mutiny of legions, 51-53, 55; in Syria, 88, 89, 94, 100, 102, 104; at Germanicus' funeral, 106; angered by Plancina's acquittal, 115; party of, 124-26; plots opposed by Sejanus, 125-30; insults Tiberius, 131-32; plans accession of Nero, 134-36; denounced by Tiberius, 137-40; exile and death, 140; significance of career, 140-41

Ahenobarbus, Lucius Domitius, 65
Ahse river, 69
Alexandria, 96, 193, 241
Aliso, 69
Alme river, 69
Alps mountains, 6
Amorgus, 176
Amyclae, gulf of, 133
Andecavi, 198
Angrivarii, 70, 73, 74, 75
Antioch, 98, 100, 211, 247, 251
Antium, 155
Antonia, 123, 146-47, 153
Antonius, Marcus, 88, 90, 200
Aphrodite, temple of, 247
Apicata, wife of Sejanus, 122, 123, 149
Appuleius, Sextus, 14
Apicius, Marcus Gabius, 116
Apollo, temple of, 147
Apronius, Caesianus, 184
Apronius, Lucius, 61, 79, 183, 184, 208
aquae et ignis interdictio, 168
Archelaus, king of Cappadocia, 201-202, 217
Ariobarzanes, king of Armenia, 81
Armenia, 6, 8, 165, 195, 196, 200, 251; Augustus' policy in, 80-81; Tiberius' diplomacy with, 81; Germanicus' policy in, 91-92
Armenia Minor, 200
Arminius, 60, 62, 64, 67, 71, 73, 77
Arno river, 226
Arpus, 69
Arruntius, Lucius, 31-32, 128, 145-46, 226
Arsaces, 195
Artabanus, Parthian usurper, 81, 84, 93, 94, 195, 196, 197
Artaxata, 92

INDEX

Artaxias III, king of Armenia, 92, 195
Asclepius, temple of, 210
Asia, province of, 184, 185, 200, 203, 209; economic conditions, 239-40, 249, 250, 252
Astrologers, 172, 173
Ateius, Marcus, 209
Athens, 89, 90
Artogerassa, 81
Augustodunum (Autun), 198, 199
Augustus (Octavian), 24, 26, 27, 28, 31, 34, 36, 42, 47, 48, 62, 77, 79, 80, 81, 84, 87, 95, 96, 116, 127, 131, 133, 137, 161, 164, 165, 170, 173, 190, 191, 201, 205, 211, 214, 216, 217, 221, 223, 230, 236, 241, 246, 247, 248, 250; character, 1; early policies, 1-2; his abdications, 2-3; proconsular and tribunician powers exercised, 3-4; plans for succession, 4-6; relations with Tiberius, 6-8; designates Gaius and Lucius as successors, 8; takes Tiberius as colleague and successor, 10; death, 12-13, 15, 16; will, 18-19; funeral, 20-21; deification, 21
Auzea (Aumale), battle of, 188-89
Aventine hill, 227
Aviola, Acilius, 198

Baetica, 252
Batavia, 69
Batavians, 70, 71
Bato, chief of Breuci, 9
Bato, chief of Desidiates, 8, 9
Belgians, 52
Belgica, 197
Bithynia, 170, 206
Blaesus, Junius, 37, 39, 40, 118, 185, 186, 187, 188
Bovillae, 17
Braga, 211
Breuci, 8, 9
Bribiesca, 211
Britain, 75
Brixia, 212
Bructeri, 58, 62, 63
Brundisium, 107
Brutus, 127
Byzantium, 90

Caecina, Aulus, 77, 174; campaigns in Dalmatia, 9; suppresses mutiny of legions, 45-46, 49, 54; participates in German campaigns, 58, 60, 61, 63, 65-67, 68
Caelian Hill, 227, 246
Caesar, Julius, 1, 3, 20, 26, 127, 154, 170, 216
Caesian Forest, 57
Camillus, Furius, 182-83
Campania, 235
Campus Martius, 20, 230
Cantabrians, 6
Capito, Ateius, 174, 219, 226
Capito, Lucilius, 203, 205
Cappadocia, made Roman province, 92, 200-202; financial administration, 202, 217; economic conditions, 240, 248, 249, 250, 256
Capri, 29, 123, 132, 142, 144, 145, 146, 147, 149, 162, 163, 180, 208, 220, 222; Tiberius withdraws to, 133-34; Sejanus visits, 136, 137; last years of Tiberius on, 153-56
Carrhae, battle of, 6
Carthage, 239
Casius, 141
Cassius, 127
Cassius, Lucius, 154
Castronius, Gaius, 53
Cato, Porcius, 128
Catus, Firmius, 171
Catwalda, 78
Celsus, 178
Cenithians, 182
Cestius, 151
Chaerea, Cassius, 46
Chariovalda, 71
Chatti, 60, 69, 75
Chaves, 211
Chersonese, Thracian, 250
Cheruschi, 60, 61, 62, 71, 72-73, 74, 78
Chiana river, 226

INDEX

Cibyra, 209
Cietae, 202
Cilicia, 94, 201
Cilicia Trachea, 200
Circus Maximus, 227
Cirminium, 212
Cirta (Constantine), 187
Clarian Apollo, oracle of, 90
Claudia, 155
Claudius, emperor, 118, 211, 230, 247
Clemens, 17, 25
Coelaletae, 193
coinage, Tiberius', 252-54, 256
Cologne, 46, 48, 49, 50
Colophon, 90
Columella, 233-34
Comitia Tributa, 3, 4, 223
Commagene, 92, 201
commerce, expansion of, 234-35; Spain, 237; Africa, 239; Syria, 240; Egypt, 241-42
Concord, Temple of, 148
Coptos, 212
Cordus, Caesius, 206
Cordus, Cremutius, 127
Cornutus, Caecilius, 175
Cos, 210, 240
Cotys, king of Thrace, 190-92, 193
Crassus, 6, 80
Crete, 127, 175, 206
Crispus, Sallustius, 15, 17
Ctesiphon, 197
cura legum et morum, 4
Cyclades, 90, 200
Cyrene, 206
Cyrene Edicts, 3
Cyrrus, 94
Cythanus, 205
Cyzicus, 210

Daesitrate, 211
Dalmatia, 7, 8-9, 107, 211-12
Damascus, 240
Danube river, 8, 43, 212
Dardania, 195
Decrius, 183
delators, see, *maiestas*
Denderah, temple at, 213, 247

Desidiates, 8, 9
Dialogue on Orators, 160
Digest, 168-69
Dii, 193
Dio, Cassius, 101, 246, 252; reports death of Augustus, 12; describes Tiberius' plan to partition empire, 30-31; portrays Tiberius' character, 157
Ditionum, 211
Dolabella, Publius, 188-89, 204-205, 208, 220
Domitian, emperor, 160-61
Drave river, 7, 10
Drusian Fosse, 69
Drusilla, 154
Drusus, brother of Tiberius, 5, 6, 7, 10, 61, 69, 79, 117
Drusus, son of Germanicus, 124, 135, 149, 152, 153, 200, 219; involved in Agrippinian plots, 140; exile and death, 141-42
Drusus, son of Tiberius, 59, 76, 78, 84, 89, 106, 107, 124, 125, 128, 135, 149, 152, 159, 173, 174, 180, 224, 230; suppresses Pannonian mutiny, 36-45; altercation with Sejanus, 120-21; death, 122, 123

Economic conditions, Roman empire, 233-56. See also, agriculture, coinage, commerce, industry, taxation
Eder river, 61
Egypt, reorganized by Augustus, 1, 2; Germanicus' visit, 95-97; economic conditions, 241, 247, 250, 252, 253, 255
Elbe river, 7, 8, 57, 72, 73, 77, 79
Eliso river, 69
Ems river, 7, 49, 62, 63, 64, 65, 69, 70, 75, 77
Ennius, Lucius, 174
Ennius, Manius, 49-50, 55, 219
Ephesus, 210, 240
equites, 17, 95, 118, 154, 229
Etruria, 116
Euboea, 89

INDEX

Eudemus, 122, 123
Euphrates river, 196

Falanius, 170
Fezzan, 187
Fidenae, 227
fiscus, 204, 247. See also, taxation
Flaccus, Pomponius, 192, 193
Flaccus, Vescularius, 171, 178
Florus, Julius, 197, 198
Forum Julium (Frejus), 78
Frisia, 63, 78-79
Fundi, 133

Gades, 237
Gaetulicus, Lentulus, 152, 208
Gaius (Caligula), 177, 201, 251; with Agrippina, 51, 52; eulogizes Livia, 137; lives with Tiberius, 142; ordained pontiff, 145, 146, 147; plot against, 150; sole heir of Germanicus, 152, 153; made quaestor, 154-55; death of Tiberius, 156
Gaius, grandson of Augustus, 6, 7, 8, 29, 81, 84, 116, 129
Galerius, Caius, 97
Gallia Lugdunensis, 197, 212
Gallitta, Cosconia, 116
Gallio, Junius, 154
Gallus, Aelius, 177
Gallus, Asinius, 214, 215; proposals for Augustus' funeral, 20; offends Tiberius, 31; Augustus' opinion of, 32; accused of illicit relations with Agrippina, 125; leader of Agrippinian faction, 128; desire of Agrippina to marry, 130; asks Tiberius to denounce Agrippinians, 136; condemned, 141; in Senate debate, 221; proposes new plan for the magistracies, 224-25; recommends consultation of Sibylline Books, 226; opposes sumptuary legislation, 228
Gallus, Togonus, 154
Garamantians, 188, 189
Garovilla, 212

Gaul, 57, 67, 68, 78, 243, 249, 251, 252, 255; status under Augustus, 2; Tiberius in, 6; Sacrovir war, 197-200, 206; economic conditions, 236-37
Geminius, 178
Geminus, Fufius, 143, 152, 178
Gemonian stairs, 149
Germanicus, 13, 18, 23, 25, 32, 109, 111, 112, 115, 118, 120, 122, 124, 132, 135, 138, 140, 153, 154, 157, 158, 159, 163, 164, 165, 173, 202, 219, 224, 230, 243, 245, 250; campaign in Dalmatia, 9; adopted by Tiberius, 10; quells mutiny of Rhine legions, 45-56; offered throne by legions, 47-48, 50; criticism of his conduct during mutiny, 54-55; campaigns in Germany, 57-79; celebrates a triumph, 59; campaign of A.D. 14, 56-59; campaign of A.D. 15, 60-68; visits Teutoberg forest, 63-64; victory at Idisiaviso, 72-74; wreck of fleet, 74-75; recalled by Tiberius, 75-77; triumph in A.D. 17, 76; in East, 80-102; nature of eastern mission, 82-83; character, 83; relations with Silanus, 84; authority in East, 87; journey to Syria, 89-91; in Armenia, 91-92; quarrel with Piso, 93-96; visits Egypt, 95-97; undermined by Piso, 98; illness, 98-102; death, 102, 103, 104; funeral, 106, 107, 108
Germany, 135, 152, 165, 198; Drusus' campaigns in, 7; Tiberius' campaigns in, 9, 10; rebellion of legions, 36-56; Germanicus' campaigns in, 57-79
Getae, 43
Gotones, 78
Greece, see, Achaea
Gyarus, 204

Hadrian, emperor, 195
Hamm, 69
Haterius, Quintus, 32, 215, 228

INDEX 275

Hera, temple of, 210
Hermunduri, 78
Herod, 249
Hiero, Parthian satrap, 197
Hispania, see, Spain
Hortalus, Marcus, 221
Hunse river, 68

Idisiaviso, battle of, 72-74
Illyria, 7, 10, 13, 78, 89
imperator, praenomen, 23, 73, 187
imperial cult, 22
imperium, 3, 5, 10, 103
Indus, Julius, 198
industry, prosperity of, 234; Italy, 235-36; Gaul, 236; Spain, 237; Sicily, 238; Africa, 239; Egypt, 241-42
Inguiomerus, 67, 73
Ionian sea, 89
Isis, cult of, 218, 232
Italy, 109, 248, 250, 252, 254-55; status under Augustus, 2; Tiberius in, 5; offers help to Germanicus, 68; administration by Tiberius, 155; *imperium* in, 215; astrologers and magicians banished, 218; imperial relief of, 226; maintenance of order, 229; economic conditions, 235-37. See also, Rome, city

Jerusalem, 230, 247, 248
Jews, 218, 230-32
Josephus, 231-32
Juba II, king of Mauretania, 187
Judaea, 243, 247, 248, 249
Julia, daughter of Augustus, 5, 7, 10, 31, 165
Julia, daughter of Drusus, 142
Julia, daughter of Germanicus, 154
Julia, daughter of Livilla, 135

Labda, 187
Labeo, Pomponius, 194, 206
Labienus, Titus, 127
Laco, Graecinius, 147, 148, 150
Latiaris, Latinius, 128, 150
Lepcis, 239

Lentulus, Gnaeus, 43, 204
Lepidus, Manius, 111, 174
Lepidus, Marcus, 184, 185
lèse majesté, see, *maiestas*
Lex Cornelia de Maiestate, 168
Lex Julia, 168, 169, 170, 179
lex sicariis, 109
Libo, 171-72, 217
Lippe river, 57, 63, 69
Livia, 12, 134, 143, 158, 164, 165, 173, 175, 177, 219, 225, 245, 250; marriage to Augustus, 5; urges Tiberius' return from Rhodes, 7-8; facilitates Tiberius' accession, 13; responsibility for murder of Agrippa Posthumus, 15-16; named Augusta, 18; honors received, 21-22, 25; intercedes for Plancina, 112; relations with Agrippina, 125; death, 137
Livilla, daughter of Germanicus, 89
Livilla, wife of Drusus, 106, 122-23, 125, 128-30, 132, 135
Lombards, 78
"Long Bridges," 65, 77
Lucius, grandson of Augustus, 6, 7, 8, 29
Lygdus, 122, 123
Lyons, 253

Macedonia, 194, 200, 202-203, 219, 239, 243
Macro, Naevius Sertorius, 147, 149, 150, 154, 156, 163, 178
Magnesia, 208, 210
maiestas, 127-28, 155, 204, 206, 218, 220
maius imperium, 86
Marcellus, nephew of Augustus, 5
Marcellus, Granius, 170, 206, 219
March river, 78
Marcomanni, 78
Marinus, Junius, 152, 178
Marobodus, 77
Marsh, F. B., quoted, 181
Marsi, 58, 60, 66, 75
Martene, 107
Mauretania, 182, 187-88, 252

Maximus, Fabius, 12
Mazippa, 182
Megalopolis, 243
Merida, 211
Mesopotamia, 197, 200
Messalinus, Cotta, 138, 150-51, 177, 220
mimes, 229
mines, Spain, 237; Sicily, 238; Greece and Macedonia, 239; owned by Tiberius, 250-51
Misenum, 156
Mithridates of Iberia, 196
Mithridates, king of Pontus, 90
Moesia, 194, 208, 212; imperial legate in, 191-92; Pomponius Flaccus in, 193, 194; Roman expansion in, 195; grouped with Achaea and Macedonia, 202; maladministration in, 206
Montanus, Votienus, 134, 176
Monumentum Ancyranum, 4
Mount Eryx, 213, 246
Mount Taunus, 60
Musulami, 182, 188
mutiny, of legions, 37-56

Nabat, 94
Nauportus, 40, 212
Nedda river, 61
Neopolis, 96
Nero, emperor, 22, 211
Nero, son of Germanicus, 84, 124, 125, 126, 127, 142, 219; plans to usurp throne, 134-36; denounced by Tiberius, 137-40; exile and death, 140; significance, 141
Nero, Tiberius Claudius, see, Tiberius
Nero, Tiberius Claudius, father of Tiberius, 5
New Carthage, 237
Nicaea, 240
Nicopolis, 89, 200, 212
Niger, Bruttedius, 203-204
Nile river, 97, 241
Nis, 195
Nola, 12, 13, 14, 17, 23, 133
Noricum, 6, 251

North sea, 65
Numidia, 182

Odrysae, 193
Ollius, T., 152
Opsius, Marcus, 128
Oracles II, king of Parthia, 80
Orodes, 196
Ostia, 17
Otho, Junius, 203

Paconianus, Sextus, 150, 179
Paconius, Marcus, 203
Paderborn, 69
Pagyda (Pazida) river, 183
Palatine hill, 147
Palmyra, 240
Pandateria, 140
Pandusa, Latinius, 191-92
Pannonia, 7, 8-9, 36-45, 55, 60, 117, 184, 208, 251
Parthia, 165, 195, 196; Augustus' policy in, 80-81; Tiberius' diplomacy in, 81-82; approves actions of Germanicus, 91-92
Pater Patriae, title accepted by Augustus, 4
Pedo, Albinovanus, 62-63
Percennius, 37, 43, 44
perduellio, 168
Pergamum, 205
Perinthus, 90
Petronius, Publius, 228
Pharasmanes, 196
Philip, brother of Herod, 249
Philippolis, 193
Phraates IV, king of Parthia, 6, 80, 195
Phraates, Parthian satrap, 197
Phraates, son of Phraates IV, 195, 196
Piso, Gnaeus, 163, 171, 217, 220, 221; consul with Tiberius, 7; appointed governor of Syria, 83; early career, 85; character, 85-86; instructed by Tiberius, 86-87; criticism of his appointment to Syria, 87-88; journey to East, 90-91; refuses to send le-

gions to Germanicus, 92-93;
quarrels with Germanicus, 94-
96; undermines Germanicus, 98;
conduct during Germanicus' ill-
ness, 98-100; suspected of poi-
soning Germanicus, 99-102;
seizes Syria, 103-104; attacked
by Sentius, 105; returns to
Rome, 107-108; trial, 108-115;
suicide, 114
Piso, Lucius, 85, 111, 175, 204, 225-
26
Piso, Marcus, 114
Planasia, 12
Plancina, wife of Gnaeus Piso, 88-
89, 91, 94, 101, 103, 112, 114-18
Plancius, Munatius, 50, 51
Pliny the Elder, 67
Pollentia, 229
pomerium, 2
Pompeius, 178
Pompeius, Sextus, 14, 184
Pompey the Great, 230
Pontevedra, 211
Pontia, 140
Porta Capena, 230
Praetorian Guard, 14, 19, 38, 41,
115, 117-18, 119, 143, 144, 145,
149-50, 154, 222, 229
princeps, 12, 169, 189, 199
princeps senatus, 1-2
Priscus, Ancharius, 206
Priscus, Clutorius, 173
proconsular powers, 2, 3, 5, 10, 26
Proculus, Considius, 178
Proculus, Gaius Cominius, 176, 220
procurator a rationibus, 251
provinces, administration, 182-213
Ptolemy, king of Mauretania, 188
Publicola, Gellius, 203
Pulchra, Claudia, 131
Pyrenees mountains, 211

Quirinus, Sulpicius, 84

Ratiaria, 194
Reate, 226
Red sea, 212

Regulus, Livineius, 111
Regulus, Memmius, 147, 148, 151
religion, changes by Tiberius, 230-
32. See also, Isis, Jews
Res Gestae Divi Augusti, 19
Rhaeti, 6, 53
Rhaetia, 6
Rheine, 63
Rhescuporis, 190-93
Rhine river, 7, 9, 36, 45, 53, 55, 60,
61, 62, 65, 67, 69, 75, 77, 198
Rhodes, 7, 8, 10, 29, 90, 91, 134,
201, 240
Rhoemetalces, king of Thrace, 9,
190
Rhoemetalces II, king of Thrace,
193, 194
roads, 210-12
Rome, city, 104, 153, 154, 155, 163;
return of Augustus to, 1; funeral of Augustus, 17, 20-21; recruits sent to legions, 46; sons
of Phraates of Parthia sent to,
80; dearth of grain, 96; honors
to Germanicus in, 105; return
of Piso to, 107, 108; attitude toward Sejanus, 120; Tiberius refuses to visit, 136; riot in, 138-
39; letters from Tiberius arrive,
144; plan of Tiberius to visit
announced, 145; trial of Rhescuporis, 191, 192-93; trial of
Archelaus, 201; fires in, 227-28;
games and shows curtailed, 229;
Jews banished, 230-31; worship-
pers of Isis banned, 232; financial panic in, 244; grain supply
of, 247-48. See also, Italy, Tiberius
Rostovtzeff, M. I., 251-52
Rubrius, 170
Rufilla, Annia, 218
Rufus, Petilius, 128
Rufus, Trebellenus, 193
Rusticus, Junius, 138

Sabinus, C. Calvius, 208
Sabinus, C. Poppaeus, 194, 200,
208

Sabinus, Titius, 126, 127-28, 175, 179
Sacrovir war, 174-75, 197-200, 249, 252
Salamanica, 211
Salonae, 8, 9, 211
Saltus Aurasius, 182
Samos, 89, 210
sanctuary, rights of limited, 210
Sardinia, 231
Sardis, 209
Saturninus, Gaius, 8
Scaurus, Mamercus, 32, 178
Scipio, Cornelius, 187
Scribonia, 5
Scythians, 191
Secundus, Pomponius, 177
Secundus, Satrius, 146
Segestes, 60, 61, 62
Sejanus, Aelius, 84, 106, 115, 159, 163, 178, 179, 180, 185, 204, 220, 222, 245; aids in suppression of Pannonian mutiny, 41; ancestry, 116; commands Praetorian Guard, 117-18; administrative aid to emperor, 119; honored by Tiberius, 119; altercation with Drusus, son of Tiberius, 120-21; alleged plot to poison Drusus, 122-23; opposes Agrippina, 124-30; seeks marriage with Livilla, 128-30; profits by Agrippina's rashness, 132; rescues Tiberius, 133; frustrates conspiracy of Nero, son of Agrippina, to seize throne, 135-36; procures Agrippina's ruin, 137-40; responsibility for condemnation of Drusus, son of Agrippina, 141-42; at height of his power, 142-43; receives additional honors from Tiberius, 143-44; secures proconsular powers, 145; harried by Tiberius, 146-47; denounced by Tiberius, 148; death, 149; children slain, 149; memory defamed, 150; supporters prosecuted, 150-52; estimate of, 152-53

Seleuceia, 98, 196-97, 240
Semonones, 77
Senate, Roman, 54, 156, 157, 158, 164, 199, 205-206, 242, 245, 254-55; relations with Augustus, 1-3, 4; banishes Agrippa Posthumus, 12; sessions after Augustus' death, 18-35; mutiny of legions referred to, 42; sends embassy to Rhine legions, 50; grants *imperium* to Germanicus, 86; tries Piso, 109-15; honors Livia, 137; opposes condemnation of Agrippina and Nero, 138-39; reverses its policy, 139-40; condemns Sejanus, 147-49; defames memory of Sejanus, 150; tries Sejanus' adherents, 150-52; discusses award of African command, 184-85; tries Rhescuporis, 194; provincial administration by, 207; deliberates about rights of sanctuary, 210; relations with Tiberius, 214-23; *Acta*, 216-17; legislation, 218-19; jurisdiction in criminal cases, 219-20; freedom of debate enjoyed by, 220-21
Sentius, 104-105, 107
Sequani, 199
Serenus, Vibius, 175-76
Seriphos, 175
Servaeus, Quintus, 108, 151
Servilius, Marcus, 221
Severus, Caecina, 185
Severus, Cassius, 127, 175
Sibylline Books, 226, 230
Sicily, 212, 237-38, 246-47, 250
Silanus, Creticus, 83-84
Silanus, Gaius, 203, 205
Silanus, Marcus, 155
Silius, Gaius, 68, 69, 126-27, 198-99, 206
Sirmium, 9
Siscia, 9
Smyrna, 240
Sophene, 200
Sosia, 126, 127, 174-75

INDEX   279

Spain, 6, 8, 68, 247, 250, 251; under Augustus, 2; roads, 211; economic conditions, 237
Stertinius, Lucius, 63, 71, 72-73
Stoicism, 161
Strabo, Seius, 14, 41, 116
Subura, 230
Suebi, 77
Suetonius, 13, 208, 215-16, 219, 246, 249, 251; quotes letters of Augustus, 10; describes Tiberius' accession, 25, 29, 33; describes Germanicus' death, 100, 101; depicts Tiberius' character, 155-57
Suevi, 53
Sugambri, 6
Suillius, Publius, 176
Sulla, 3, 168
sumptuary legislation, 218, 228-29, 242
Syria, 107, 163, 200, 255; Augustus' powers in, 2; arrival of Vonones in, 82; Piso appointed governor, 83; arrival of Piso in, 91; legions honor Piso, 93; Germanicus undermined by Piso, 97; seized by Piso, 103-104; reconquered by Sentius, 105; trial of Piso, 109, 111, 114; Vitellius in, 196; flight of Tiridates to, 197; public works, 212; economic conditions, 241; asks diminution of tribute, 243; gifts to legions, 245; taxes, 248, 249; coinage, 252

Tacfarinas, 252; organizes African rebellion, 182-83; defeated by Caesianus, 184; sends embassy to Tiberius, 186; checked by Blaesus, 187; renews war, 188; defeated at Auzea, 188-89; death, 189
Tacitus, 28, 29, 30, 31, 32, 33, 66, 67, 68, 70, 71, 73, 75, 132, 136, 201, 207, 216, 217, 227, 231, 235-36, 246; description of Augustus' visit to Planasia, 12; description of death of Agrippa Posthumus, 15-16; discusses Tiberius' reluctance to rule, 24, 25; description of mutiny, 36-56; criticizes Tiberius' conduct during mutiny, 55-56; accuses Tiberius of jealousy of Germanicus, 59-60; criticizes Tiberius' recall of Germanicus from Germany, 96; description of Germanicus' death, 99-102; discussion of Piso's trial, 106, 109, 112, 114, 115; interpretation of ruin of Agrippina, 137-39; portrayal of Tiberius' character, 157-62; discussion of *maiestas* prosecutions in Tiberius' reign, 166-67; account of Libo's conspiracy, 171-72. See, Agrippina, Germanicus, Sejanus, Tiberius
Taurus mountains, 202
taxation, in Roman empire, 244-52
Tencteri, 6
Terentius, Marcus, 151, 152
Terni, 226
Teutoberg Wood, battle of, 6, 9, 60, 63, 77
Thala (Haidra), 183
Thapsus, 239
Theater, Pompey's, 246
Thermus, Minucius, 151
Thrace, 250; Germanicus in, 89-90; conquest, 190-94
Thubuscum (Tiklat), 188
Tiber river, 128, 149, 218, 226
Tiberius, 36, 37, 41, 42, 47, 57, 59, 60, 73, 80, 82, 101, 104; parentage, 5; early life, 6; early campaigns in Spain and Gaul, 6; relations with Augustus, 6-8; divorce from Vipsania, 7; victories in Pannonia, 7; withdrawal to Rhodes, 7-8; victories in great Pannonian war, 9; tribunician powers renewed, 9-10; accession to throne discussed, 12-35; responsibility for death of Agrippa Posthumus, 14-16; curbs Livia's honors and titles, 21-22; accepts titles, 22-23; reluctance to accept ruling powers, 24-33;

INDEX

Tiberius (*continued*)
acceptance of ruling authority, 33-34; sends Drusus to Pannonia, 41; criticism of his policy during mutiny, 55-56; disapproves Germanicus' acts at Teutoberg Wood, 64; recalls Germanicus from Germany, 75-77; his later policy in Germany, 77-79; his policy in Armenia, 81-82; sends Piso to Syria, 83-85; instructions given to Piso, 86, 87; criticism of Piso's appointment, 87-88; pleased by Germanicus' policies in Armenia, 95; censures Germanicus for his visit to Egypt, 97; honors Germanicus, 105-106; conduct at Germanicus' funeral, 106; supervision of Piso's trial, 107-115; confidence in Sejanus, 118-20; reaction to death of his son, Drusus, 123-24; succession plans after Drusus' death, 124-25; denies Sejanus' request for Livilla's hand, 128-30; insulted by Agrippina, 131-32; withdraws to Capri, 133-34; learns of Agrippina's plots, 135-36; conduct after Livia's death, 137-38; denounces Agrippina and Nero, 137-39; prosecutes Agrippina and Nero, 139-40; estimate of his attitude toward Agrippina, 141; bestows added honors upon Sejanus, 143-44; honors his grandson, Gaius, 145; harries Sejanus, 146; learns of Sejanus' alleged plots, 147; orders overthrow of Sejanus, 148; authorizes Senate to try Sejanus' adherents, 150-52; last years at Capri, 153-55; death, 156; character according to Suetonius, 156-57; character according to Dio, 157; character according to Tacitus, 157-62; author's estimate of character, 162-65; *maiestas* cases in reign, 170-81; estimate of cases, 179-81; policy in Africa, 182-90; policy in Thrace, 191-94; relations with Parthia, 195-97; suppression of Sacrovir revolt, 199-200; acquires Cappadocia, 200-202; punishes extortion in provinces, 203-207; prolongs provincial commands, 207-208; limits asylum rights, 210; building projects in provinces, 211-13; shares administration with Senate, 214-23; policy in regard to elections, 223-25; relief policies in Italy, 226-29; policing of Italy, 229-30; religious changes in reign, 230-32; economic conditions in reign, 233-56; as financial administrator, 244-48; taxation, 248-50; estates owned, 250-51; coinage issued in reign, 252-54; deals with financial panic, 254-55; estimate of economic policies, 255-56. See also, Agrippina; Drusus, son of Tiberius; Germanicus; Livia; Sejanus; Tacitus

Tigranes III, king of Armenia, 81
Tigranes V, king of Armenia, 201
Tigranes II, king of Parthia, 6
Tiridates, Parthian usurper, 80
Tiridates, son of Phraates IV, 196, 197
Trajan, emperor, 211
Travastere, 230
Trebia, 219
Treveri, 51, 197
Treves, 55, 198
tribunician powers, Augustus', 3, 5; Tiberius', 7, 18, 23, 32, 169, 215
Trio, Fulcinius, 108, 111, 115, 151, 171, 178
Troy, 90
Tubantes, 58
Tubero, L. Seius, 116
Tunis, 183
Turoni, 198
Turranius, Gaius, 14
Tusculum, 155
Tuy, 211
Tyre, 240

INDEX

Urgulania, 225
Usipites, 6, 58

Vaga, 212
Varilla, Appuleia, 172, 220
Varro, Roman consul, 126, 199
Varus, 6, 52, 57, 63
Vellaeus, Publius, 193
Velleius, 242
Veranius, Quintus, 92, 108
Vespasian, emperor, 197
Vestal Virgins, 18, 230
Vibilius, 78
Vibulenus, 40, 41, 43, 44
Viminacium, 195
Vindelici, 6
Vinicius, Marcus, 154
Vipsania, 7, 31
Vistilius, Sextus, 152, 177-78
Vitellius, emperor, 248
Vitellius, Lucius, 196

Vitellius, Publius, 67-68, 111, 151, 177
Vitia, 178
Volsinii, 116
Vonones, king of Parthia, 80-81, 82, 84, 93, 94, 95, 251

Wag river, 78
Wed Bedja, 212
Weser river, 8, 49, 69, 70, 72, 77, 79

Xanten, 49, 54

Yssel river, 69

Zeno, king of Armenia, 82, 201
Zeno, son of Polemo of Pontus, 82, 91, 92, 93. See also, Artaxias III
Zuyderzee, 63, 69

FUNDERBURG LIBRARY
MANCHESTER COLLEGE

937.07
Sm 53t